No Time to Sew

Fast & Fabulous Patterns & Techniques for Sewing a Figure-Flattering Wardrobe

Sandra Betzina

Rodale Press, Inc.
Emmaus, Pennsylvania

OUR PURPOSE

*"We inspire and enable people to improve
their lives and the world around them."*

If you have any questions or comments concerning the editorial content of this book, please write to:

Rodale Press, Inc.
Book Readers' Service
33 East Minor Street
Emmaus, PA 18098

Library of Congress Cataloging-in-Publication Data

Betzina, Sandra.
    No time to sew : fast & fabulous patterns
& techniques for sewing a figure-flattering wardrobe
/ Sandra Betzina.
        p.   cm.
    Includes index.
    ISBN 0–87596–744–2 (hardcover : alk. paper)
    1. Tailoring (Women's) 2. Machine sewing. I. Title.
TT519.5.B47 1997
646.4'04—dc20   96–32382

Distributed in the book trade by St. Martin's Press

2 4 6 8 10 9 7 5 3 1 hardcover

NO TIME TO SEW EDITORIAL AND DESIGN STAFF

Editor: *Susan Huxley*

Interior and Pattern Envelope Design and Layout:
    Nancy Smola Biltcliff

Interior Illustrators (electronic): *Sue Gettlin,
    Kristin S. M. Kohuth, Jane D. Ramsey, Joyce A. Robinson,
    Annie Tregay Segal, Marla Stefanelli,
    Kathryn Wager Wright*

Interior Illustrators (traditional): *John Gist ("Welcome to My
    Studio" and "The Sewing Basket"), Amy J. Talcott (fashion
    illustrations)*

Cover and Interior Photographer: *John Hamel*

Cover and Interior Photo Stylist: *Pamela Simpson*

Makeup Artist: *Colleen Kobrick*

Cover Designer: *Mary Ellen Fanelli*

Technical Artist: *Tanya L. Lipinski*

Project Coordinator: *Patricia Field*

Copy Editor: *Nancy N. Bailey*

Manufacturing Coordinator: *Patrick T. Smith*

Indexer: *Nan N. Badgett*

Editorial Assistance: *Nancy Fawley, Rebecca S. McElheny,
    Jen Miller, Susan Nickol, Jodi Rehl, Lori Schaffer*

Garment Construction: *Elke Haines*

Pattern Testing: *Karen Coughlin, Marcia Ferris,
    Jacqueline Lukity, Jane Merkel, Mary Frances Salines,
    Rita Schmell, Helen Snell, Cathie Werner*

Garment fabric courtesy of Stonemountain & Daughter
    Fabrics, 2518 Shattuck Avenue, Berkeley, CA 94704
    (Call 1-510-845-6106 for information on their swatch
    service.)

Garments were photographed on location at Bridgewater
    Commons, Bridgewater, New Jersey; Brookside Country
    Club, Macungie, Pennsylvania; and South Mountain
    Center at Rodale Press, Inc., Emmaus, Pennsylvania

RODALE HOME AND GARDEN BOOKS

Vice President and Editorial Director: *Margaret J. Lydic*

Managing Editor: *Cheryl Winters Tetreau*

Art Director: *Paula Jaworski*

Associate Art Director: *Mary Ellen Fanelli*

Studio Manager: *Leslie Keefe*

Copy Director: *Dolores Plikaitis*

Production Manager: *Helen Clogston*

Office Manager: *Karen Earl-Braymer*

*To all of the women who have
read my sewing column,
attended my lectures, tried
on my clothes, and described
to me the timeless shapes
they seek in patterns.*

Contents

Full Pull-On Pants 2

A Flattering Style for All Figures

Easy to make and wear, comfortable, feminine pants flatter all figures. Cut from one pattern, this garment features a single leg seam and a shirred waistband.

The Next Step:

Slim Pull-On Pants 28

The Ultimate Wardrobe Extender

A lean silhouette is the dominant detail of this versatile garment. These pants have an elasticized waistband and a single leg seam.

The Next Step:

Coordinating Vest 48

The Essential Third Piece

Wide shoulders and curve-conscious shape define a flattering silhouette. This garment has a rounded hem and an optional single closure at the center front.

The Next Step:

Oversize T-Shirt . . . 72

Easy, Fast, and Stylish

A trendy topper for either organza full pants or denim shorts depends on your fabric choice. Set-in sleeves cover the upper arm, and shaped side seams complement your figure.

The Next Step:

Tuxedo Shirt 92

Goof-Proof and Versatile

Clean lines and slimming style add up to an irresistible cut. The curved, faced hem dips toward the side seams, while the wing-tip collar treatment draws the eye up to the face.

The Next Step:

Shawl Collar Jacket 116

A Simply Great Garment

Roomy, cut-on sleeves make this jacket easy to sew and easy to wear. Change the fabric and design details for a totally new look.

The Next Step:

Gored Skirt 144

The Perfect Pattern

Celebrate the soft drape of a feminine skirt. Offered with 6 or 12 panels, this garment features a lapped zipper and shirred waistband.

The Next Step:

Raglan-Sleeve Dress 164

A Dress Code You'll Love

The raglan sleeve conforms to the body, making alterations largely unnecessary. Cutoff lines at the hips, knees, and ankles offer several length options.

The Next Step:

Oblong Scarf 186

Your Number One Accessory

Draw the eye up to your face, break horizontal lines, and add polish to any outfit. Every wardrobe should include several scarves.

The Next Step:

Putting It All Together 194

The Ultimate Wardrobe

Timely advice makes the ultimate wardrobe accessible. Learn to combine the garments you've made, select the right fabrics and colors for your complexion and figure, and organize your closet.

Acknowledgments

Because of the tireless enthusiasm and patience of my editor, Susan Huxley, *No Time to Sew* is the best it could possibly be. Susan's sense of humor, tact, and kindness not only kept me on track but also inspired me to be more explicit and more creative, finding words for every step of the construction process. I also want to thank Rodale Press not only for believing in the *No Time to Sew* concept but also for realizing the importance of including the patterns.

Without my assistant, Karie White, *No Time to Sew* would still be in yellow notepad format. Not only did she type the manuscript but she also did all the preliminary artwork—no small task in a project this size. I want to thank my best friend, Helen Snell, who tested patterns, gave suggestions, and bolstered my energy. I want to thank Susan Steinberg from Stonemountain & Daughter Fabrics for her unbridled generosity in donating 95 percent of the fabric for the model garments, which gave me unlimited resources to create each model garment as though it were my own.

Once the patterns were perfected, Elke Haines was the dressmaker responsible for working in a tight time frame while still maintaining high standards for all of the model garments.

I also want to thank my three friends, Marcy Tilton, Margaret Islander, and Clotilde, for taking what little free time they have to review this book.

Last, but not least, I want to thank my husband, Dan, and children, Kim, Shaun, Monique, and Justin, for not making me feel guilty when this book assumed top priority and for sharing with me the pride in producing a book and patterns I hope you'll love.

It was very exciting working with the models. I was thrilled to see my designs come to life when the ladies put on the garments. At every photo shoot, I added the finishing touches to the outfits. In fact, you'll see pieces of jewelry from my personal collection in many of the photographs.

Introduction

As the pace of the world quickens and our lives become busier, "I've got no time to sew" is a familiar remark uttered among even the most dedicated sewing enthusiasts. "I don't even have time to peruse the pattern books anymore," says one. "Ready-to-wear has so many simple figure-flattering styles; why can't I find patterns for those?" asks another. This book is in response to the needs of busy people who want to sew but rarely have more than an evening at their disposal.

In *No Time to Sew*, you'll find very simple but flattering patterns that are sized realistically in small, medium, and large. The clothes are modeled by women in all three size ranges, so that you can see—whatever your size—how great you'll look in these styles. (It's difficult to imagine how a real person will look in a pattern modeled by a tall, skinny model.) Even if you're much larger or much smaller in certain areas, you'll be able to customize each multisized pattern to fit your measurements for different parts of your body. Let's face it, few people fit within a single size range from head to toe!

Forget your worries about wasting good fabric on pattern hopefuls. These patterns work. They've been tried on by women of all sizes and shapes. Patterns in *No Time to Sew* are foolproof. You're making a garment that you'll love, from a pattern you'll use again and again. I have nine pairs of full pull-on pants in my wardrobe, six pairs of slim pull-on pants—I just made two more recently—three jackets, two dresses, one tunic, and one lounge robe (the last two from the dress pattern), five T-shirts, four tuxedo shirts, and too many vests to count.

What I love about these patterns is that they're so versatile—merely by changing the fabric, you have a whole new look. My suggestions for suitable fabrics for each garment are easy to find at the beginning of each chapter.

You want and deserve success each time you sew. That's what this book is all about—success the first time, in shapes you'll love so much that you'll keep making them over and over. To spark your creativity, look for "The Next Step" at the end of each chapter. There you'll find creative alternatives for the same pattern.

In addition to guiding you effortlessly through the construction of each piece, I have tried to teach you techniques that you can use in a variety of garments, not just the ones in this book.

No Time to Sew offers pleasurable sewing that will result in some very special garments—garments that I hope you'll enjoy making and wearing as much as I do!

Sandra Betzina

The Sewing BASKET

What You Need to Sew Your Garments

Every chapter of *No Time to Sew* includes a list of supplies that you need to make the featured garment. In addition to these items, you need some basic supplies, which I have listed here. I suggest that you assemble these supplies, and put them in a sewing basket so that you'll have them on hand when you're ready to start sewing. There's nothing worse than wasting 30 minutes looking for your scissors, pins, and other notions every time you sit down to sew.

- Clear ruler
- Dressmaker's chalk
- Dressmaker's pins
- Dressmaker's tissue paper
- Dressmaker's tracing paper and tracing wheel, or a water- or air-erasable marking pen
- Hand sewing needles
- Pencil
- Point turner
- Press cloth
- Rolled towel or sleeve roll
- Seam ripper
- 7-inch or 8-inch shears
- Sharp scissors
- Tailor's clapper
- Tailor's ham
- Tailor's square (an L-shaped ruler)
- Tape measure
- Thimble
- Transparent tape

Sandra says

STOCK UP Once I start sewing, I hate to leave the house for anything, especially thread. So once a year I take a thread inventory, drawing up a list of colors that I'm low on or no longer have. On my next trip to the fabric store, I buy the items on my list. And no, I don't care if I use a thread that isn't an exact color match with my fabric.

Welcome to My Studio

One of the keys to sewing faster and better is an organized and well-equipped sewing space. I've sewn in a wide variety of circumstances, including all of the hotel rooms that I stay in when I'm on tour. While you may not have the luxury of converting a loft in your home as I did 14 years ago, I do hope that you can use some of my time saving ideas.

1 These are cardboard patterns. For easy access I hang them up next to my other bulky items, such as drafting paper and rolls of tracing paper.

2 It always pays to have extra thread in a variety of colors. Fabric and thread don't need to be an exact match, so I buy most of my thread (and extra zippers) during one annual shopping trip. By avoiding trips to the fabric store for forgotten notions, I have saved lots of time.

3 Buttons and trims go in these four drawers. I always consider using something from my "collection" before I buy new notions.

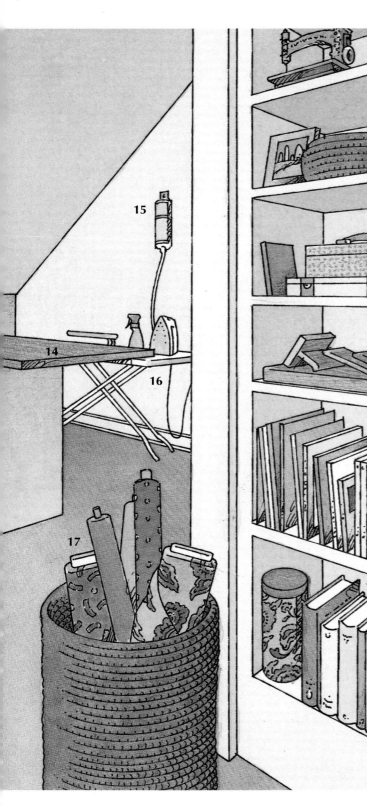

6 This is where I like to spend my time . . . in front of a sewing machine. Manufacturers lend me their machines to try so that I can answer students' questions about specific brands.

7 A little basket holds equipment that I need while sewing. I don't have to search for a seam ripper, small scissors, chalk, beeswax, hand sewing needles, or a 6-inch (15-cm) ruler.

8 Storage space is important, even though I'm not a "neatnik." The drawer under my sewing machine holds bobbins, zippers, and alternate presser feet.

9 My pressing surfaces are always set up. This is my Elnapress, which I use to fuse interfacing to fabric because it fuses large areas quickly.

10 I'm not a "fabrica-holic." When I finish a garment, I throw out my fabric scraps. I only keep shoulder pads, interfacing, and some extra lining.

11 Scissors are always handy in this container. I don't waste time searching for pairs that "disappear" while I'm sewing.

12 Patterns go in these two drawers. I keep only the ones that I love. I throw out the "dogs" so I can forget about the time I wasted on them.

13 I make fewer mistakes when I don't have to strain to see what I'm doing, so there's spot lighting at the cutting table and at the machines.

14 When I get in the mood to cut fabric (one of my least favorite sewing tasks), I do several garments at once. My cutting table is 40 inches (100 cm) high, and the surface is 49 × 93 inches (124.5 × 236 cm).

15 My steam iron is always on when I sew so I don't have to wait for it to heat up when I want to press something. I like the instant response of a gravity-fed system that has a wall-mounted water bottle.

16 I use a Shirtmaker ironing board, which I love because it's a wide 21 inches (53 cm) and it's sturdy.

17 This basket holds fabric that I love but haven't dedicated to a particular project. Keeping the material in a visible place prevents me from forgetting about it.

4 If you don't have a serger, you should think about getting one. You won't spend nearly as much time pinking or turning under seam allowances.

5 Some sewers toss scraps on the floor as they sew, then sweep them up later. Not me. I keep a wastebasket right beside me in my sewing area.

Full Pull-On PANTS

Flattering Style for All Figures

*I*f you think full pants aren't flattering on you, I urge you to give this pair a try. I have a long waist and short legs so I'm very sensitive to anything that might make my legs look shorter and me wider. For the longest time I thought that full pants would be the worst possible style for me. I avoided them until I inherited a pair from my "twenty-something"-year-old daughter. They hung in my closet for the longest time until one day I gave the full pants a try because I had a sweater that was a perfect match. Not only did I receive lots of compliments, but the mirror also told me they looked good.

I was hooked.

Now I own lots of pants in this style. If the garment fabric is drapey, these pants are flattering on everyone. I think that you'll also love their versatility. As far as I'm concerned, they are a real wardrobe basic. The full pants can be worn with a jacket, a loose sweater, a vest, or an overblouse. Slimmer gals have even more choices because the pants look good with short sweaters and tucked-in shirts or bodysuits.

The best part of these stylish pants is that you can sew up a pair in three hours or less—and this includes the time you'll spend cutting out the pattern pieces.

This is no ordinary shirred waistband. Usually the waistband is finished, and then separate pieces of elastic are inserted into each of three channels. But there's a faster method. In this chapter you'll learn to sew in a single length of elastic at the same time that you finish the waistband. Topstitching the elastic while you stretch it gives the shirred effect.

What You Need

The amount of fabric that you need to make these full pants is the same, regardless of your size, fabric nap or print, and material width. This makes it so easy to shop because you don't have to refer to the yardage table every time you find something that you like.

"One of the things I like about full pants is that I feel feminine in them, almost as though I'm wearing a skirt. And since full pants in drapey fabrics are now a classic, I always feel in fashion. You can also use my pattern to make shorts by simply using the cut-off line in the pattern."

Fabric Yardage for Full Pants

Fabric width	Small	Medium	Large
All fabric widths	2⅝ yards (2.4 m)	2⅝ yards (2.4 m)	2⅝ yards (2.4 m)

Fabric Yardage for Shorts

Fabric width	Small	Medium	Large
All fabric widths	1¾ yards (1.6 m)	1¾ yards (1.6 m)	1¾ yards (1.6 m)

Appropriate Fabric

When choosing fabric for full pants, your goal is to find soft fabric that hangs gracefully in small vertical folds that are close to the body. Good candidates are wool jersey, imported cotton knit, rayon velvet, velour, 2-ply and 3-ply silk crepe de chine (4-ply is too heavy), rayon crepe, rayon challis, fluid polyester georgette, or a double layer of chiffon.

Sandra says

BAN THE REST Ban-rol Stretch Elastic is the only elastic I've used that doesn't lose its "oomph" when top-stitched. This monofilament nonroll elastic comes in several widths. Choose the 1½ inch (1 cm) wide if you want the look of ready-to-wear.

TRY BEFORE YOU BUY

Sandra says

Before you purchase fabric, go to a mirror and unravel several yards of fabric. Gather the fabric in your hands and drape it on your body. If the fabric hangs in soft folds, it's a keeper. But if the fabric forms large folds that stand away from your body, put this bolt back. Full pants in this fabric will make you look heavy and you'll never wear them.

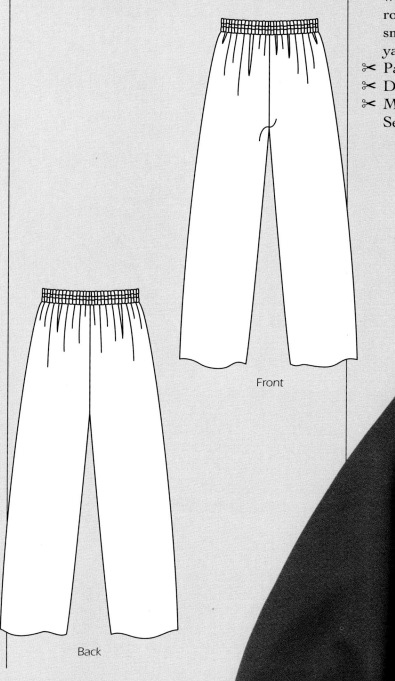

Front

Back

Notions

- ✂ Matching thread: fine machine embroidery for chiffon or georgette, all-purpose polyester or cotton thread for other fabrics
- ✂ Sewing machine needles: 10/70H for silk, rayon crepe, and challis; 10/70HS for knits; 8/60H or 9/65H for chiffon and georgette
- ✂ 1-inch (2.5-cm)-wide or $1\frac{1}{2}$-inch (3.5-cm)-wide nonroll monofilament elastic, such as Banrol Stretch Elastic: $\frac{3}{4}$ yard (0.7 m) for size small, $\frac{7}{8}$ yard (0.8 m) for size medium, and $1\frac{1}{4}$ yards (1.1 m) for size large
- ✂ Package of $\frac{1}{2}$-inch (1-cm)-wide Seams Great
- ✂ Double or twin needle (for hemming)
- ✂ Miscellaneous supplies, as listed in "The Sewing Basket" on page ix

Fit Your Full Pants Pattern

Altering a pattern sure is intimidating, isn't it? But without making it perfect for your body, you'll be disappointed with the results. Luckily, you'll need to do very little to my patterns for the Rodale Designer Collection because they're made to fit and flatter many body types.

Get Started

Select your pattern size according to your hip measurement; see the size table on page 208. Since the patterns in the Rodale Designer Collection are multisized, you don't need to spend a lot of time altering them. You make adjustments by using the cutting lines for the larger and smaller pattern sizes, according to your figure variations. For example, if your hip measurements match the size small pattern but you have large thighs, you use the size small cutting lines through the hips and the size medium cutting lines in the thigh area. (See the Quick Class "Get Real" on page 8 for more advice on adjusting pattern sizes.)

LOOK IN THE MIRROR
Having a large seat is different from having a protruding seat. A woman may have 50-inch (127-cm)-wide hips but her bottom may be flat. If you suspect this is your problem, the easiest way to confirm it is to inspect your body's silhouette. Turn to your side and look at your seat in the mirror.

If you're a size large and feel that your seat protrudes excessively, add 1 inch (2.5 cm) or more to the pattern, as explained in "Protruding Seat" on the opposite page. My fitting method is so simple because I have an easy way of dealing with any extra fabric. If you have added so much that you end up with horizontal wrinkles under your seat, you can always cut it off when you fit the pants.

Flat Seat

How do you know if you have a flat seat? Any ill-fitting pants have quite a bit of excess fabric under the seat, which forms horizontal wrinkles, if you have a flat seat. If the pants have darts, there's excess fabric at the end of the darts since there isn't any body to fill it up.

Cut your full pants back one size smaller along the back inner leg starting at the crotch and continuing to the hem. For example, if you're cutting a size medium pattern, use the cutting line for small on the back inner leg only.

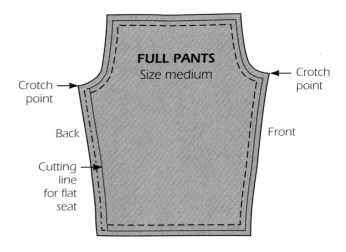

If you are using a size small, simply cut ¼ inch (5 mm) less on the back inner leg. But you don't want to narrow the leg all the way to the hem if you also have well-developed calves. In this case, cut a size smaller on the back inner leg at the crotch and taper to the original cutting line at the knee.

Protruding Seat

If you have a protruding seat that causes your pants to "cup" in the back so that the fabric follows the shape of your seat and then scoops in toward your thighs, you need this pattern adjustment. The back is trying to find more fabric so it's pulling some fabric from the front of the pants. If you are using a size medium pattern, for example, cut your full pants back one size larger along the back inner leg.

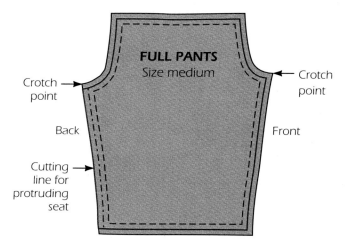

If you're using the size large pattern and need to make the pattern larger, tape tissue paper (or butcher's paper) to the back inner leg of the pattern. Add ½ inch (1 cm) to the leg from the crotch point to the bottom of the pants. This should be enough because the pants are loose-fitting.

Full Thighs

If you have full thighs, your pants are overly fitted across the front thighs, often causing a horizontal wrinkle in this area. Cut your full pants front one size larger along the front inner leg. For example, if you're using the size medium pattern, use the cutting line for size large on the front inner leg.

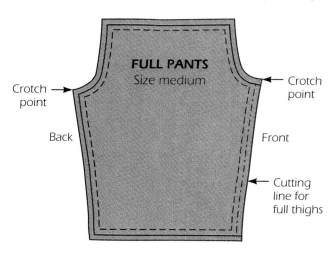

If you're following size large for all the other cutting lines, simply add ½ inch (1 cm) to the outside of the size large cutting line on the front inner leg. You can add more in this area if you like. It all depends on how close you want the fit. If you're worried about the fit, make your pattern out of an inexpensive fabric and try the pants on before you sew them from the fashion fabric. You can also refine the amount you want after you make your first pair of full pants.

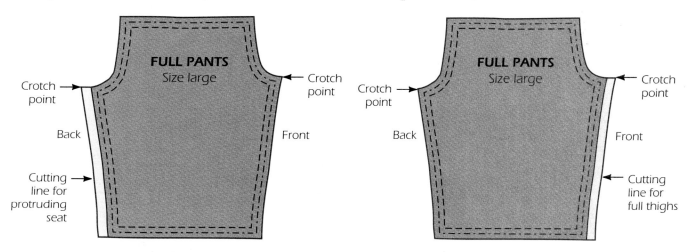

Crotch Length

Since taking this measurement is so difficult for most people, let's take a shortcut. The following pattern adjustments will get you into the ball game. You can make further refinements after you make your first pair of full pants.

If the pants you buy tend to be long in the crotch, shorten the full pants pattern on the lengthen/shorten line between the crotch point and the waistline. Draw a line 1 inch (2.5 cm) above and parallel to the lengthen/shorten line on the pattern. Fold the pattern along this line, bringing the fold down on the lengthen/shorten line. While the alteration is 1 inch (2.5 cm), the fold on the pattern is only ½ inch (1 cm) wide.

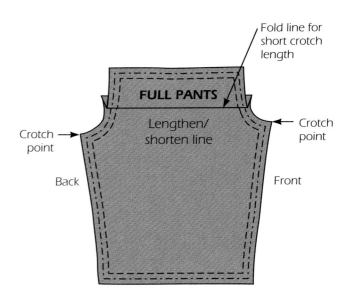

Fold line for short crotch length

FULL PANTS

Lengthen/ shorten line

Crotch point

Crotch point

Back

Front

QUICK CLASS

Get Real

Don't feel discouraged if you think you have a problem figure. All real people have problem areas. This is no big deal. I've been teaching sewing for 20 years and I have found only one individual who didn't need pattern adjustments. She fit perfectly into a size 10. (I might add that she was 5'9" and 21 years old!)

Because my patterns are multisized and based on more realistic body measurements than many commercial patterns, you'll find fitting these pants easy. Full pants are more figure- and fit-forgiving than tailored ones, so just relax and take the alterations step by step. Don't try to second-guess me because I've simplified the process for you. By the time you make your third pair of these wonderful pants, all of this will be second nature to you.

How to Choose and Adjust Your Pattern

1 To solve the problems, see where your measurements fall in the size table on page 208.

2 Use the cutting lines for whatever size matches your measurements for that part of the pattern and body. You may use one size at the waist and another size at the hips, for example.

3 If your tummy measurement is bigger than your hip measurement or within 3 inches (7.5 cm) of it, use the larger measurement in the waist, tummy, and hips. The pants will be slightly fuller over the tummy and, consequently, more flattering. They won't overfit your tummy and make this portion of your body obvious.

If the pants that you buy tend to be short in the crotch, lengthen the pattern on the lengthen/shorten line between the crotch point and waistline by 1 inch (2.5 cm).

Cut the pattern on the lengthen/shorten line and tape a piece of paper to the top half of the full pants pattern. Measure 1 inch (2.5 cm) down from the line. At this distance draw a line on the paper that is parallel to the lengthen/shorten line. Tape the lower part of the pants pattern along the line that you drew.

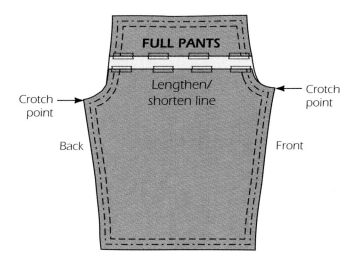

Leg Length

If you made adjustments to the crotch length, the overall length is affected. So make the overall leg length adjustments last. Your pants should end under the ankle bone. Since the legs on my full pants in the Rodale Designer Collection are straight, you can save time by making an easy length alteration at the hem.

You can determine the correct pants length by measuring from your waistline, down the side of your leg, to under the ankle bone.

Another reliable method to determine your desired length is to copy a favorite pair of pants. Measure along the side seam from under the waistband to the hemline.

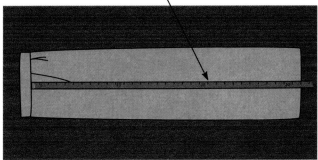

Measure from waistline to hem

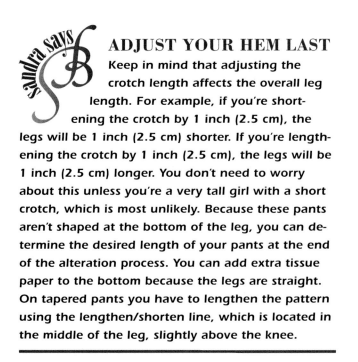

ADJUST YOUR HEM LAST
Keep in mind that adjusting the crotch length affects the overall leg length. For example, if you're shortening the crotch by 1 inch (2.5 cm), the legs will be 1 inch (2.5 cm) shorter. If you're lengthening the crotch by 1 inch (2.5 cm), the legs will be 1 inch (2.5 cm) longer. You don't need to worry about this unless you're a very tall girl with a short crotch, which is most unlikely. Because these pants aren't shaped at the bottom of the leg, you can determine the desired length of your pants at the end of the alteration process. You can add extra tissue paper to the bottom because the legs are straight. On tapered pants you have to lengthen the pattern using the lengthen/shorten line, which is located in the middle of the leg, slightly above the knee.

Compare your desired length to the pattern length. The finished lengths of the full pants pattern are listed in "Finished Length and Hem Widths" on page 208. Remember that the full pants pattern length is longer than the finished length because it includes a 1-inch (2.5-cm) allowance for the hem. Also, the measurement is taken over the hip, rather than along the leg inseam.

Tape extra dressmaker's tissue paper to the bottom of your pants pattern if you need to add length, or cut the desired amount off the bottom of the leg if you have shorter legs. The length of the full pants pattern should be 1 inch (2.5 cm) more than the measurement of your favorite pants. If the pattern length is more than 1 inch (2.5 cm) longer than the length of your favorite pants, cut the difference from the pattern.

Cut Out Your Full Pants Pattern Pieces

30 MINUTES

You'll be surprised at how little time it takes to cut out this garment. Since there aren't any side seams, there's only one pattern for the pants and another for the waistband. I don't like cutting out patterns, but I didn't mind doing this one at all.

The First Steps

1 The full width of the fabric is needed for all of the fabric widths and all of the pattern sizes.

2 If you're making shorts, cut off the bottom of the pattern, as indicated by the cutoff line printed on the pattern tissue.

3 Refer to the pattern layouts on the opposite page to position your patterns on the fabric according to your size and the width of the material.

4 Pin the pattern pieces to the fabric by placing pins in all the corners, with other pins spaced along the gaps. Cut them out.

Layout for Napped or One-Way-Design Fabrics

1 A one-way design has an obvious top and bottom. Nap refers to fabric like microfiber or one with a pile like velvet. Plan to cut the pattern through one fabric thickness for the first leg, and then flip the pattern over to cut the second leg. Otherwise you won't have mirror images, and you'll end up with two right (or left) legs.

2 Straighten the cut ends of the fabric by pulling a thread close to each edge. If it breaks, just pull on the thread next to it until the fabric puckers along the width. Cut the fabric along this pucker, so that you have a straight edge that is on grain.

3 Lay the fabric flat. Place the full pants pattern on this single layer of fabric so that the grainline printed on the pattern is parallel to the selvages. (The selvages are the tightly woven edges that run along both lengthwise edges of your fabric.) Scoot the pattern close to one selvage. Cut out the pattern. Don't cut out the waistband yet.

4 Flip the pattern over and cut it out of the remaining fabric. To ensure that the fabric nap goes in the same direction on both pattern pieces, make sure the hem is pointed in the same direction as the pattern piece that you cut out in Step 3.

5 Because the waistband is shirred, it isn't necessary to worry about the nap. If you're short on yardage after you cut out both full pants pattern pieces, fold the remaining fabric in half. Lay the waistband pattern on the fabric with one short edge on the fold. Cut out the pattern.

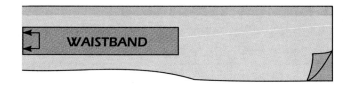

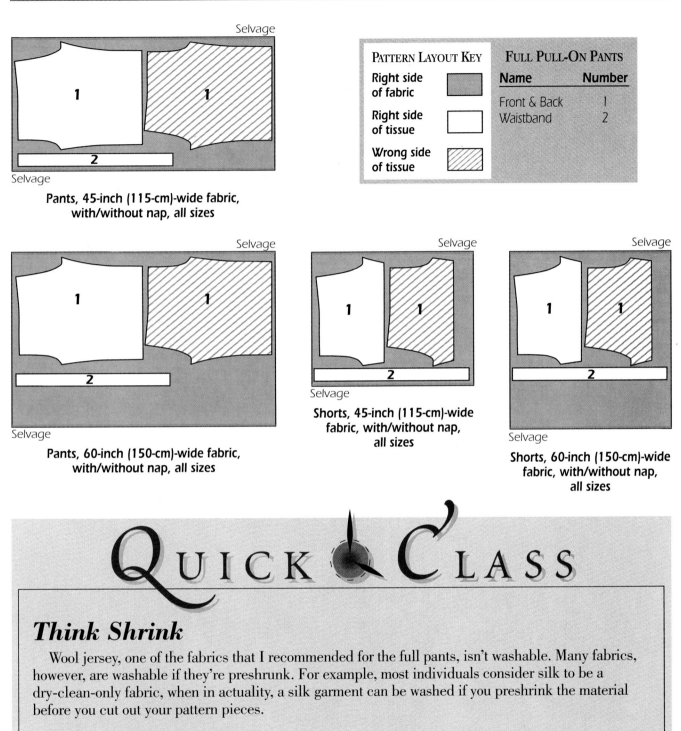

Pants, 45-inch (115-cm)-wide fabric,
with/without nap, all sizes

PATTERN LAYOUT KEY

Right side
of fabric

Right side
of tissue

Wrong side
of tissue

FULL PULL-ON PANTS

Name	Number
Front & Back	1
Waistband	2

Pants, 60-inch (150-cm)-wide fabric,
with/without nap, all sizes

Shorts, 45-inch (115-cm)-wide
fabric, with/without nap,
all sizes

Shorts, 60-inch (150-cm)-wide
fabric, with/without nap,
all sizes

QUICK CLASS

Think Shrink

Wool jersey, one of the fabrics that I recommended for the full pants, isn't washable. Many fabrics, however, are washable if they're preshrunk. For example, most individuals consider silk to be a dry-clean-only fabric, when in actuality, a silk garment can be washed if you preshrink the material before you cut out your pattern pieces.

How to Preshrink Silk

1 Preshrink your silk by hand washing the fabric in warm water with two capfuls of shampoo.

2 Let it air-dry. The best way to do this, and avoid wrinkles, is to hang the fabric over a shower curtain rod.

3 When you're ready to launder your finished garment, remember to wash and dry it in the same way that you pretreated it. This will prevent disappointment later because the fabric may shrink yet again. Then the garment won't fit and the seams will probably be puckered.

Layout for Other Fabrics

1 Straighten the cut ends of the fabric by pulling a thread close to each edge. If it breaks, just pull on the thread next to it. The idea is to draw the thread until the fabric puckers. Now cut the fabric along this pucker, so that you have a straight edge that is on-grain. It's important to start with fabric that has a straight grain because the fabric pattern pieces need to be cut on-grain. This will ensure that the finished garment hangs correctly.

2 Place the full pants pattern on the fabric so that the grainline printed on the pattern is parallel to the selvages. Scoot the pattern closer to one of the selvages so that you have enough room to cut the waistband along the opposite edge of the fabric. Place the waistband pattern on the fabric with one lengthwise edge at the selvages. Pin the patterns to the fabric. Use only enough pins to hold the pattern in place.

3 Cut out your full pants and waistband patterns from the fashion fabric. As you cut, stabilize the pattern by placing one hand on it.

QUICK CLASS

"Waist" Your Selvage

Sometimes when you sew, you are confronted with either not enough time to finish the waistband or not enough fabric to cut out a waistband. But by cutting your waistband in a specific way, you can prevent these problems before they happen.

How to Cut Your Waistband to Save Time or Fabric

1 If you don't want to bother finishing one long edge of your waistband by turning it under or serging it, then cut out the waistband with one long edge on the selvage. Since a selvage has tightly woven threads, it won't fray. The selvage provides a nice edge that will be visible on the pants when they are finished.

2 If you're running low on fabric, don't worry. Place your waistband on the crosswise grain, running from selvage to selvage. Since the waistband on your full pants is shirred by elastic, you won't need the stability that you would get by cutting on the lengthwise grain, which is parallel to the selvage.

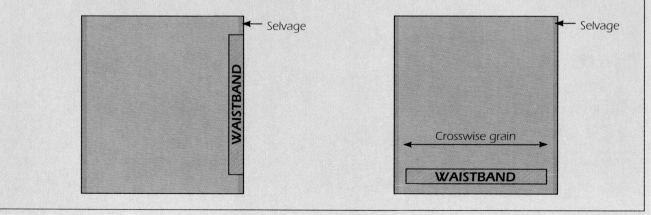

Construct Your Full Pants

2 1/2 HOURS

*O**nce you make your first pair of full pants, you'll be knocking out another
pair in two hours or less. They're so comfortable and versatile, you'll want
lots of them in your wardrobe. Each pant leg is constructed separately,
joined with a crotch seam, and then hemmed.*

Sew the Inner Leg Seam

1 All the seam allowances are 5/8 inch (1.5 cm) wide and the stitch length is medium (10 to 12 stitches per inch or 2.5 on a 0-to-4 stitch length setting), unless otherwise indicated. If you own a serger, serge the cut edges of each leg separately through a single layer of fabric.

2 Fold one of the full pants pattern pieces in half lengthwise with the right side of the fabric inside. Pin together the cut edges of the inner leg seam. The front and back legs are not exactly the same length. You have to distribute the extra fabric along the seam so that they're the same length when the seam is completed. Sew the pants pattern piece with the longer side against the feed dogs. The "teeth" of the feed dogs will help to ease the larger side to the smaller. Sew the inner leg seam.

3 Press the inner leg seam allowances open. If desired, place a rolled towel or sleeve board under the seam. This will help the seam allowances stand upright, thereby making it easier for you to open them in order to press them flat. Sew and press the remaining leg seam in the same manner as the first.

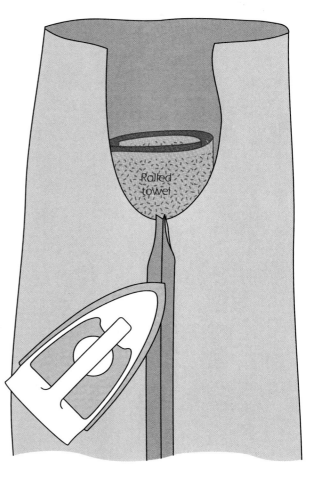

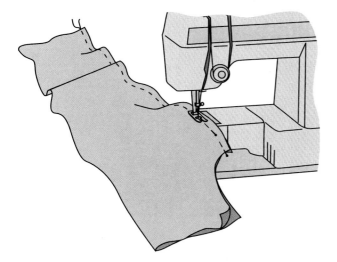

Sew the Crotch

1 Turn one of the legs right side out. Insert this right-side-out leg into the wrong-side-out leg. Pin the crotches together, matching the inner leg seams and notches. The crotch seam looks like a horseshoe. Sew the crotch seam, starting at either the front or the back crotch.

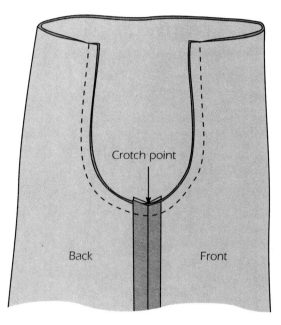

Crotch point

Back   Front

2 Clip into the seam allowances of the crotch curve. Make a cut 3 inches (7.5 cm) away from both sides of the inner leg seam.

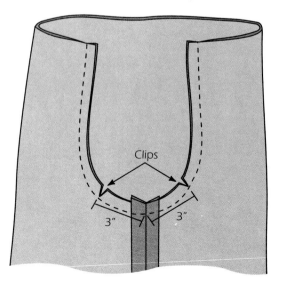

Clips

3"   3"

LENGTH MATTERS You can easily find the back of your pants by comparing the length of the front and back of the crotch. The back crotch seam is always longer than the front crotch seam.

3 Trim the seam allowances between the clips in the lower crotch curve to $1/4$ inch (5 mm). Zigzag or serge together the reduced seam allowances in the lower crotch curve.

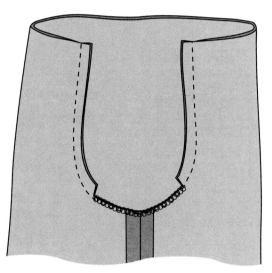

4 Press the remaining crotch seam allowances open. If desired, zigzag or serge the remaining seam allowances, but do each one separately. Turn the pants right side out.

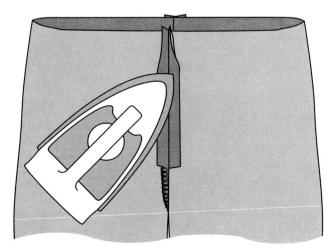

Make the Waistband

1 If you didn't cut your waistband on the selvage, serge or pink one long edge to give it a finish that won't ravel.

Serged edge

Pinked edge

2 Sew the waistband in a circle by joining the short ends with right sides together. Press the seam allowances open, and trim them to 1/4 inch (5 mm).

AVOID THE STRAIGHT AND NARROW If you're using a stretch fabric, sew the inner leg seam with a narrow width zigzag stitch of a medium length (10 to 12 stitches per inch or 2.5 on a 0-to-4 stitch length setting). This stitch will give a slight stretch to the seam, allowing it to relax with the fabric.

Apply the Waistband

1 Pin the unfinished long side of the waistband to the top of the pants, positioning the waistband seam at center back. Place the right side of the waistband against the right side of the pants.

2 The waistband and the pants should be the same size. If the waistband is too small, piece it in back so that it fits. (To piece a waistband, simply sew together several shorter pieces of the fabric to obtain the desired length.) If the waistband is a bit too large, you can ease the pants slightly to fit the waistband, just as you eased the inner leg seam. (See Step 2 on page 13.)

3 Sew the waistband to the pants. Press the seam allowances toward the waistband.

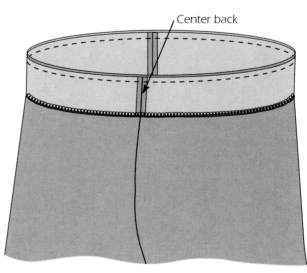

Center back

---

thread TALES

I've been teaching pants fitting for years, but the day I discovered a pattern that really worked, I was looking at a side view of myself in the mirror. I realized that the front and back halves of my body should be on different people!

I now cut a size 14 front and a size 10 back for my pants. They fit like a dream. Because I want to make sewing fun and easy, I took care of this figure dilemma when I designed the pants patterns for the Rodale Designer Collection.

Sandra

Join and Insert the Elastic

1 Cut a piece of elastic the length of your honest waist measurement minus 4 inches (10 cm). The elastic is cut smaller than your waist because elastic stretches slightly as it's topstitched. If your fabric is slightly heavy, like velvet or velour, cut the elastic 5 inches (12.5 cm) smaller than your honest waist measurement. If you have a small waist and large hips, with a difference of 10 inches (25 cm) or more between the two measurements, for example, you need to experiment to make sure that the elastic cut to fit your waist will stretch over your hips. If it doesn't, cut the elastic a little longer. Also, when you sew the waistband, eliminate the topstitching rows. Since topstitching makes the elastic lose some of its elasticity, this ensures that the elastic maintains maximum stretch so that it can go over your hips and still fit your waist.

2 Now join the ends of the elastic together to make a circle. To eliminate elastic bulk at the seam, butt the elastic ends together over a 2-inch (5-cm)-wide piece of scrap fabric that's cut twice the width of the elastic. Zigzag the ends of the elastic to the fabric scrap. Be sure that the elastic ends are butted together, not overlapped. Fold the fabric scrap over to enclose the elastic ends. Zigzag the scrap in place. This prevents the ends of the elastic from poking through the waistband.

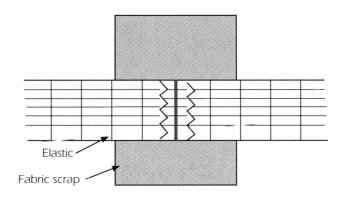

Elastic

Fabric scrap

QUICK CLASS

Measurable Results

Your waist size is one of the most difficult measurements to be honest about, especially if it's over 30 inches (76 cm). In fact, many women don't even realize that they're "cheating" when they take this measurement. I have a quick trick: Hide the inches so that you're forced to be honest.

How to Measure Your Waist

1 Turn the measuring tape over so that the metric side is out. This is the side that you're going to use to take your waist measurement.

2 Wrap the measuring tape around your waist. Cinch the tape so that it's snug but not uncomfortable. Hold the tape measure so that a finger is between the tape and your body.

3 With the tape measure still wrapped around your waist, sit down. Is the tape still comfortable? If it doesn't feel quite right, perhaps a bit snug, then let it out a little.

4 Now open up the tape with your thumb on the centimeter marking for your waist measurement. Look at the inch side. The number at your thumb is your correct waist measurement.

TALK'S CHEAP Don't get hung up on the "right" words when you're reading sewing instructions. We all have different names for the same procedures. For example, years ago I apprenticed with a woman who had worked in a couture house. She felt strongly that the term "stitch-in-the-ditch" was uncouth and insisted that I substitute "well" for "ditch." After two years, I was totally brainwashed.

3 Fold the elastic in half along the seam that you made in Step 2. This seam is center back; center front is the fold at the opposite end of the elastic. Mark center front on the elastic with a pin.

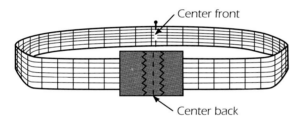

Center front

Center back

4 Position the circle of elastic on the wrong side of the waistband at the waistline seam, between the waistband and the seam allowance of the waistline seam that joins the waistband to the pants. Position the elastic's seam at the waistband's center back seam.

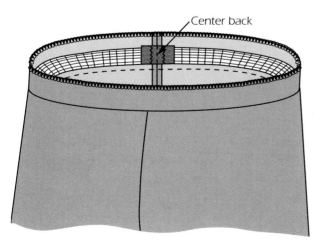

Center back

5 Anchor the elastic to the waistband by sewing through the waistband and the elastic in the "well," or "ditch," of the center back seam.

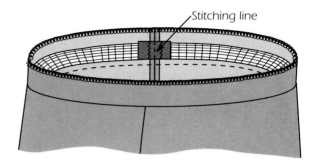

Stitching line

Complete the Waistband

1 Bring the waistband up away from the pants and wrap it around the elastic and into the inside of the pants so that the long finished side extends past the waistline seam by about $1/4$ inch (5 mm). The waistband wraps around the elastic for a pretty snug fit.

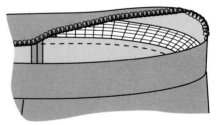

2 The waistband is sewn down in sections. Start by pinning the waistband in the well of the waistline seam from the right side of the pants. Wrap the waistband around the elastic along its length as far as you can without stretching the elastic. This will enable you to encase the elastic while working on a flat surface. The pants will be bunched up at the far end since there's more fabric there than relaxed elastic. Pin the part of the waistband that is un-bunched to the well of the seam, catching the seam allowance of the long, finished side of the waistband with the pins.

3 Install a zipper foot on your sewing machine. Now enclose the elastic in the waistband by sewing the waistband in the well of the waistline seam from the outside of the band only as far as you have pinned. Don't catch the elastic in this stitching since the elastic must be able to move freely. Backstitch and break your threads.

4 Take the pants out of the machine. Pull on the elastic so that the part of the waistband that you stitched in Step 3 scrunches up on the elastic. Keep pulling the elastic and scrunching up the band until you have enough elastic to lie flat around the waistband. Repeat Steps 2 and 3 for the remainder of the waistband until your elastic is completely enclosed.

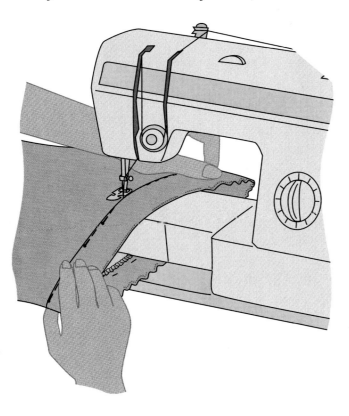

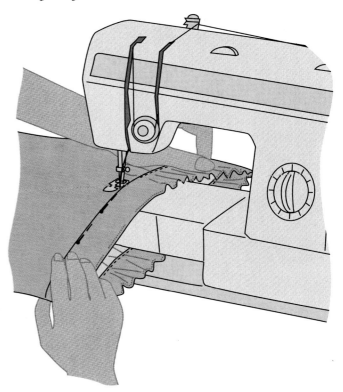

Sandra says

USE GOOD SHEARS Using sharp scissors saves time because I'm not struggling to cut through my fabric. If you don't own a good, sharp pair of scissors, you probably get very frustrated every time that you cut patterns from fashion fabric. You should treat yourself to a pair of Gingher serrated shears. They're the best that I've ever used. The 7-inch and 8-inch (17-cm and 20-cm) lengths are the best choices. They're also available in left-hand models. I own three pairs of shears but I always switch to the Ginghers if I have inadvertently picked up another pair. Unfortunately, funky old scissors are difficult to throw away because we always intend to get them sharpened but never do.

Shirr the Waistband

1 Evenly distribute the fabric gathers. Eyeball the width of the waistband and roughly divide it into thirds lengthwise. Switch to a straight-stitch presser foot.

2 Topstitch the waistband so that it's divided into thirds. The first row of stitching is 1/8 inch (3 mm) from the waistline seam. As you stitch, pull the elastic and waistband taut by grasping the material in front of and behind the needle. On velvet and velour, one row of topstitching in the middle of the band is sufficient; on heavier fabric such as these, more rows reduce the waistband's elasticity too much.

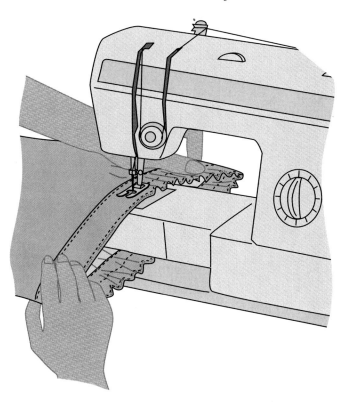

Hem the Pants

1 Turn under a 1-inch (2.5-cm) hem at the bottom of both legs. Pin the hems in position.

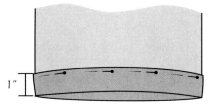

2 Try on your pants and check the length while wearing shoes. The pants should be the correct length if you altered the legs before you cut out the pattern. The correct pant length is right under the ankle bone. Adjust your hem, if necessary.

3 Lightly press just the fold on your hem, remove the pins, and open out the hem. Clean finish the bottoms of the legs by serging or enclosing them with Seams Great. Pull a strip of Seams Great until it cups around the cut edge of the bottom of the leg. Zigzag the Seams Great in place.

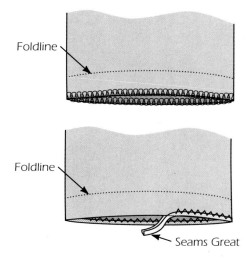

4 You now have the choice of hand hemming or machine hemming. If time is of the essence, I suggest machine hemming. However, machine hemming napped fabrics like velvet and velour isn't a good idea. They look nicer hand stitched. (See "Hand Hemming" on page 27.)

Machine Hemming

1 In my opinion, the fastest and most professional hems are done with the double, or twin, needle. If your machine has a zigzag stitch, it can accommodate a double needle. These needles come in a variety of widths, with the width being the spacing between the needles. My favorite double needle width is the Schmetz 4.0/100.

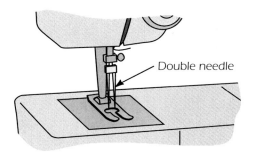

2 To use a double needle, you must have thread feeding from two separate sources. If your machine spindle isn't long enough to hold two spools of thread, wind thread onto a bobbin and position the bobbin underneath the spool on the spindle.

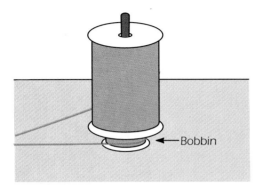

← Bobbin

3 Both top threads go through the same thread guides. For smooth stitches, put one thread on either side of the tension disk, then continue threading through the guides to the needles.

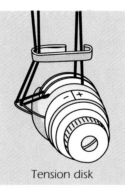

Tension disk

4 Topstitching using a double needle and a straight stitch forms two rows of parallel stitching on the right side and a zigzag stitch connecting the two rows on the wrong side.

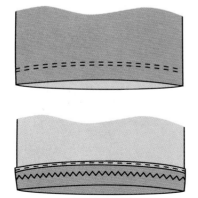

5 Because the topstitching is sewn from the right side of the garment, approximately 1/4 inch (5 mm) down from the top of the hem, position the pins with the heads facing you and the bulk of the pants to your left. This will enable you to remove pins easily as you sew. Pin on the outside of the garment.

6 Using a straight stitch (9 stitches per inch or 3 on a 0-to-4 stitch length setting) and working from the right side, topstitch the hem in place between 3/4 inch and 7/8 inch (2 cm and 2.25 cm) from the creased edge. If you have difficulty eyeballing a uniform distance for the topstitching, mark the desired sewing line with dressmaker's chalk or a sliver of soap. Start and stop the topstitching at the inner leg seam. Press the hem flat.

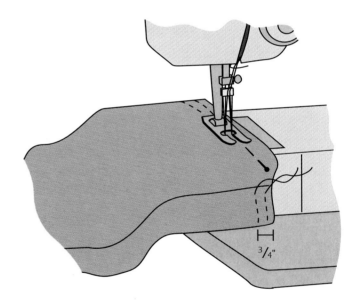

3/4"

A FREE ARM SAVES TIME

If you have a free arm on your sewing machine, topstitching the hem is a snap. You can slide the entire bottom of a leg over the free arm, which is easier than fussing with the fabric on a standard bed to make sure that the hem is flat.

Reversible Full Pants

4 HOURS

Traveling light? How about adding a pair of reversible silk pull-on pants to your wardrobe? Since the pants are reversible, wrinkling is kept to a minimum because the second layer acts as a lining. And dry cleaning costs are reduced since you can reverse the pants for additional wear.

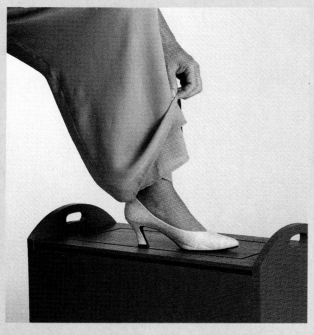

When I teach, I wear pants made in a current pattern, and often they're reversible. I make one layer slightly longer than the other since it's hard to get them even.

Add to Your Shopping List

Reversible pants are essentially two pairs of pants that are sewn together at the waist. You need to select two fabrics, and buy the amount of yardage that is listed in the following table for each one.

Fabric Yardage for Reversible Pants

Fabric width*	Small	Medium	Large
45 inches (115 cm)	2⅝ yards (2.4 m)	2⅝ yards (2.4 m)	2⅝ yards (2.4 m)
60 inches (150 cm)	2⅝ yards (2.4 m)	2⅝ yards (2.4 m)	2⅝ yards (2.4 m)

* If you select fabric with a one-way design or a nap, you won't need extra fabric for any pattern size or fabric width.

Appropriate Fabric

Double-layer pants in chiffon or georgette are a great addition to a wardrobe. Choose colors of the same value to eliminate "show through." For example, one black fabric and one white fabric won't work as reversible pants because the black layer will show through the white layer. On the other hand, a mint green layer on one side and a taupe layer on the other is quite compatible. Fabrics that convey different moods are great wardrobe extenders. Sandwashed silk on one side and chiffon or georgette on the other gives you a more casual option for day and a dressy option for night. A chiffon pair of reversible pants, with both layers in black, has a beautiful effect and limited transparency.

Notions

Use the same notions listed on page 5. Chiffon or georgette seams are less visible if you use a 60/8H or a 65/9H needle and fine machine embroidery thread.

Construct the Pants

1 Pretreat your fabric, alter the pattern, and cut out your pants pattern pieces. Don't cut out the waistband. Sew each pair of pants separately, following the steps on pages 13–14, stopping after completing Step 4 of "Sew the Crotch" on page 14. Don't attach the waistband to the pants. To prevent the vertical seams from drawing up the chiffon or georgette fabric, use a zigzag stitch on the narrowest possible width and a medium length for elasticity in the finished seams. Also pull the fabric taut at the front and back as you sew. Consider using French seams, as discussed in the Quick Class "A 'Seamless' Finish" on page 26.

2 Slip one pair of pants inside the other with wrong sides together. Machine-baste the layers together at the waist, using 6 or fewer stitches per inch or 4 on a 0-to-4 stitch length setting.

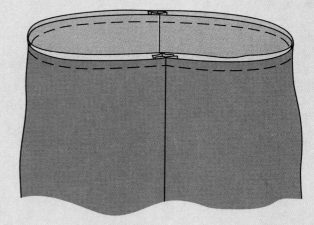

3 Cut one long strip of each of the fashion fabrics. Cut each one 3¼ inches (8 cm) wide if you're using 1½-inch (3.5-cm)-wide elastic, or 2¾ inches (7 cm) wide if you're using 1-inch (2.5-cm)-wide elastic. Use the waistband pattern to determine the length of your waistband pieces.

4 Sew the two strips of fabric together along one long edge with right sides together. Press the seam allowances open and trim them to ¼ inch (5 mm).

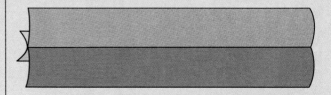

5 Press under a ⅝-inch (1.5-cm) seam allowance on one long edge of the waistband. Sew the short ends together, with right sides facing, so that the waistband forms a circle the

same circumference as the pants waistline. Open up the previously pressed edge before stitching so that the seam extends the entire width of the waistband. Let it fold again after the seam is finished. Press the seam allowances open and trim them to ¼ inch (5 mm).

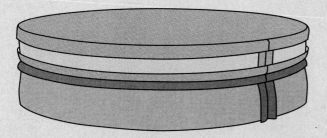

6 Fold the waistband in half along the long seamline with wrong sides together. The edge with the seam allowance that is folded under will be shorter than the other cut edge. Press. Topstitch ⅛ inch (3 mm) from the seamed edge. To make the stitching appealing, thread the top of the machine with a thread that matches the fabric you place face up on the sewing machine bed. Use thread that matches the other fabric in the bobbin. This second fabric will be face down and closest to the feed dogs.

Sandra says **CONSIDER PINKING** If you don't own a serger, cut out your full pants pattern with pinking shears or use flat fell seams. If you want to learn my fast method for making flat fell seams, see the Quick Class "The Fastest Mock Flat Fell Seam" on page 39.

7 Unfold the waistband along the seamline that you just made. With the seam at center back and right sides together, pin the wider side of the waistband to the pants at the waistline, matching the fabric on that side of the waistband to the pants fabric. Sew the waistband to the pants.

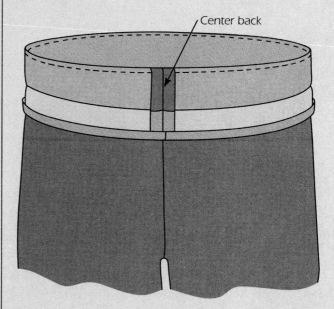

Center back

8 Press the seam allowances toward the waistband. Fold the waistband in half along the long middle seam, with wrong sides together. The loose side of the waistband and the second pants fabric now match. Enclose the waistline seam allowances over the waistline seam by pinning the edge that was turned under.

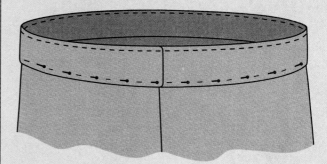

9 Topstitch, leaving a 2½-inch (6-cm) opening at center back for inserting the elastic. The color of the top thread must match the fabric next to the presser foot. The color of the bottom thread must match the fabric next to the feed dogs.

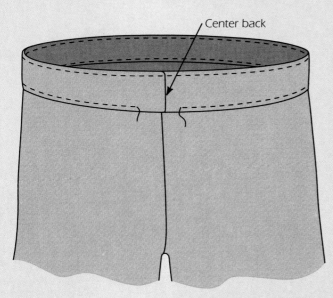

Center back

10 Insert your waistband elastic and finish the waistband, as explained in "Shirr the Waistband" on page 18.

Sandra says

CORRECT THE LENGTH
Chiffon loses some of its length in loft since it hangs slightly away from the body. So hem chiffon pants ½ inch (1 cm) longer than you do similar pants in another fabric so that they'll be the correct length when you wear them.

Hem the Pants

1 Hem the layers separately using a hand-rolled hem or a machine-stitched edging.

2 Since it's impossible to have reversible pants always hang correctly at the bottom without the inside layer showing, favor one layer by hemming it ½ inch (1 cm) longer than the other layer. The longer length of one side of the pants will add a nice contrast when you wear the pants with the shorter side facing out.

Machine-Stitched Rolled Hem Edging for Sheer Fabrics

1 This machine hem for sheers is not only "un-bulky," as I would say, but also fast and professional-looking. You don't use a rolled hem foot or a special hemming stitch setting. At the bottom of the leg, press ½ inch (1 cm) to the wrong side. Using your narrowest zigzag width setting and smallest stitch length, sew along the fold so that one side of the stitches goes off the fold.

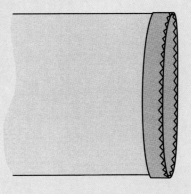

2 Sewing on the fold is usually quite sufficient to prevent stretching. But if the fold is stretching as you sew, you can prevent the fabric from coming out of the presser foot too quickly by placing a finger on the fabric behind the presser foot. Let the fabric build up for a few inches before releasing it. Repeat.

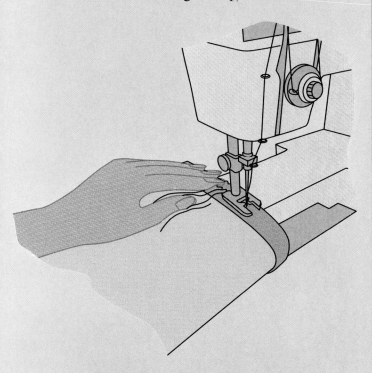

3 Trim away the excess fabric beyond the stitches at the fold using sharp scissors. Press flat.

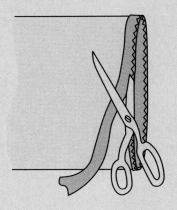

SHOP WISELY Don't you hate it when you make a pair of pants from a gorgeous fabric, and then discover that the fabric is too scratchy or doesn't hang right? Believe me, it happens to the best of us. Since I've made so many pairs of full pants, I know what fabrics will work best for the garment.

What do the fabrics of my favorite full pants have in common? All of my favorites are made with drapey material. I also like fabrics that are soft to the touch. I have a trick for deciding if a fabric is soft enough for me. You should try it the next time you're in a fabric store: Rub the inside of your wrists against the fabric that you're thinking of buying. If it's scratchy, chances are you'll never wear it.

You should also carefully consider the fabric's color before taking the bolt to the cutting table. Why would you want to make a pair of pants that won't match any of your blouses? (Unless you're looking for an excuse to sew some tops to match the pants.)

What colors are your favorite items? Most of us tend to gravitate toward colors that look flattering on us. If you only wear gray, white, or black when you are well rested—and you're never well rested—why put any more items in these colors in your wardrobe?

In the last chapter in this book, I explain how to coordinate the colors in your wardrobe as well as how to use a color wheel. You may want to read "Putting It All Together," starting on page 194, before you buy fabric to make your full pants.

QUICK CLASS

A "Seamless" Finish

I find that garments made of sheer or fine fabrics look best with French seams. Such a treatment encloses the seam allowances so that the cut edges don't show through to the right side of the garment.

How to Make a French Seam

1 Pin the wrong sides of your fabric together with the cut edges of the seam allowances even. Sew a seam with ⅜-inch (9 mm) seam allowances. Use tiny-width zigzag stitches if your fabric is stretchy.

⅜"

seam allowances are visible at the seamline, sew another line of tiny zigzag stitches with a slightly deeper seam allowance.

2 Press the seam allowances closed. Fold the fabric along the seamline with right sides together, enclosing the seam allowances. Press. Sew a line of stitching a scant ¼ inch (5 mm) from the fold, completely enclosing the seam allowances.

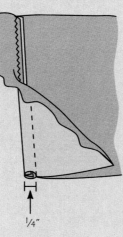

¼"

A French seam makes the inside of a pant leg look almost as good as the outside. There is a seam allowance but no visible cut edges. As you can see, I used a rather large hem on this pant leg to give it some weight.

3 After a few inches of stitching, check to make sure no loose threads from the trimmed seam allowances protrude from the most recent line of stitching. If the

Hand Hemming

1 To make the hand-hemming process easier, I sew a row of machine stitches 1/4 inch (5 mm) from the bottom of each leg. All of the legs are sewn separately. Simply let the edge of the presser foot ride along the cut edge of the fabric. If you cannot change the needle position, simply sew a little farther away from the edge of the fabric. This prevents the needle from pushing fine fabric, like chiffon, down into the bobbin thread hole.

2 At the pressing surface, use the stitching line as a "pulling point" to roll the cut edge of the fabric approximately 1/4 inch (5 mm) to the wrong side of the fabric.

3 After you complete one roll, make a second roll that encloses the cut edge of the first roll. Little by little, pin the second rolled edge to the pressing surface cover and press down the second crease. If you are working on a natural fiber like silk, the crease stays in position without pinning. Complete all four legs in this manner.

Sandra says

PREVENT FRAYING

Once in a while I notice that tiny "hairs" ravel away from a trimmed edge. When this happens, I seal the edge with a liquid seam sealant, such as Fray Stop Spray or Fray Check. Both are commonly available in fabric stores.

4 Find yourself a comfortable chair with good lighting. Start by hiding the knot in your thread under the inside leg seam. Slide the needle along the fold for 1/4 inch (5 mm) and bring the needle and thread up out of the fabric. Take a stitch in the leg, then slide the needle back into the fold, progressing 1/4 inch (5 mm) farther. Continue around the leg in this manner. At the end, take a few tiny stitches and break your thread. If necessary, press once more.

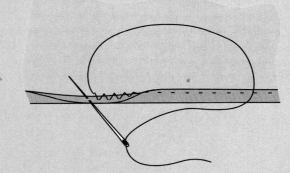

Slim Pull-On
PANTS

The Ultimate Wardrobe Extender

Think of these pants as "wardrobe extenders"—ways to take pieces you already own and make them work in today's fashion picture. They're comfortable and stylish. They can be worn with many tops and sew up really quickly. Even fitting the pattern is a breeze. With my system, it won't take you more than an hour to adjust for your figure variations.

These pants are easy to make because they only have a few seams, fitting is minimal, and you don't need to thread a serger. After I made my first pair, I couldn't stop. I made four more pairs over the next four weeks. I made so many because I had some terrific tops that cried out for mates.

What makes these pants work is that they make you look thin. Impossible? Try a pair with a long, loose top and see how pleasing the proportions are. If you think that slim pants are only for women with perfect figures, think again. Anyone can wear slim pants if they're paired with a top that covers figure faults. The slim pants look best with a top— whether it's a big sweater, big shirt, jacket, or vest—that's crotch length or longer. If your thighs are large, wear your top a little longer.

After you've made your first pair, try the more advanced project featured in "The Next Step" on page 45, where I explain how to make a vented hem.

The waistband on my slim pants for the Rodale Designer Collection is slightly smaller than the circumference of the pants' waist. After it's sewn onto the pants, an elastic circle is inserted, and the waistband is wrapped around the elastic and is secured by stitching the "well" of the waistband seam. There's no hand sewing!

What You Need

These pants require fabric that has some stretch. But don't let the thought of sewing this type of fabric intimidate you. I have plenty of tips that'll help, like using woolly nylon on the bobbin, plus there are only three seams and two hems in the entire garment!

❝ *I own seven pairs of slim pants: black, brown, charcoal, gray, olive, burgundy, and off-white. They're so comfy and versatile that I wear them with T-shirts in the summer and sweaters in the cooler months. Because these pants don't hug my calves and ankles, they have a slimming effect. I like to add a vent to the hem; instructions for this treatment are featured on page 45.* **❞**

Fabric Yardage for Slim Pants

Fabric width	Small	Medium	Large
60 inches	2¼ yards	2½ yards	2¾ yards
(150 cm)	(2 m)	(2.25 m)	(2.5 m)

Note: This pattern is only suitable for stretch fabric that's 60 inches (150 cm) wide.

Appropriate Fabric

The absolute first choice for these pants is wool double knit. It has a nice weight, doesn't wrinkle, and most importantly, has great resiliency. Pants made from this fabric return to their original shape after hanging overnight. Other good fabrics are stretch velour, wool and Lycra blends like stretch wool crepe, and stretch denim. You might find a cotton knit that has enough Lycra to prevent the knees and seat from bagging. Before you buy, stretch the fabric on the crosswise grain. If it returns to its original shape, you have a winner. If the edges of the fabric curl, put the bolt back.

Sandra says

SEW FAST I don't always use the right notion. There are times when being precise isn't important. For example, I can never find my chalk. When I'm marking a waistband, I'll just stick a pin in center front rather than going on a treasure hunt.

Notions

- ✂ One spool of woolly nylon thread, off-white or black, whichever blends best with your fabric
- ✂ Matching sewing machine thread
- ✂ 1-inch (2.5-cm)-wide Action Elastic, Ban-rol Stretch Elastic, or No-Roll Elastic
- ✂ 3 inches (7.5 cm) of ribbon or seam tape, any width
- ✂ Double needle, size 4.0/100
- ✂ Miscellaneous supplies, as listed in "The Sewing Basket" on page ix

TRY MY WOOLLY IDEA

You don't need a stretch stitch to make these slim pants from a stretchy fabric. Instead, use a very narrow zigzag stitch, regular sewing thread for the needle, and woolly nylon on the bobbin.

Woolly nylon is commonly used on sergers but that doesn't mean you can't use it on your sewing machine. The only thing you need to remember is to wrap it on to the bobbin by hand so that it doesn't lose its stretch. Yes, this takes more time than winding it with your sewing machine, but you'll be much happier with the results. I save time by winding several bobbins at a time while I'm talking on the phone. You can even watch TV while doing this task.

Woolly nylon is also good for double-needle hemming. Since it's only used on the bobbin, its color doesn't have to match the fabric exactly. I own two spools of woolly nylon, one black and one off-white. One of these will work as the bobbin thread whenever I need stitching that stretches.

Front

Back

Fit Your Slim Pants Pattern

This pattern doesn't have side seams. Consequently, the sizing is done through the crotch. All of the alterations are simple, regardless of your figure problem. Together we'll tackle your problem, whether it's your seat, thighs, crotch, or waist.

Get Started

Determine your correct size by matching your hip measurement to the size table on page 208. All the patterns in this book are multisized so you can use different sizes for different parts of your body. In each of the categories below, I show you how to determine if you have a particular problem and explain how to adjust your slim pants pattern to accommodate your body shape.

Protruding Seat

A woman with a protruding seat looks better in pants than women with other figure types. However, if a woman with a protruding seat wears ill-fitting pants, they "smile" under the seat and overfit the area. The smile wrinkle forms because the pants are grabbing fabric from the front to accommodate the larger seat.

This figure problem is often confused with a long crotch. (See "Short or Long Crotch Length" on page 34.) You know that you have a protruding seat rather than a long crotch when crotch length is added to front and back and the front crotch on the finished garment is too long to fit you nicely. In other words, there's extra fabric that hangs too loosely between your legs. If you've never altered a pattern, you can still determine if you have a protruding seat by noting how your ready-to-wear pants fit. Only the back of your pants will pull down.

To fix this problem, all you need to do is cut a size larger on the back inner leg of the pattern. If your hips are size large and you have a protruding seat, cut ½ inch (1 cm) or more beyond the size large line. Experiment with your first pair of pants until you get the fit you want. Do this by cutting a wide seam allowance on the back inner leg so that you'll have more fabric to let out if the amount that you added to the pattern isn't enough.

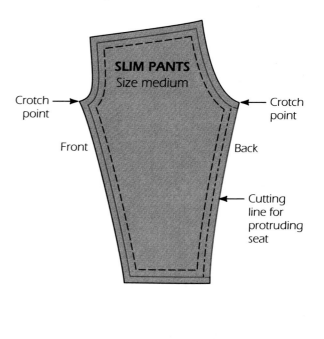

Crotch point · Crotch point

SLIM PANTS
Size medium

Front · Back

Cutting line for protruding seat

SUBSTITUTIONS ABOUND

Sandra says

Don't spend hours trying to find a press cloth. A lightweight cotton dish towel or linen napkin works just as well. A press cloth is important because the iron will scorch the fabric if left in one place too long.

Flat Seat

You have a flat seat if your pants bag under the seat. Posture also can create a flat seat. If you lock your knees and tuck in your seat, fabric wrinkles under the seat because it catches on your calves.

To accommodate this problem, cut the pattern a size smaller on the back inner leg. For example, if your hip measurement is size medium, cut the waist, front crotch, back crotch, front inner leg, and hem on the size medium lines. Cut the back inner leg on the size small line. If you're a size small with a flat seat, cut the inner leg ½ inch (1 cm) inside the size small cutting lines.

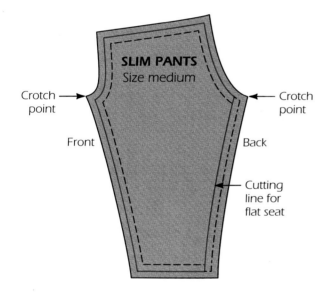

Full Thighs

Pants that don't fit often form horizontal wrinkles over and above full thighs. These wrinkles are caused because the pants are looking for more fabric to go over the thighs. Once you enlarge the full thigh area of your pattern, the pants will hang straight.

To do this, cut your pattern a size larger on the front inner leg. If you wear a size large and have large thighs, cut ½ inch (1 cm) or more beyond the size large line on the front inner leg of the pattern. Experiment with your first pair of pants until you

get the fit you want. Do this by cutting a wide seam allowance on the front inner leg so that you have more fabric to let out if the ½ inch (1 cm) that you added to the pattern isn't enough.

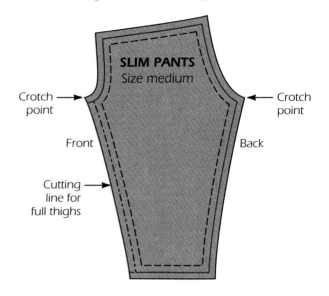

Slim Thighs

If your thighs are slim, vertical wrinkles form in the front near the inner leg seam. Cut a size smaller on the front inner leg pattern to prevent the vertical wrinkles on the finished pants. If you're a size small, cut ¼ inch (5 mm) inside the cutting line on the front inner leg.

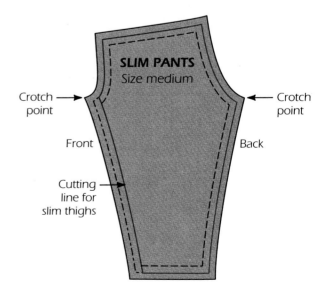

Short or Long Crotch Length

This problem is hard to diagnose, but the pattern alteration is very easy.

You can tell that you have a short crotch if you always want to roll over the waistband on your pants. You have a long crotch if the crotch seam is too high for comfort. Another figure variation, a protruding seat, is often confused with a long crotch.

Before you decide whether you have a short or long crotch, read through the description for a protruding seat on page 32.

To alter slim pants for a long crotch, cut your pattern one size larger at the waist at the top of the pants. On a size large, a long crotch is created by drawing a new cutting line ½ inch (1 cm) above the size large waist.

If you're short in the crotch, cut one size smaller at the waist at the top of the pants. On a size small, you reduce the crotch length by cutting ½ inch (1 cm) inside the size small cutting line printed on the pattern.

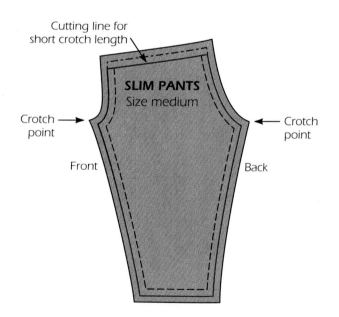

Cutting line for short crotch length

SLIM PANTS
Size medium

Crotch point — Front — Back — Crotch point

Because your slim pants fabric stretches, it isn't necessary to pay close attention to matching the crotch length on your pattern to your body's crotch length. It can be adjusted during the first fitting, before you attach the waistband.

YOU CAN HAVE BOTH Some figures are long in the crotch *and* have a protruding seat. If you're unsure about your figure variation, alter for a protruding seat and a long crotch. Any discrepancy can be corrected by trying on the pants before sewing the elastic into the waist. Your exact crotch length is determined during the first fitting. If you're not sure about this alteration, use the size large cutting lines. You can always cut off the excess fabric later.

Small or Large Waist and Tummy

If you have a small waist, pants that fit your hips are too big at the waist. If you have a large waist, you have trouble doing up the waistband button even though the pants fit at the hips.

Using the cutting lines for your pattern size, measure the slim pants pattern in the tummy area 2½ inches (6 cm) down from the waist, from cutting line to cutting line. I recommend measuring at the tummy rather than at the waist because this assures that the amount of fabric around the waist is sufficient to go over your tummy when you pull on the finished pants. Any extra fabric at the waist is drawn in by the elastic.

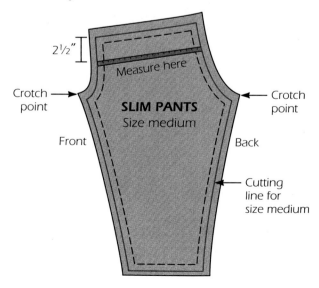

2½"

Measure here

Crotch point — Front — **SLIM PANTS** Size medium — Back — Crotch point

Cutting line for size medium

Subtract 1¼ inches (3.2 cm) from this measurement because this is the amount that will be used for the seam allowances. Since this pattern is only half of the garment, multiply your resulting measurement by 2. This is the amount of room that your pants will have.

Tie a string around your waist. Measure your tummy area about 2½ inches (6 cm) down from your natural waistline, which is where the string is positioned.

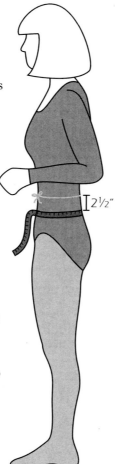

Now add 1½ inches (3.5 cm) to this measurement for ease. The ease is the amount of extra fabric you need at the tummy so that your pants aren't skintight.

Compare your pattern measurement to your tummy measurement with ease added. The difference is the amount you must alter the pattern. If you need less, use the cutting lines for a smaller size. If you need more, use the cutting lines for a larger size. Blend this new cutting line into the size that you measure at the hips.

If the amount you need at the tummy is bigger than the largest size, cut a central vertical line from the waist to the hem. Place tissue paper under your pattern.

Since the pattern is half of the pants, spread it so that the gap at the tummy is half the amount that you need to add. For example, if you need 3 more inches (7.5 cm) at the tummy, spread the pattern 1½ inches (3.5 cm). This gives you 1½ inches (3.5 cm) on each side.

Tape the pattern to the tissue paper and trim the tissue paper so it doesn't jut out.

This alteration adds fabric at the waist and the tummy. The elastic will draw in any excess fabric at the waist.

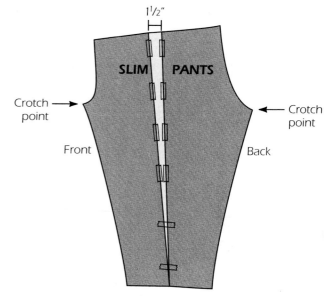

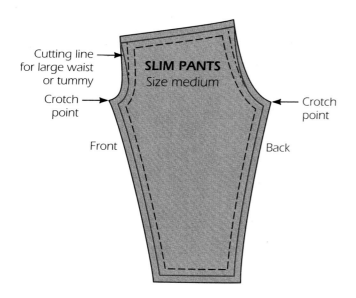

Leg Length

Measure the side of your leg from your waist to just below the ankle bone for your pants length.

If you plan to wear your pants with panty hose, make the pattern 1 inch (2.5 cm) longer than your desired pants length. Slim pants worn with panty hose have a tendency to creep up the leg a little.

Compare your desired pants length to the finished length of the pattern. (See "Finished Lengths and Hem Widths" on page 208.)

Lengthen Your Pattern

Cut through the pattern horizontally at midleg. Place tissue paper under the pattern and spread it the amount desired. Don't add more than 2 inches (5 cm). If necessary, slash and spread again 5 inches (12.5 cm) higher. Straighten the seamlines.

Shorten Your Pattern

Make a fold in your pattern at midleg. The fold's width should be half the overall amount that you want to subtract from the length. Don't subtract more than 2 inches (5 cm) in one place. If necessary, fold again 5 inches (12.5 cm) above the first fold. Shortening in this manner maintains the pants' style. Straighten the seamlines.

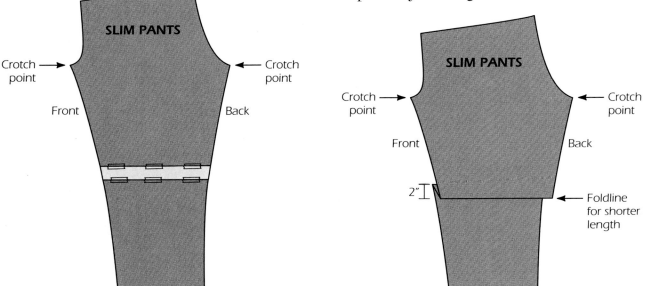

Cut Out the Pants Pattern Pieces

15 MINUTES

This is a very fast process because there are only two pattern pieces to cut out. Don't you just love that? If your time is limited, I suggest that you use the same "trick" that I have found so useful: Cut out your slim pants one evening, and sew them together the next.

1 Fold your fabric in half crosswise so that the selvages are on both sides of the fabric. (The selvages are the tightly woven edges that run along both lengthwise edges of your fabric.)

2 Place the pattern on the fabric with the grainline parallel to the selvage. Pin the pattern to the fabric by positioning pins in each corner and along the sides.

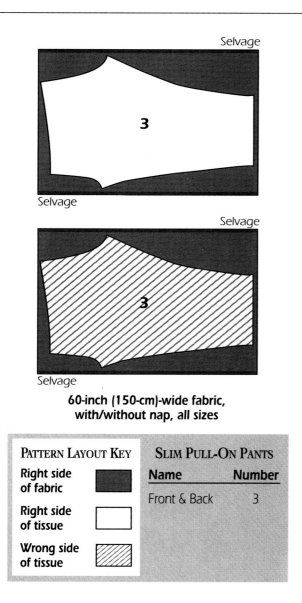

Selvage

Selvage

Selvage

Selvage

60-inch (150-cm)-wide fabric, with/without nap, all sizes

PATTERN LAYOUT KEY		SLIM PULL-ON PANTS	
Right side of fabric		**Name**	**Number**
Right side of tissue		Front & Back	3
Wrong side of tissue			

3 It's very important to make notches on the back crotch of your pattern piece. This makes it much easier and faster for you to assemble the pants. Although the back crotch is a bit longer than the front crotch, they're hard to tell apart without the notches.

4 No waistband pattern is provided. To cut a custom-fit waistband, you need to make a "pattern" for your fabric. On the crosswise grain, cut a 4-inch (10-cm)-wide strip of fabric that's 4 inches (10 cm) smaller than your honest full hip measurement. If you're very tall and have added length to the pattern, cut out your slim pants and waistband patterns at the same time.

First refold the fabric so that only one layer of fabric is at one end of the fabric. Since you cut only one waistband, a single fabric layer is all that's necessary.

Crosswise grain

4"   WAISTBAND

Hip measurement minus 4"

Selvages

Construct Your Slim Pants

2 HOURS

Since these pants have only one leg seam, they're easy to sew. Plus, the assembly instructions in this section include my "quickie" technique for getting a great fit through the crotch by adjusting the crotch length before you sew on the waistband.

Sew the Inner Leg Seam

1 All the seam allowances are ⅝ inch (1.5 cm) wide, and the stitch length is medium (10 to 12 stitches per inch or 2.5 on a 0-to-4 stitch length setting), unless otherwise indicated. Fold one pattern piece in half lengthwise with the right sides together so that the cut edges of the inner leg are even. Pin from the back of the pants. Match the top and bottom of the seam, distributing the extra fabric in the front between the pins. The front leg is slightly longer than the back inner leg so that the pants fit well under the seat. The feed dogs will ease in the excess fabric as you sew.

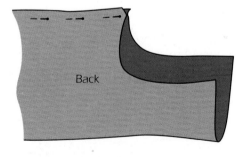

2 Put the leg under the presser foot with the front against the feed dogs. The feed dogs will ease the slightly longer front leg to the back leg. To put some stretch into the seam, sew it with a very narrow, medium-length zigzag stitch.

3 Place your seam, wrong side up, on top of a rolled towel or sleeve roll. Press the seam allowances open. Make the inner leg seam allowances into a mock flat fell seam, as shown in the Quick Class "The Fastest Mock Flat Fell Seam" on the opposite page.

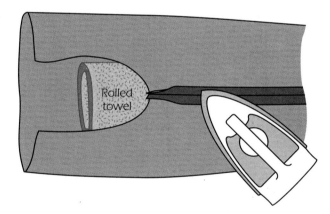

4 Sew the inner leg seam on the remaining leg, following Steps 1 through 3 on this page.

AVOID THE STRETCH STITCH Except for the hem, all the sewing on these pants is done with a little zigzag stitch. I don't use the stretch stitch provided on most sewing machines because this stitch puts too much thread in the fabric, causing the seam to stretch and curl. (See "Try My Woolly Idea" on page 31.)

QUICK CLASS

The Fastest Mock Flat Fell Seam

A flat fell seam is so versatile that you often see it in ready-to-wear clothes. It's suitable for almost any straight or slightly curved seam, and it's perfect for your slim pants.

I'm going to give you a shortcut. Because creating a flat fell seam the traditional way is a bit fussy, I'm going to use a mock flat fell seam, which accomplishes the same result, working from the right side of the garment. As well as being faster and easier, this technique reduces bulk.

How to Make the Seam

1 With right sides together and cut edges even, sew your seam with 5/8-inch (1.5-cm) seam allowances. Press them open.

2 Trim the seam allowance for the portion of the garment that is closest to the front (for your slim pants, trim the seam allowance for the front pattern piece) to 1/4 inch (5 mm).

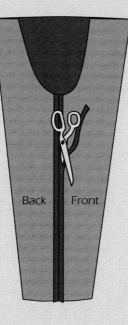

4 Turn the pants right side out. Topstitch along the seamline an even 3/8 inch (9 mm) from the seamline, as measured from the seamline to the slim pants front. As you sew, ensure that both seam allowances are smooth and flat.

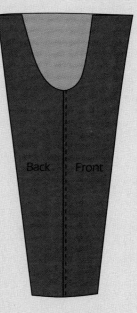

5 Turn the pants wrong side out. Trim off the excess seam allowance close to the top-stitching.

3 Flip the back seam allowance over the trimmed front seam allowance. Press.

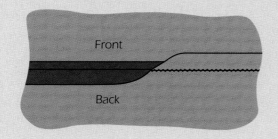

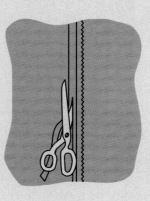

Sew the Crotch

1 Turn one leg right side out. Insert this leg
into the other leg, which is still wrong side
out. Match the inner leg seams and the notches
for the front and back crotch. With cut edges
even, pin together the horseshoe shape, which is
the crotch seam.

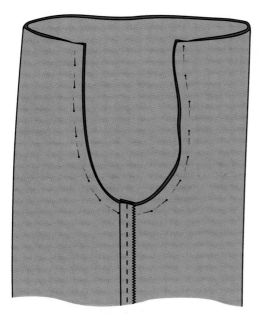

2 Sew the crotch seam with tiny zigzag
stitches. Finish the seam with a mock flat fell
seam, as explained on page 39.

Mark the Waist and Hem

1 Turn the pants right side out. Pin up a 1-inch
(2.5-cm) hem allowance, and try on the pants
while wearing shoes. Tie a piece of elastic around
your waist, and slip the top of your pants underneath it. Adjust the pants by pulling up the waist
here and there until the pants look the way you
want them to. The fit through the crotch should
be pretty close. Run dressmaker's chalk around
the pants at the bottom of the elastic.

Sandra says

NOBODY'S PERFECT Don't
be surprised if you pull up more fabric
in certain areas of your waist than in
other spots. Completely horizontal waist-
lines are in the minority.

2 Step out of the pants and lay them on a table. Connect the chalk marks to indicate your waistline. Cut off any excess fabric that's more than 5/8 inches (1.5 cm) above the chalk line.

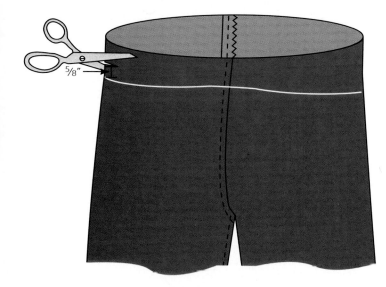

Apply the Waistband

1 To eliminate bulk, you're applying a separate waistband that's slightly smaller in circumference than the pants.

2 Sew the waistband in a circle by joining the two shorter ends. Press the seam allowances open and trim the width of each one to about 1/4 inch (5 mm). Divide the waistband in half along the width so that the seam that you just made is at one end. Make a chalk line at the other end of the waistband. This chalk mark indicates the position of center front on the waistband. The seam indicates the position of center back.

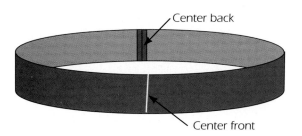

Center back

Center front

TRY BEFORE BUYING Do you end up with a lot of fabric that's beautiful but doesn't go with anything you own? When you "fall in love" with a fabric, buy 1/8 to 1/4 yard (0.1 to 0.2 m) only. Take the strip home and hang it in your closet. See what it goes with. Let it hang there for a few days, and see if you have enough items that will work with it so that you aren't committing yourself to accessorizing another entire color scheme. If I can't decide between two fabrics, no, I don't buy them both. I buy strips of each and hang them in my closet. Within a day or two, one of them is clearly "the chosen one."

3 Place the right side of the waistband against the right side of the pants, matching the waistband seam to the center back seam on the pants and also matching the center front chalk mark on the waistband with the center front seam on the pants. You can find the back of your pants by comparing the length of the front and back crotch seams. The back crotch seam is always longer than the front crotch seam. Also, the back crotch has notches. Pin the waistband to the pants. You have to stretch the waistband slightly to get it to fit the pants.

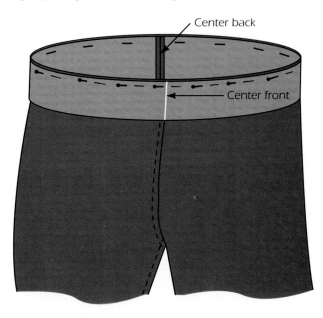

Center back

Center front

4 Sew the waistband to the pants, once again using a narrow zigzag stitch with a medium length. This will give the seam some elasticity so that you can pull the pants over your hips.

5 Cut a length of the elastic to match your honest waist measurement minus 4 inches (10 cm). (See the Quick Class "Measurable Results" on page 16.) The waistband on these pants needs to be a bit tight to keep the pants in place as you walk and sit.

Join and Insert the Elastic

1 Now join the ends of the elastic together to make a circle. To eliminate bulk caused by overlapping the elastic at the seam, butt your elastic ends together over a piece of ribbon or seam tape, which acts as a support strip. Zigzag or straight stitch each side of the elastic to the strip.

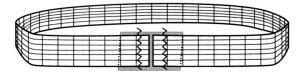

2 Sandwich the elastic between the waistband seam allowance and the waistband, matching the elastic joint with center back.

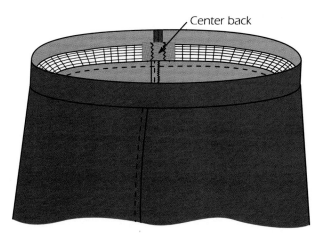

Center back

3 Wrap center back of the waistband around the elastic to the inside of the pants so that the loose lengthwise edge extends past the seamline and the waistband wraps snugly over the elastic. Using a straight stitch on the outside of the pants, sew up and down in the "well" of the waistband seam through the elastic and through both sides of the waistband. This vertical stitching through the elastic and waistband will prevent the elastic from twisting.

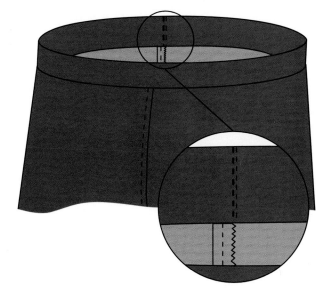

4 Working all around the waistband, wrap the waistband around the elastic. To do this, bring the waistband to the inside of the pants, extending the cut edge past the seamline on the inside of the pants. Tuck the seam allowances inside the waistband. On the right side of the pants, insert pins in the well of the seam. The pins should go through all of the layers of the fabric, including the waistband on the inside of the pants. It's not necessary to distribute the pants' and waistband's fullness evenly at this step. You adjust this after the waistband is securely anchored all around the pants.

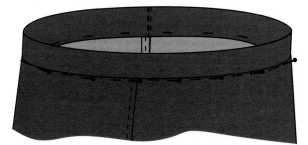

5 Stretching the pants at the waist as you go, topstitch in the well of the seam using a tiny zigzag stitch. Don't sew through the elastic.

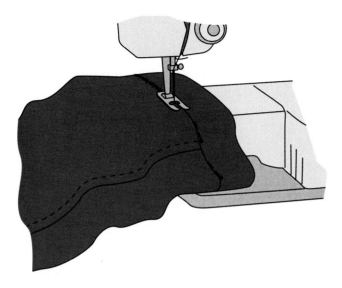

6 Remove the pants from the bed of the sewing machine. On the inside of the pants, trim away the excess waistband fabric that hangs below the stitching line. If your pants are made with a fabric other than a knit, trim the fabric with pinking shears.

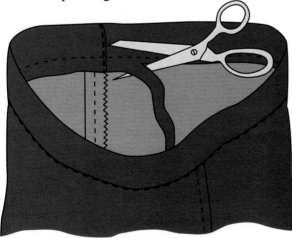

7 Adjust the fullness evenly around the waist. Don't bother to shift the fabric along the elastic. The fastest way to distribute the fullness is simply to stretch the waistband. This almost always results in gathers that are equally spaced around the entire waistband.

 STRETCH TIME In the chapter "Full Pull-On Pants," I explain how to join your waistband elastic by butting the ends, wrapping them in a fabric scrap, and seaming the edges together. Sometimes it is necessary to match your notions so that they "work well" together. For example, I wrap ribbon rather than fabric around Ban-rol stretch elastic. I save time assembling the slim pants by replacing the fabric scrap with ribbon. It isn't necessary to measure and then cut out a bit of fabric because I'm using Ban-rol for the slim pants. This elastic doesn't have the little nylon "pokies" that always stick out, so ribbon can be used to join the ends of the elastic. When you're sewing, keep in mind that using quality products can often save time.

Hem Your Pants

1 You already folded up a 1-inch (2.5-cm) hem. Pin it from the pants side, not the hem side, of the leg. Press up the hem allowance.

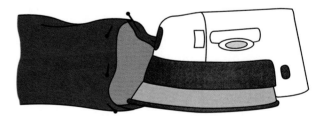

2 Install a double needle in your machine, woolly nylon thread on your bobbin, and regular sewing thread in the needles. Woolly nylon thread is often used on a serger but works just as well on the bobbin of a conventional sewing machine. It's ideal for these pants because it gives stretch to the stitching line. Be sure to hand wrap the thread around the bobbin. If you let the machine wind the bobbin, the taut winding process takes all of the stretch out of the thread.

Sandra says

DO DOUBLE TIME Hemming by machine is fast and easy when you use a double needle. If you look at many ready-to-wear garments, you'll notice that two lines of topstitching are often used to finish hems. So if you use a double needle, the hem on your slim pants will look very professional. The double needle creates two rows of parallel stitching simultaneously on the top, with zigzag stitches connecting the rows on the wrong side of the fabric. Even the most basic of sewing machines can handle a double needle because the only requirement is that your machine be capable of making a wide zigzag stitch.

3 Topstitch the hem in place, with the needle closest to the hem's crease positioned ³/₄ inch (2 cm) from the crease. Start and end the stitching at the inner leg seam. Use a medium-length straight stitch when topstitching with the double needle. Since the pants are narrow and the fabric has some stretch to it, stretch the topstitching a little as you sew. This prevents snapped stitches when you slide your foot in and out of the bottom of the pants.

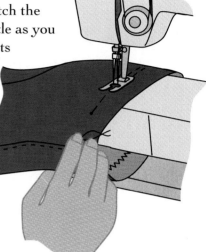

QUICK CLASS

Two Spools in One

I recommend that you use a Schmetz 4.0/100 double needle. If your sewing machine doesn't have two spool pins, you can still use a double needle.

How to Thread a Double Needle

1 Wind some matching thread on to a bobbin. Place the bobbin on the spool pin with the spool of thread on top.

2 Both threads go through all the same thread guides except at the tension disks, where the threads split. One thread goes on each side of the tension disk.

3 Threads go their separate ways one last time when they go through the two needle eyes.

Tension disk

The Next Step

Vented Hem for Slim Pants

45 MINUTES

_In just a few minutes, you can upgrade your pants with a designer
detail for the hem. The following instructions show you how to create an
angular or curved vent. Because you're adding a facing, you don't need to
fuss with a curved hem or mitered corner._

You must be certain that you have the correct length for
your slim pants because you won't be able to make adjustments after you cut out your pattern pieces. To create this
detail, you cut the hem allowance off the pattern and add
a shaped facing before cutting your fabric. If you aren't
confident about the finished length, cut a hem allowance.
After fitting, if you don't need the extra length, cut off the
excess hem allowance before attaching the facing.

Design a Facing Pattern

1 You need to adjust the pattern before you
cut the pattern pieces from your fabric. The
pattern has a 1-inch (2.5-cm) hem allowance.
Fold up 3/8 inch (9 mm) at the bottom of the
pattern. This leaves a seam allowance 5/8 inch
(1.5 cm) past the desired pants length.

2 Fold the pattern in half lengthwise, and
mark the center of the leg. This location is
halfway between the cut edges on the hem
bottom.

Center of pant leg

3 Open the pattern. To mark to position on
the vent, make a 1/4-inch (5-mm)-deep
notch in the hem at the fold.

4 Cut out a 3-inch × 11-inch (7.5-cm × 27.5-cm) strip of paper. Place the pants pattern on a table, and slide the paper underneath the revised bottom, which is now ³⁄₈ inch (9 mm) shorter than the original pants pattern.

5 Trace the shape of both sides of the pants leg onto the strip of paper. Transfer the halfway mark at the bottom of the hem onto the paper strip.

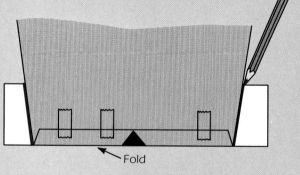

Fold

6 Remove the pants pattern and cut the excess paper away from the traced shape on the new pants facing pattern. Draw a grainline parallel to the long sides of the pattern.

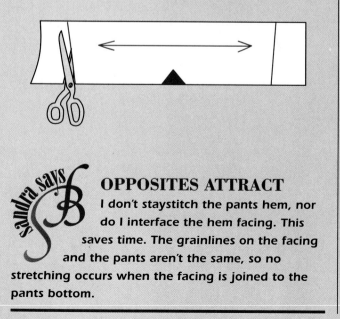

OPPOSITES ATTRACT

Sandra says

I don't staystitch the pants hem, nor do I interface the hem facing. This saves time. The grainlines on the facing and the pants aren't the same, so no stretching occurs when the facing is joined to the pants bottom.

7 Decide whether you prefer a rounded or an angular vent. Draw your shape accordingly at the center of the facing pattern, ending the vent detailing ³⁄₄ inch (2 cm) from the top wide edge of the pattern and allowing a ⁵⁄₈-inch (1.5-cm) seam allowance at the bottom.

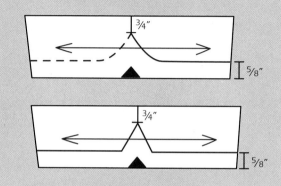

Cut Out the Pattern

1 Decide how long your pants will be, and make sure that the hemline on the leg falls in the correct spot. The hemline is 1 inch (2.5 cm) above the cutting line at the bottom of the leg. Lengthen the leg, if necessary.

2 Using the facing pattern, cut two facings (one for each leg) on the lengthwise grain of the fabric. The slim pants pattern is also cut lengthwise, so that the crosswise grain on the finished pants wraps around the leg. On the other hand, the lengthwise grain on the facing wraps around the leg.

3 Transfer the facing shape to the facing fabric with tracing paper and a tracing wheel.

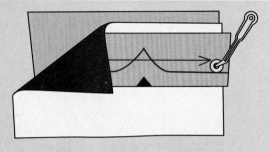

Construct the Vent and Pants

1 Sew the vent before the inner leg seam. With right sides together, pin the facing to the pants bottom.

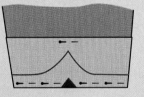

2 Use the vent detailing lines that you drew (and transferred) as the sewing lines. Straight stitch along these lines with small machine stitches, about 15 to 18 stitches per inch or 2 on a 0-to-4 stitch length setting. Whether the vent is round or angular, hand walk two small stitches at the top of the vent. (See the Quick Class "Let Your Fingers Do the Walking" on page 191.)

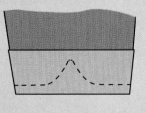

3 Cut into the vent opening to within ¹/8 inch (3 mm) of the stitching at the point. Press the seam allowances toward the facing side. Trim the seam allowances to ¹/4 inch (5 mm).

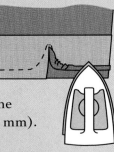

4 Fold one pants leg so that the cut edges of the inner leg are even and the right side is together. Sew the inner leg seam with tiny zigzag stitches, starting at the crotch. Fold down the facing and finish the inner leg seam. Complete the inner leg with a mock flat fell seam. (See the Quick Class "The Fastest Mock Flat Fell Seam" on page 39.)

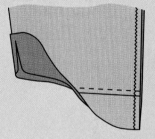

5 Now that the leg seam is completely sewn, fold the facing at the bottom of each leg to the wrong side of the pants.

6 From the outside of the pants, anchor the facing and inner leg seams together by stitching in the well of the inner leg seam through the pants and the facing. Press and pound the seam flat with a tailor's clapper.

7 Topstitch the bottom of both legs ¹/4 inch (5 mm) away from the bottom of the pants. Use a double needle and follow the shape of the vent. (See the Quick Class "Two Spools in One" on page 44.)

Coordinating VEST

The Essential Third Piece

I think of this garment as the essential third piece because it plays such an important role in a wardrobe. It "pulls together" a top and bottom, and it's a terrific jacket substitute. In addition, a vest is slimming if it's coordinated with the color of your pants or skirt. You'll notice that this vest has broad shoulders, which also creates a slimming silhouette by making the bottom half of the body appear smaller.

In this chapter you'll learn how to make lined, quilted, and reversible vests plus learn how to add design details like decorative pocket flaps and a buttonhole window.

The cut edges of all of the vests are trimmed with either bias-cut fabric strips or purchased bias binding. This is a very easy way to assemble a vest and offers a lot of design options.

Your vest will look like a million dollars if you use a synthetic leather like Fabuleather for the trim. You'll need a little bit more yardage if you select Ultrasuede, but the results are well worth the extra cost.

Another neat idea is to use striped fabric to create your trim. I just love the multicolor effect that this gives. It's especially attractive when you use bias-cut strips because the strips end up on an angle.

Although this vest looks as if it's quilted, I just used a purchased quilted fabric to line it. A lining eliminates the need for finishing seams and hides the interfacing. The technique for lining my vest in the Rodale Designer Collection is so simple and fast that anyone can do it. In fact, I bet that you'll make your first lined vest in less than three hours.

What You Need

You can make this vest from any fabric, depending on the look you want. Material with body and substance is the most attractive, unless you want a softer look. In this case your best bet is to use wool jersey or sandwashed silk.

"*I chose a shiny fabric for this vest because it looks nice when quilted, a technique I explain on page 62. The general instructions, which start here, feature a lined, unquilted vest. To make it, consider using canvas, medium- to heavy-weight wool, melton, mudcloth, or tapestry.***"**

Fabric Yardage for Vest

Fabric width	Small	Medium	Large
45 inches (115 cm)	1½ yards (1.3 m)	1⅝ yards (1.5 m)	1¾ yards (1.6 m)
60 inches (150 cm)	⅞ yard (0.8 m)	1 yard (0.9 m)	1 yard (0.9 m)

Additional fabric	Small	Medium	Large
Lining	1½ yards (1.3 m)	1⅝ yards (1.5 m)	1¾ yards (1.6 m)
Fusible knitted tricot interfacing*	⅞ yard (0.8 m)	1 yard (0.9 m)	1 yard (0.9 m)

Fabric for trim†	Small	Medium	Large
Contrasting fabric, all widths	¼–½ yard (0.2 m–0.4 m)	¼–½ yard (0.2 m–0.4 m)	¼–½ yard (0.2 m–0.4 m)
Fabuleather‡	¼ yard (0.2 m)	¼ yard (0.2 m)	¼ yard (0.2 m)

* *You need to purchase more interfacing if you decide to interface the entire surface of the pattern pieces. For further information on yardage requirements for the interfacing, see "Appropriate Fabric" and "Interfacing Adds Body" on the opposite page.*

† *The yardage required for the trim will vary, depending on the type of fabric that you select. For further information on yardage requirements, see the Quick Class "Bound to Succeed" on page 58. If you prefer to buy trim, see "Buy Your Trim" on page 59.*

‡ *To order Fabuleather, call Donna Salyers Fabulous Furs at 1-800-848-4650.*

Appropriate Fabric

A vest can be made in almost any fabric and lined with a slippery fabric like Ambiance rayon (a lightweight Bemberg rayon lining) or China silk, or else with flannelette or a lightweight cotton.

You can purchase bias tape for your trim or make your own from a contrasting fabric or synthetic leather. Wool jersey and cotton knit, cut on the crosswise grain for maximum stretch, are inexpensive choices since less than 1/4 yard (0.2 m) of one of these is needed to trim the whole vest.

A striped knit or woven fabric, cut on the bias, creates dramatic trim. Although the maximum stretch on a knit is on the crosswise grain, you can use strips of bias-cut knit for the trim because it'll still have plenty of stretch to conform to the vest's curves. I especially like to use black and white stripes for bias-cut or crosswise-grain knit trim.

Be sure to choose a trim fabric that doesn't fray when it's cut on the bias because the cut edge will be exposed on the inside of the finished vest.

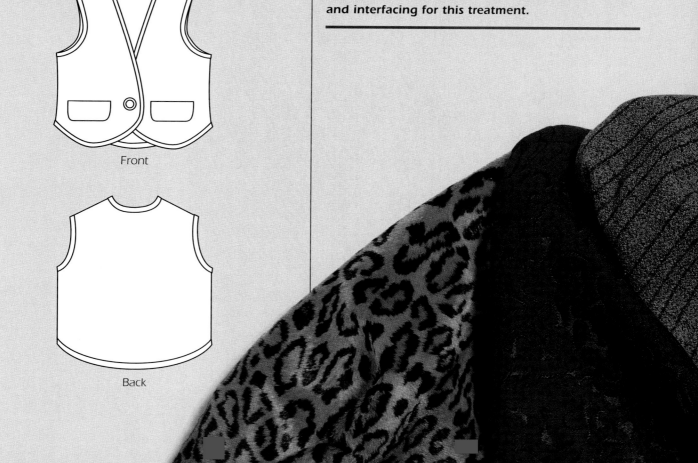

Front

Back

Notions

- ✂ Matching thread
- ✂ Three packages of wide bias tape or a bias-tape maker to make bias tape with a pressed width of 1 inch (25 mm), if you prefer to use contrasting fabric for the neck trim
- ✂ Large button, 1 1/2 inches (3.5 cm) or larger
- ✂ Appliqué scissors
- ✂ Miscellaneous supplies, as listed in "The Sewing Basket" on page ix

Sandra says

INTERFACING ADDS BODY If you like a crisper-looking vest, interface the entire vest fronts and back. This will give your fabric more body and help the vest maintain its shape. I do this whenever I want to make a vest from a fabric that's too drapey for my taste. To determine the amount of interfacing that you'll need, just refer to the yardage requirements for the fashion fabric. You'll need to use the same amount for both fabric and interfacing for this treatment.

Fit Your Vest Pattern

This is a very loose-fitting vest, so chances are good that you won't need to make any alterations at all. The only exception is if you have a small frame for your size, for example, a narrow upper chest. But even if you have to make this alteration, you'll only spend a few minutes doing so. Don't you just love it?

Get Started

All my patterns are multisized so you can cut different sizes to fit different parts of your body. Choose your pattern size by comparing your bust measurement across the fullest part to the size table on page 208. Then adjust the pattern to fit the parts of your body that are larger or smaller than the size you selected. Each of the categories in this section explains how to make any necessary adjustments.

Full Back

When you're full in the back, jackets often feel tight, and your sleeves may tear away from the armholes.

If you're one of the many women who have a fuller back than front, you need to cut the vest back a size larger above the armhole. For example, if you selected size medium to match your bust measurement but have a full back, use the size large cutting lines above the armholes.

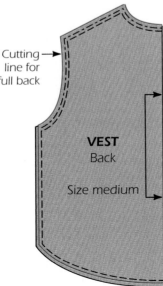

Cutting line for full back

VEST Back

Size medium

If you wear a size large, you are in luck because I made this vest quite roomy. It's very unlikely that you'll need to increase the pattern width above the armholes.

If you have broadened the back or narrowed the front shoulder, the top of the shoulder on the vest back pattern is now larger than the top of the shoulder on the vest front pattern.

The width in the back is needed only below the shoulder. Don't cut off the excess on the back shoulder. Instead, use a dart to take out the excess at the shoulder while retaining the fullness at the upper back.

At the center of the shoulder, draw a dart that's ¹/₂ inch (1 cm) wide at the shoulder seam and tapers to a point 3 inches (7.5 cm) into the pattern.

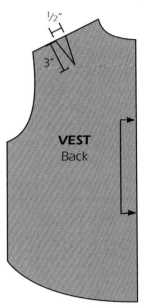

¹/₂"

3"

VEST Back

Narrow Upper Chest

A narrow upper chest is indicated on your ill-fitting garments by vertical wrinkles between the shoulder and the bottom of the armhole. The shoulder seam falls onto the arm. A person with a narrow upper chest can also have a broad back, which is why you may have problems finding a pattern that fits.

If your upper chest is small and the rest of your body fits a larger size, cut the vest front smaller above the armhole. Below the armhole, follow the cutting line that fits your bust measurement.

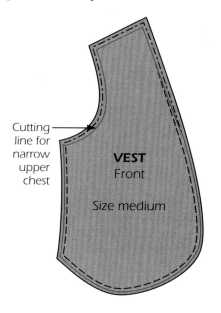

Cutting line for narrow upper chest

VEST
Front

Size medium

Body Length

The length of this pattern is flattering, but if you're very tall or very short, feel free to use the length for a size larger or smaller than what you're using for the rest of your body.

COPY READY-TO-WEAR

The best way to determine the most flattering length for your vests and jackets is to try on a bunch. Go to a store and work your way through a rack of them. Find one that suits you and measure it at center back from the neck to the hem. Do this in the dressing room or you may no longer be welcome at that dress shop.

QUICK CLASS

The Choice Is Yours

Some people wash and dry their fabric before they cut out their pattern pieces. Others don't. The main reason that fabric is "pretreated" is to shrink it so that the finished garment won't lose length or have "scrunched-up" seams after it's washed for the first time. Some fabrics don't need to be pretreated because they have such minimal shrinkage. It all depends on the type of fiber used to make the fabric as well as the way the fabric was handled before it left the mill.

How to Pretreat Your Fabric

1 Handle your fabric the same way that you plan to clean the finished garment. If dry cleaning is your choice, you can eliminate the preshrinking process. The exception is wool crepe, which must be processed first at the dry cleaner.

2 Pay attention to the lining you buy for your garment. Since a lining can't be removed when a garment is washed, select a lining

and fabric that have the same care instructions and pretreat them in the same manner.

3 I usually cut my interfacing with the pattern grainlines "on the bias"—that is, at a 45-degree angle to the selvages—so it isn't necessary to preshrink it. If you don't preshrink it **or** cut it on the bias, the fused interfacing will draw up the fabric and make your pattern piece slightly smaller.

Cut Out the Vest Pattern Pieces

25 MINUTES

If you're a confident sewer, you may want to cut out the lining and the fabric at the same time. I fold the fabric according to the layout diagram, and then place the lining, folded in the same manner, on top. Of course, this only works if your lining and fabric are the same width.

1 Straighten the fabric's cut ends, which are perpendicular to the selvages, by pulling a thread close to each cut edge. (The selvages are the tightly woven edges that run along both lengthwise edges of the fabric.) If a thread breaks, just pull on the thread next to it. The idea is to draw the thread until the fabric puckers slightly. Now cut the fabric along this pucker so that you have straight edges that are on-grain and at right angles to the selvages.

2 Fold your fabric in half lengthwise so that the selvages are together. When they're together, you'll know that the fold is probably on-grain.

3 Place the patterns on the fabric so that the grainline printed on each pattern is parallel to the selvages. Scoot the front close to the selvages so that you can place the back with center back on the fold. Place pins in the corners of your patterns and spaced along the gaps.

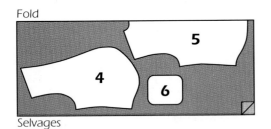

45-inch (115-cm)-wide fabric or lining (use this layout for both), with/without nap, all sizes

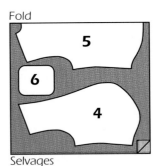

60-inch (150-cm)-wide fabric, with/without nap, all sizes

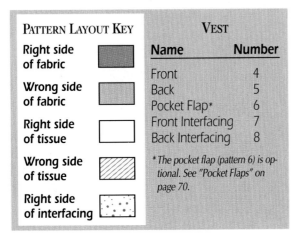

PATTERN LAYOUT KEY		VEST	
Right side of fabric	▨	**Name**	**Number**
Wrong side of fabric	▨	Front	4
Right side of tissue	▢	Back	5
		Pocket Flap*	6
Wrong side of tissue	▨	Front Interfacing	7
Right side of interfacing	▨	Back Interfacing	8

The pocket flap (pattern 6) is optional. See "Pocket Flaps" on page 70.

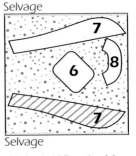

25-inch (65-cm)-wide interfacing, all sizes

4 Cut out your patterns through both layers of fabric. Also cut a vest back and two vest fronts from the lining fabric. As you cut, use smooth, long motions whenever possible, holding the pattern flat against the fabric with your opposite hand. The pocket flap is optional.

5 If you want decorative pocket flaps for your vest, mark the pocket flap placement on both fronts, using tracing paper and a tracing wheel or tailor's tacks. Tracing paper isn't always faster than my "quickie" tailor's tacks; see the Quick Class "A Tailor-Made Solution" on this page. Tailor's tacks are easier to find, and you don't have to worry about making a mark that won't come off.

If you added darts at the shoulders of the back, make tailor's tacks at the bottom (the widest part) and the apex (the point) before removing the back pattern from the fabric pattern piece.

FLIP-FLOP YOUR PATTERNS Whenever you're cutting through a double thickness of fabric, which is 90 percent of the time, you can place the pattern right side up or right side down, whichever way fits onto the fashion fabric or lining better.

Since you're usually cutting two fabric pattern pieces at once, you end up with a left and a right pattern piece.

But if you're cutting through a single thickness of fabric, be sure to turn the pattern over when you cut the second pattern piece from the fabric or interfacing. This will give you one left and one right side. They'll be mirror images. If you forget to flip the pattern over, you'll end up with two left or two right pattern pieces.

QUICK CLASS

A Tailor-Made Solution

The fastest way to mark placement lines and darts on your fabric pattern pieces is with dressmaker's tracing paper and a tracing wheel. Tracing paper or a water- or air-erasable marking pen works on most fabrics, but sometimes only a tailor's tack will show up.

How to Make a 1-Minute Tailor's Tack

1 Thread a hand sewing needle and make the ends of the thread even lengths, with the needle in the center. Don't knot the ends.

2 Insert the needle and double thread through the pattern and fabric at the place you want to mark. Leave a 2-inch (5-cm)-long double-thread tail on top of the pattern.

3 Close to the point where it just came through, insert the needle and thread back through the fabric and pattern from back to front, leaving a large loop in the thread. Clip the thread, leaving a second thread tail that's at least 2 inches (5 cm) long. Clip the threads so that no loops remain on the top of the pattern.

4 Gently pull the pattern away from the fabric. The threads remain in the fabric layers. Gently separate the fabric layers about 1 inch (2.5 cm). Clip the threads between the fabric layers.

Interface the Vest Pattern Pieces

10 MINUTES

After cutting out your pattern pieces, you apply interfacing to the neckline. Remember to apply the interfacing to the vest fabric, not to the lining. If you choose to make this vest without a lining, don't interface the pattern pieces. It will be exposed on the inside of your unlined vest.

1 Preshrink your fusible interfacing, unless you plan to cut it on the bias. Cut out the patterns, referring to the layouts on page 54.

2 Fuse the interfacing pattern pieces to the wrong side of the fabric pieces. (See the Quick Class "Fast and Easy Fusibles" on this page.)

3 Set the bond by pressing one more time from the front side. Lay the pattern piece on your pressing surface wrong side down, so that the interfacing is the bottom layer. Cover the pattern piece with a damp press cloth. Press, allowing the iron to stay in one place for about ten seconds.

Fast and Easy Fusibles

I use fusible interfacing whenever possible because applying it is so much faster than hand basting sew-in interfacing. Test-fuse your interfacing on the back of a scrap of fabric to make sure that you like the amount of stiffness that the interfacing gives your fabric. Change to a lighter weight interfacing or a sew-in if you aren't happy with the results.

How to Apply Fusible Interfacing

1 Position the interfacing with the resin, or "glue," side against the wrong side of the corresponding fabric pattern piece. Make sure that the cut edges match.

2 Place the interfacing and fabric together on a pressing surface so that the shape of the pattern piece isn't distorted and the interfacing is on top. Cover the inter-

facing and fabric with a press cloth. Spray lightly with water.

3 Set the iron to medium high and steam, then fuse, using a press-and-lift motion. Don't slide the iron because this stretches the interfacing. Let the iron rest in one area for about ten seconds. Lift the iron, move it to the next area, and repeat.

Construct Your Vest

2 HOURS

Even though this is a lined vest, there is absolutely no hand sewing (unless you add a button). The lining and fabric pattern pieces are machine-basted together, then secured when the trim is sewn on. To save time, sew the trim to the inside of the vest by stitching in the well of the seam.

Join the Vest Fronts and Back

1 All the seam allowances are ⅝ inch (1.5 cm) wide and the stitch length is medium (10 to 12 stitches per inch or 2.5 on a 0-to-4 stitch length setting), unless otherwise indicated. If you adjusted your vest back pattern to accommodate a full back, you added darts to the shoulders. Fold one back shoulder right side together matching the marks on each side of the dart. Sew from the wide end to the skinny end. To eliminate puckering at the point, sew almost on the fold for the last ½ inch (1 cm). Do the same to the lining pieces.

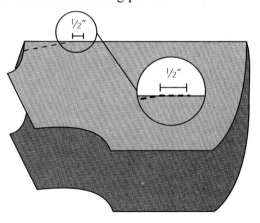

2 With right sides facing, sew the vest fronts to the vest back at the shoulder and side seams, matching the notches. Sew the lining together in the same way. Press the seam allowances open over a rolled towel or seam roll.

Easestitch the Armholes

1 A large bust or rounded back causes gaping at the armholes. This problem is corrected by easestitching on the seamline in the problem area and by slightly stretching the trim as you apply it. Sew ¾ inch (2 cm) in from the cut edge on the lower two-thirds of the armhole, doing only the front of the armholes for a large bust and only the back for a rounded back. Easestitch the armholes on the lining pattern pieces in the same manner.

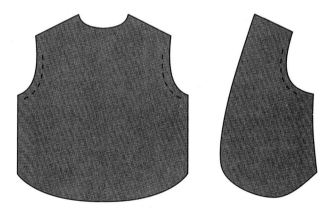

2 Slip the lining inside the vest with the wrong side of the vest and the wrong side of the lining together and the cut edges even. Pin the layers together at the armholes and outside edges. Try on your vest, then pin the vest and the lining together at the hem. The hems may not be properly aligned until each fabric has a chance to hang.

QUICK CLASS

Bound to Succeed

To finish the edges of the vest, you'll need a 1-inch bias-tape maker and ¼ yard (0.2 m) of fabric, if it's cut on the crosswise grain, or ½ yard (0.4 m), if it's cut well off-grain or on the bias. (See "Buy Your Trim" on the opposite page for the amount of bias tape to buy, if you prefer not to make your own.)

How to Make Bias Tape

1 Straighten a cut end of your fabric by pulling a thread close to a vertical edge. If it breaks, just pull on the thread next to it. The idea is to draw the thread until the fabric puckers slightly. Now cut the fabric along this pucker. This will result in a straight edge that is on-grain and perpendicular to the selvages. Strips cut from most fabrics are easier to shape around curves when they're off-grain or on the bias. So it's important that you establish the location of the grainline before you make your trim.

2 Fold the fabric diagonally by matching up the crosswise edge of the fabric with one of the selvages. Press the fold lightly. This fold is on the fabric's true bias.

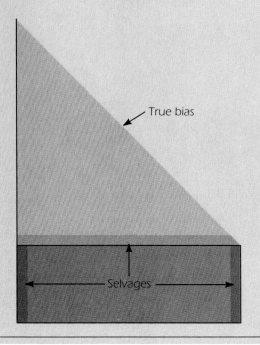

True bias

Selvages

3 Open the fold. Using a clear ruler and dressmaker's chalk, mark diagonal lines 2 inches apart on the fabric parallel to the true bias. Cut the fabric along these lines. Regardless of the desired finished width of your bias tape, cut your bias strips 2 inches (5 cm) wide.

4 Cut the short ends of each strip so that they're square. If you are using a striped fabric or want to piece the strips at an angle to cut down on bulk, follow the instructions in the Quick Class "Easy Pieces" on page 138.

Cutting line

5 Sew the strips together to make one length. To join two strips, pin together a short end from each strip with right sides facing and cut edges even, and sew. Press the seam allowances open, and trim them to ¼ inch (5 mm).

6 Cut an angle at one end of your bias strip. This makes it much easier to feed your bias strip into a metal bias-tape maker. Following the instructions that come with your bias-tape maker, make your bias tape. It's easier to perform this task at your pressing surface.

Staystitch the Curves

1 Sewing through both the lining and vest fabric, sew around the armholes and the outside edges of the vest ¾ inch (2 cm) in from the cut edges.

¾"

2 Trim off ⅝ inch (1.5 cm) from the armholes and outside vest edges that you just staystitched. Don't cut off the staystitching, however. It remains as a stabilizer for your trim and secures the lining so that the trim can be easily applied.

Apply the Trim

1 First decide how wide you'd like the trim on your finished vest. To do this, cut a 2 × 6-inch (5 × 15-cm) fabric scrap. Wrap it around the armhole of the outer edge of the vest so that ½ inch (1 cm) shows on the right side. Now shift the scrap so that ¼ inch (5 mm) shows. Regardless of how wide you'd like the finished trim to be, start with the same width of trim. You'll cut away any excess after it's attached.

2 If you're making your own trim, cut 2-inch (5-cm)-wide fabric strips, join them, and use a bias-tape maker to create it. (See the Quick Class "Bound to Succeed" on the opposite page.) Refold

and press the tape so that one side is ⅛ inch (3 mm) wider than the other. Now unfold one side of the trim. Starting at the right side seam, place the right side of the trim against the right side of the vest with the cut edges even. Pin the first few inches of the trim to the vest by inserting the pins from the inside of the vest. This positioning is important because you place the trim against the feed dogs when you sew this seam. This will ease the trim to fit the vest edge, thus preventing the vest edges from curling.

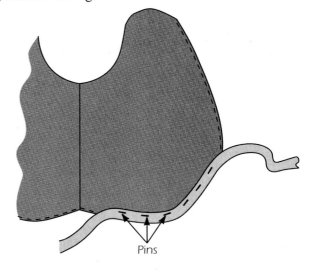

Pins

3 Install a straight-stitch presser foot on your machine. Place the side seam of the vest, with the start of the trim pinned in place, under the presser foot with the trim against the feed dogs. (If your machine has differential feed, make sure that it's off.) Sew the trim on, starting about 1 inch (2.5 cm) from the end of the trim. Use a ¼-inch (5-mm) seam allowance if you want the finished width of your trim to be ¼ inch (5 mm) on the outside of the vest. Use a ½-inch (1-cm) seam allowance if you want the finished width to be ½ inch (1 cm).

Sandra says

BUY YOUR TRIM If you're really in a hurry, you may want to trim your vest with purchased double-fold bias tape that has a finished width of ½ inch (1 cm) rather than make your own. **You need three packages to cover all of the cut edges.**

4 As you sew, continue to position the edge of the trim against the edge of the vest. You may need to clip the edges to help them conform to the curves of the vest. The right sides of the vest and trim are still facing and the trim is against the feed dogs. Sew the trim to the vest's back hem, left front, neckline, and right front. Stop sewing 3 inches (7.5 cm) away from where you started.

5 Stop stitching and remove the vest from under the presser foot. Pin the remaining trim to the garment so that the trim ends meet. Where the trim ends meet, with right sides facing, join the trim with a pin inserted parallel to the ends, taking care not to stretch the trim.

6 Remove the pins that join the trim to the vest. Sew the trim ends together, stitching ⅛ inch (3 mm) inside the pin holding the ends together.

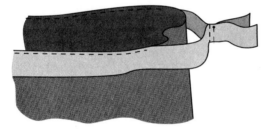

7 Press the seam allowances open and trim to ¼ inch (5 mm). At the machine, place the vest against the presser foot, and finish sewing the trim.

8 Wrap the trim to the inside of the vest, snugly covering the seamline. From the outside of the vest, pin the trim in its finished position. The cut edge of the trim isn't turned under. Change the thread on your machine and bobbin to match the trim.

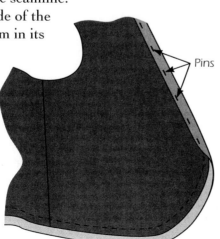

Pins

9 From the right side, attach the trim by sewing in the well of the previous seamline.

10 Open the vest and turn it wrong side up so that you can see the underside of the trim. Using appliqué scissors, cut off the excess trim close to the stitching line. The cut edges of the trim aren't turned in, which saves time that would be spent hand sewing.

Trim the Armholes

1 This procedure is much the same as attaching the trim to the rest of the vest. But you place the vest closest to the feed dogs so that the armhole will curve in to your body. With right sides together, pin a few inches of the trim to the armhole, but this time place the pins on the trim side.

2 Sew with the trim side up and the vest closest to the feed dogs. This will slightly stretch the trim, causing the armhole to pull in. Stop sewing when you are 3 inches (7.5 cm) from the start.

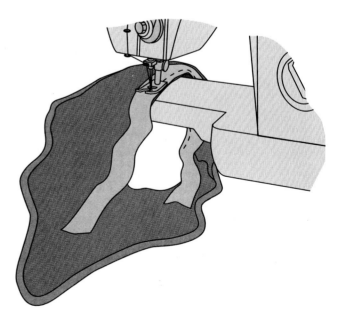

3 Join the ends of the trim, and sew it to the vest, as explained in Steps 5 through 10 on this page. Press, and pound the trim flat with a clapper.

Add a Closure to Your Vest

15 MINUTES

While I'm offering you some advice on buttons and buttonholes, you can spice up your vest by using a fabric loop or a frog. I always try to choose a closure that suits the personality of the fabric. For example, my vest with the oriental motif in the photo on page 48 has a frog closure.

1 You can sew the buttonhole with just about any needle, but if you want the best results, use a 10/70 H-J sewing machine needle to make it easier to sew over bulky areas. You'll also save time because you won't struggle to get it right.

2 Position your button on the right front so that the button's edge is ³/₄ inch (2 cm) from the edge. Place a pin in the fabric at the center of the button. Remove the button. This pin marks the start of your horizontal buttonhole. Set the buttonhole length to ¹/₄ inch (5 mm) longer than the button diameter. For example, if you're using a 1¹/₂-inch (3.5-cm)-diameter button, the buttonhole is 1³/₄ inches (4.5 cm) long and the end of the buttonhole is 3¹/₄ inches (8 cm) from the vest's edge.

3 If you're using a 1¹/₂-inch (3.5-cm)-diameter button, place the edge ³/₄ inch (2 cm) from the finished edge. Sew the button on the left front.

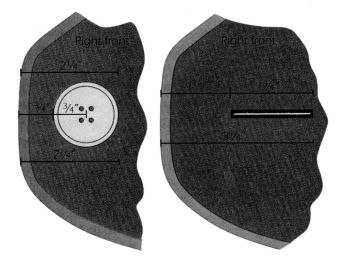

THE NEXT STEP

Quilted Vest

3 HOURS

A vest is an ideal machine-quilting project since the pieces are manageable. The process is easy because the pattern pieces are quilted before they are sewn together. Just remember: Don't use interfacing and don't choose a batting that's too bulky.

The quilted vest in this photo is satin on one side and cotton on the other. The satin fabric really shows off the highs and lows of the quilting.

Sandra says

IT'S A SNAP Sulky and Madeira carry threads for machine embroidery and topstitching. Use an N topstitching needle with rayon thread and an HE Metafil needle with metallic thread to avoid thread breakage.

Add to Your Shopping List

Your yardage requirements for the fabric, lining, and batting are the same as for a regular lined vest. The yardage for the trim varies, depending on the type of fabric that you select. See "Appropriate Fabric" on page 51 for further information.

Appropriate Fabric
Quilted stitches show up better on plain rather than printed fabric. My rule of thumb is that if topstitching doesn't look nice, the fabric won't look good when it's quilted. Velvet, for example, is a poor choice. Fabric with sheen is interesting because the raised and indented surface that's caused by quilting adds interesting shading. My favorite battings are cotton flannelette, Thermore, Thermolam, and Thinsulate.

Additional Notions
✂ Fine machine embroidery thread
✂ Darning presser foot

Prepare to Sew

1 Pretreat your fabric and lining in the same way that you plan to care for the finished vest. Battings are usually preshrunk.

2 Adjust the pattern to fit your body, following the instructions in "Fit Your Vest Pattern" on page 52.

3 Cut the vest fabric, lining, and batting 1 inch (2.5 cm) larger than the patterns around all of the outside edges. The quilting process "shrinks" pieces, so if you cut the patterns larger, you end up with a vest that's the right size. If you added darts to the shoulders of your vest back, after you cut the pattern piece out of the batting, cut out the center of the dart, leaving about 1/8 to 1/4 inch (3 to 5 mm) of batting beyond the sewing lines.

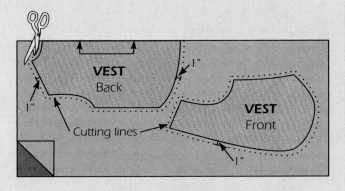

VEST Back

VEST Front

Cutting lines

1"

1"

1"

4 If you plan to add pocket flaps (see page 70), mark the flap placement on both fronts using dressmaker's tracing paper and a tracing wheel or tailor's tacks. If you adjusted your back pattern to accommodate a full back, you also added darts to the shoulders. Before removing the back pattern from the fabric pattern piece, make tailor's tacks at the bottom (the widest part) and the apex (or point) on both darts. For instructions on making tailor's tacks, see the Quick Class "A Tailor-Made Solution" on page 55.

5 Sandwich and pin the front batting between the front fashion fabric and the front lining. Hand baste the layers together 1 inch (2.5 cm) from the edges. Hand baste diagonally across the pattern piece twice, through all layers. Prepare the back in the same manner.

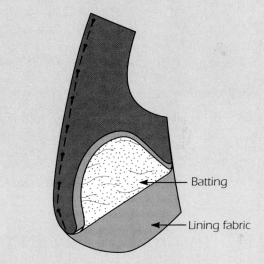

Batting

Lining fabric

Create Free-Motion Quilting

1 Experiment on a scrap of the lining-batting-fabric layer before working directly on your vest pattern pieces, then quilt your pattern pieces, as explained in the Quick Class "E'motion'al Designing" on page 64.

2 Separately quilt each of the layered pattern pieces. Because the presser foot is not putting pressure on the fabric, you won't have any difficulty keeping the layers from shifting. Begin on any one of the main spots on a vest pattern piece: the shoulder, bottom, front, or side seam. I worked back and forth across the vest.

3 After all the pattern pieces are quilted, lay each one under the matching tissue pattern. Trim off any excess fabric beyond the tissue pattern. This is necessary because variations in quilting affect the amount that the vest pieces reduce in size.

4 Remove the hand basting. Join the quilted pattern pieces together in the same way you did for the lined vest but exclude the lining and finish the seam allowances with bias tape. (See the Quick Class "Wrapping It Up" on page 126.) Attach trim to the outer edges and the armholes, following the directions starting on page 59.

Sandra says

THINK SMALL   Free-motion machine quilting is easier when you operate your machine at top speed. This is different than moving the fabric faster. Small stitches look nicer, which is the result of moving the fabric slowly and running the machine fast. Also, using a thread color that matches your vest fabric will be more forgiving of mistakes.

QUICK CLASS

E'motion'al Designing

To machine quilt, use a darning presser foot, and set the feed dogs and presser foot positions as suggested in your sewing machine manual. Thread your needle with fine embroidery thread. Wind the bobbin with metallic or regular sewing thread.

How to Create Free-Motion Quilting

1 Insert the layers under the darning presser foot. Lower the feed dogs to the correct position for your machine. You will notice that even though the presser foot is lowered, you can still move the fabric around. Bring the bobbin thread to the top of the fabric. If you forget to do this, a knot will form on the underside of the fabric.

2 Move the fabric manually when you do free-motion machine quilting. Place your hands on either side of the fabric that is under the presser foot, and begin sewing with a straight stitch. As you sew, move the fabric around. Faster movement results in long stitches. Slower movement gives you small stitches. Try different movements back and

forth as well as around in circles. Get a rhythm going, working toward achieving similar but not identical movement.

3 Fabric is easier to push around if you roll up the fabric to the right of the needle. Decide what pattern you would like to see on your vest. Experiment a little more.

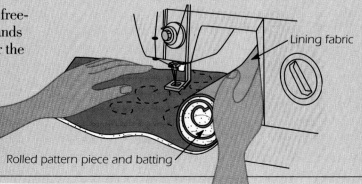

Lining fabric

Rolled pattern piece and batting

Reversible Vest

2 HOURS

There are great reversible fabrics on the market and I urge you to give one of them a try. But for a customized vest, you can create a reversible fabric by cutting a set of patterns from each fabric and basting the pieces together with wrong sides facing.

A reversible vest is a great wardrobe extender because it can be worn two ways, which makes it ideal for trips when you need to pack light. Because seams in reversible fabrics can get bulky, I use an alternative technique for seams and darts. This procedure completely eliminates bulk.

Add to Your Shopping List

Use the same amount of fabric listed in the fabric yardage table on page 50. Don't purchase interfacing and lining. Use ¼ yard (0.2 m) of wool jersey for the trim.

Appropriate Fabric
Double-faced wool is an excellent choice for a reversible vest since each side of the fabric is different. Your fabric shouldn't be flimsy.

Prepare to Sew

1 Preshrink your fabric with steam, or dry-clean it. Adjust your pattern to fit your body. Cut the pattern pieces from your fashion fabric. (See the Quick Class "The Choice Is Yours" on page 53, "Fit Your Vest Pattern" on page 52, and "Cut Out the Vest Pattern Pieces" on page 54.)

2 Cut out the vest patterns ⅝ inch (1.5 cm) inside the cutting lines so that the fabric pattern pieces don't have seam allowances. Don't cut anything off center back because it's cut on the fold.

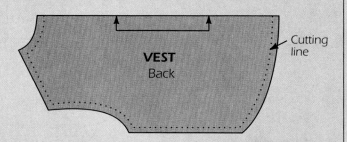

VEST
Back

Cutting line

3 Cut 2-inch (5-cm)-wide strips of wool jersey on the crosswise grain. Piece the strips end to end to measure 190 inches (4.8 m) for size small, 195 inches (5 m) for size medium, and 208 inches (5.3 m) for size large. Also, cut four more strips of wool jersey on the crosswise grain, each 2 inches (5 cm) wide and the same length as the side seam. The crosswise grain on knit fabric has the maximum stretch so it's best for making flexible trim.

Join the Fronts and Back

1 Butt together the side-seam edges of a front pattern piece and the corresponding side-seam edge of the back. Place them on the right side of a jersey strip. Both of the pattern pieces must be either right side up or wrong side up. Pin them to the jersey strip.

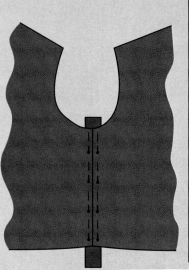

2 Using the widest feather stitch possible, join the side seam of the vest together, sewing through the wool jersey strip as you stitch.

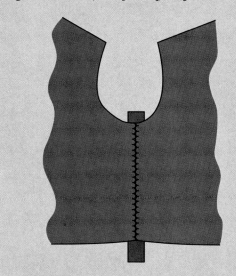

3 Flip over the vest so that you can see the wool jersey strip. Trim one side close to the feather stitching using appliqué scissors.

4 Turn under ¼ inch (5 mm) of the cut edge on the opposite side of the wool jersey strip. Fold this side of the strip over the stitching, and pin it to the vest.

5 Hand sew the strip in place. A line of feather stitches is visible on one side. The other side has a narrow, jersey-covered side seam. Press using a tailor's clapper. Join the remaining side seam and shoulder seams in the same manner.

Apply the Trim

1 Cut the short ends of each of the three remaining strips of wool jersey so that they are square. Piecing on an angle isn't necessary. It does cut down on fabric bulk but is often not worth the trouble of figuring out the angle.

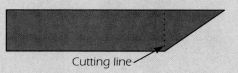

Cutting line

2 Pin together a short end from each strip with right sides facing and cut edges even, and sew. Press the seam allowances open. Join the remaining strips together. Trim the seam allowances to $1/4$ inch (5 mm).

3 Press under $1/4$ inch (5 mm) along one long edge of the trim.

4 Starting at the right side seam, place the right side of the unpressed edge of the wool jersey strip against the right side of the vest along the outside edges with cut edges even. Pin and sew the trim to the hem and neckline of the vest. Join the start and finish of the trim, as explained in Steps 2 through 7 of "Apply the Trim" on page 59.

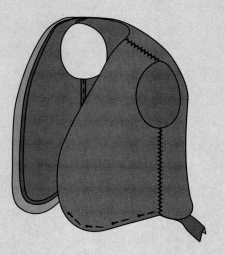

5 Enclose the cut edges of the newly sewn seam by wrapping the trim strip from the right side of the vest to the wrong side. Pin the pressed edge of the trim strip very close to the seam stitches.

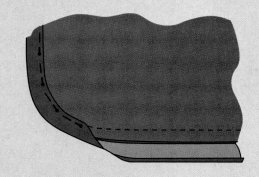

6 Blind-hem stitch the trim by hand to the seam by sliding a needle inside the trim's fold for $1/2$ inch (1 cm). Then take a stitch in the vest. Again slide the needle along the inside of the trim's fold $1/2$ inch (1 cm) further, and continue stitching back and forth in this manner. (The size of this stitch can vary according to your fabric's weight and your personal preference.) Don't pull the thread too taut. When the trim is completely attached, press and pound it with a tailor's clapper.

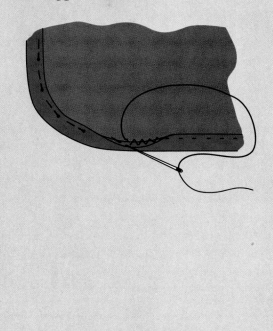

Buttonhole Window

30 MINUTES

This treatment is strong and attractive on both sides, which makes it ideal for a reversible vest. If your garment is trimmed with fake or real leather or suede or with wool jersey, this fabric should also be used for the patch because these fabrics don't ravel.

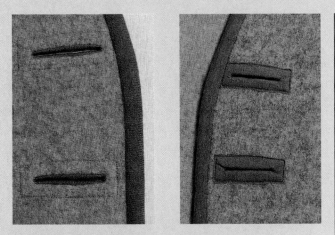

Buttonholes in a reversible or unlined garment are difficult. A machine buttonhole through a single fabric thickness will stretch or pull away from the cloth. A bound buttonhole, while attractive on one side, is quite unattractive on the other. A buttonhole window is attractive on the front (left in the above photo) and on the inside (right).

THREAD COUNTS Unless you enjoy rethreading your machine every time the thread breaks or knots in front of the needle, buy good-quality thread, like Molnlycke, Madeira, or Güttermann. These threads are consistently smooth. Spending a few additional dollars on thread is a small price to pay to eliminate the aggravation of frequent rethreading.

Prepare Your Vest

1 Mark the buttonhole placement line on both sides of the vest with dressmaker's chalk. Position the start of each buttonhole 1 inch (2.5 cm) from the finished front edge of the right vest front. To determine the perfect size for your buttonhole, experiment on a scrap first.

2 Interface the wrong side of each buttonhole with a ¹/₂-inch (1-cm)-wide strip of fusible interfacing that is 1 inch (2.5 cm) longer than the intended buttonhole opening.

3 For each buttonhole, cut a patch of trim (felt or wool jersey is suitable) 2¹/₂ inches (6 cm) wide by the button diameter plus 1¹/₂ inches (3.5 cm). The patch isn't interfaced.

Attach the Patch

1 Place the right side of the buttonhole patch against the right side of the fabric. It needs to be positioned so that the patch is centered over

the buttonhole placement line. Pin it in place. For a reversible vest, you can place the right side of the patch against either side of the vest.

2 Flip the vest over so that you can see the buttonhole placement line. Using 15 to 18 stitches per inch (2 on a 0-to-4 stitch length setting), sew a line of stitches about $1/16$ inch (1.5 mm) away from the buttonhole placement line.

3 Upon reaching the end of the buttonhole placement line, pivot and sew three small stitches perpendicular to the line of stitching that you just made. Since it's difficult to sew only three stitches with the machine foot pedal, hand walk the stitches by turning the wheel by hand. (See the Quick Class "Let Your Fingers Do the Walking" on page 191.) You have now made one long and one short side of a rectangle.

4 Sew a second line parallel to the first on the other side of the buttonhole placement line. Pivot and sew three stitches at the end of and perpendicular to the second stitching line, connecting the sewing into a narrow rectangle that's about $1/8$ inch (3 mm) longer than your button.

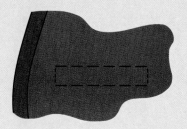

5 With sharp scissors, cut between the two long lines of stitching. Cut diagonally into the corners, close to the stitching on each end.

6 If you used a long strip for several buttonhole windows, cut the strip between each buttonhole. Pull the patch through the center of each opening.

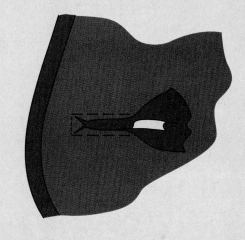

7 From the side of the garment that no longer has a patch on top of it, press the opening so that some or all of the patch is visible, as desired. Using the width of the presser foot as a guide, sew a rectangle around each of the windows, approximately $1/4$ to $1/2$ inch (5 to 10 mm) from all sides of the opening. On the other side of the fabric, trim the patch fabric close to the stitching.

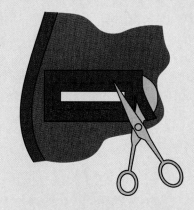

Pocket Flaps

30 MINUTES

A pocket flap isn't tough to make, especially when it's a mock version that doesn't have a pocket. I make the flaps the easy way: by sewing the shape, turning it right side out, and then attaching the finished flap to the vest front with a single line of stitching.

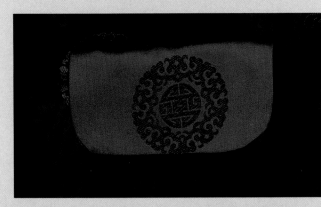

I prefer to make my flaps from coordinating fabric so that my vest has some visual interest. This red satin is a treasure that I picked up while wandering around in San Francisco's Chinatown district.

SHOP BY MAIL Mail-order shopping can be a great timesaver. Free catalogs are available from Nancy's Notions (1-800-833-0690), Clotilde (1-800-772-2891), Donna Salyers Fabulous Furs (1-800-848-4650), and the National Thread & Supply Company (1-800-331-7600). Stonemountain & Daughter Fabrics (1-510-845-6106) will send you fabric samples for a fee.

Add to Your Shopping List

- ✄ ⅛ yard (0.1 m) of trim or fabric that coordinates with the vest
- ✄ Fusible tricot interfacing, the size of one pocket flap pattern

Cut Out the Pattern Pieces

1 Cut two flap pattern pieces on the straight grain from the fashion fabric to make two flaps. Cut one flap pattern piece on the bias from the fusible tricot interfacing. See the pattern layouts on page 54.

2 Cut the interfacing flap piece in half, using the cutting line that is indicated on the pattern.

3 Fuse one piece of interfacing to the wrong side of each fabric flap. The side of the flap that is interfaced is the half that will be visible on the outside of the garment.

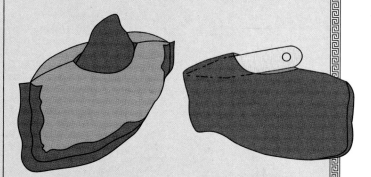

4 Cut ⅛ inch (3 mm) off all around the half that isn't interfaced so that the flap's underside won't show after it's sewn on to the vest.

5 Fold the flap in half with right sides together, matching the cut edges. The flap won't lie flat because one side was trimmed smaller. Pin the halves together from the side that isn't interfaced.

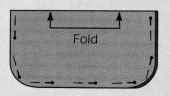

Fold

6 The feed dogs will ease the larger outside half of the flap to fit the smaller trimmed half of the flap. Using a ¼-inch (5-mm) seam allowance, sew around the flap with the interfaced half closest to the feed dogs.

7 Remove the flap from the sewing machine. Press one of the seam allowances back onto the body of the pocket flap.

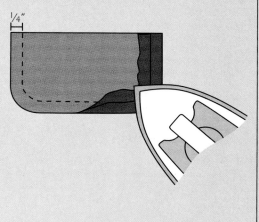

¼"

8 Make a 2-inch (5-cm) slash along the fold. Pull the flap right-side-out through the slash. Push out the corners with a point turner.

Apply the Flaps to the Vest

1 Position a flap on the right side of the vest with the round part of the flap pointed toward the shoulder and the foldline along the placement line on the front.

2 Sew along the flap fold with zigzag stitches that are ⅛ inch (3 mm) wide and 1/16 inch (1.5 mm) long. The line of zigzag stitches will go on and off the fold. This closes the slash and attaches the flap to the vest in one operation.

3 Fold the pocket down. Cover it with a press cloth, spray lightly with water, press, and pound the flap flat with a clapper. If the flap isn't completely flat against the vest, invisibly hand stitch the flap to the underside of the vest. Make and attach the remaining flap in the same manner.

Oversize
T-SHIRT

Easy, Fast, and Stylish

This T-shirt does double—and even triple—duty because, depending on the fabric that you select, it looks dressy or casual. You can wear it to the office under a suit jacket, yet it also looks great with skirts, pants, jeans, and shorts. I like combining it with shorts made from the full pants pattern.

It's also one of the fastest garments you'll ever sew. I promise that this T-shirt will take you only two-and-a-half hours to make, including the time spent cutting it out. In addition to having only three pattern pieces, this T-shirt features several timesaving assembly techniques.

The front and back are joined at only one shoulder before the neckline is finished with bias tape. This is much easier than trying to attach bias tape to a round neckline, and you don't need to fuss with the overlapping end of the bias tape.

My instructions also call for sewing in the sleeves by the flat assembly method. This is a fancy name for a very simple procedure. After the sleeve cap is shaped, it's sewn onto the body. Only then are the side seams and underarm of the sleeve sewn together.

Unlike the boxy, one-size-fits-all T-shirts that are sold in most stores, my garment for the Rodale Designer Collection is meant to flatter your body. It fits the upper chest and shoulders, and the sleeves are loose so that the T-shirt is comfortable in hot weather.

The set-in sleeves are the toughest part of this garment, and I'm giving you lots of advice so that they're as easy as possible to sew. My instructions offer a really fun way to construct this T-shirt because the side and sleeve seams are sewn at one time.

What You Need

You don't need to buy many supplies to make this T-shirt—just a short length of fabric for the body, plus some optional trim and matching thread. For the trim you can use bias-cut strips of self-fabric or purchased bias tape, if you're really eager to finish this T-shirt tonight.

"The neckline on this T-shirt is feminine, showing just enough skin to draw attention to your face. To prevent it from stretching when you apply the bias tape, I recommend stabilizing the neckline with twill tape. Complete instructions for this procedure start on page 80."

Fabric Yardage for T-Shirt

Fabric width	Small	Medium	Large
45 inches (115 cm)	2¼ yards (2 m)	2¼ yards (2 m)	2⅝ yards (2.4 m)
60 inches (150 cm)	1⅝ yards (1.5 m)	1⅝ yards (1.5 m)	1⅝ yards (1.5 m)
Contrasting fabric for trim*			
All widths	½ yard (0.4 m)	½ yard (0.4 m)	½ yard (0.4 m)

* For the neckline, if you don't use purchased bias tape.

WASH IN TIME I agree that preshrinking your fabric can be a pain. But you're better off spending time at the washer and dryer rather than spending several hours restitching hems and seams if the fabric shrinks after the garment is sewn.

Of all the suggestions in "Appropriate Fabric" on the opposite page, only wool jersey needs to be dry-cleaned. Rayon challis, acetate slinky knit, and velour can be machine washed and dried. (Don't forget to turn velour inside out when laundering it.)

Rayon velvet can also be machine washed and dried, but it takes on an antique appearance. Cut off a fabric strip and throw it in with your next load of laundry. If you like the results, wash the velvet. If not, this fabric goes into the dry-cleaning category.

The other fabrics are hand washed and air dried.

Appropriate Fabric

This T-shirt works in a wide variety of fabrics, from rayon challis, rayon velvet, silk crepe de chine, and velour to acetate slinky knit and wool jersey. Satin and tissue-weight linen are both great choices for the neckline trim.

Front

Back

Notions

- ✄ Matching sewing machine thread
- ✄ Package of 1/4-inch (5-mm)-wide twill tape (optional)
- ✄ Package of wide bias tape, or a bias-tape maker to make bias tape with a pressed width of 1 inch (25 mm), if you prefer to use contrasting fabric for the neck trim
- ✄ Woolly nylon thread, if you're using a knit (optional; an exact color match isn't necessary)
- ✄ 2.0/80 double needle for hemming (optional)
- ✄ Serger, if you're using wool jersey
- ✄ Miscellaneous supplies, as listed in "The Sewing Basket" on page ix

KNOW RIGHT FROM WRONG For ease in identifying the right and wrong sides of your fabric, place an adhesive dot or crossed pins on the wrong side of each fabric pattern piece after it's cut out.

Fit Your T-Shirt Pattern

The fit on this T-shirt is forgiving, so you'll probably need to alter very little on the pattern. And because this pattern is multisized, what you do need to adjust can be done in minutes. I alter by simply "transitioning" from one size to the next along the cutting lines.

Get Started

First determine your T-shirt size by matching your bust measurement to the size table on page 208. If necessary, adjust the pattern to fit the parts of your body that are larger or smaller than the size you selected to match your bust. Each section that follows shows how to determine if you have a particular problem and explains how to adjust your pattern to accommodate your body shape.

Disproportionate Bust and Upper Chest

You can tell that you have a narrow upper chest if purchased garments don't sit properly on your shoulders. The seams joining your sleeves to the garment's body fall onto your upper arms.

If you encounter this problem, use a size smaller at the armhole, shoulder, and neck than you're using at the bust, unless you're already

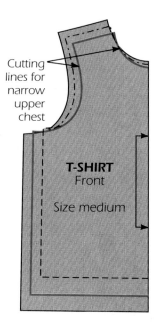

Cutting lines for narrow upper chest

T-SHIRT
Front

Size medium

using a size small, in which case you don't need to alter the pattern.

If you're large in the upper chest, your shoulders extend into the sleeve cap. Unfortunately, this prevents the sleeve from hanging properly in your ready-to-wear garments. To fix this problem, I suggest that you use a size larger at the armhole only.

Sleeve Adjustment

If you made adjustments to the bust and upper chest in the pattern, following the instructions in the previous section, you should also adjust the sleeve pattern. At the underarm on your sleeve pattern, use the same size you're using at the bust. On the sleeve cap, use the same size you're using above the armhole. This illustration is for a size medium with a narrow upper chest.

Underarm →   **T-SHIRT**
Sleeve
Size medium   ← Underarm

Large Hips or Protruding Seat

My T-shirt in the Rodale Designer Collection is designed to comfortably fit a wide range of sizes, even at the hips. Since this T-shirt is loose, it has quite a bit of ease (extra fabric so the garment isn't skintight) built into it, so you may not need to adjust the pattern at all through the hips.

Measure your hips 9 inches (22.5 cm) down from your waist. Compare this measurement to the T-shirt circumference at the hem in "Finished Lengths and Hem Widths" on page 208, and use the cutting lines for the size on the pattern that matches your hip measurement from hip to hem. Using a pencil, draw a new cutting line that transitions between the different sizes at the bust and the hips on both the front and back patterns.

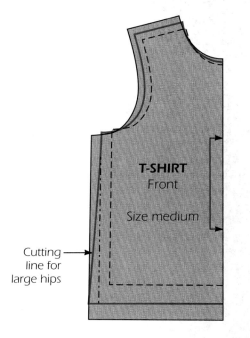

T-SHIRT
Front

Size medium

Cutting line for large hips

You may want to cut the side seams on your patterns a size larger from the bust to the hem if you have full, high hips or a full tummy. If the T-shirt is too big, you can always take it in at the side seams as you're constructing it. However, once the T-shirt pattern pieces are cut out of the fashion fabric, there's no way to obtain the extra fullness if you need it.

SHOP WISELY Note the care instructions on the fabric bolt before you commit yourself to a certain material. In particular, you should notice if the fabric is dry clean only and if it resists wrinkles.

To test, crumple a handful of the fabric and then release it. Do the wrinkles shake out? Through countless discussions with students, I've noted that favorite garments are usually made in fabrics that resist wrinkles.

Pressing is a low priority in most people's lives, including mine. So it's wise to choose low maintenance fabric. The less time you spend ironing, the more you can spend at your sewing machine.

While I'm a devotee of natural fabrics, I often spend more money on a particular fabric in order to get superior performance. I will spend $10 a yard more for a wool if it resists wrinkles. I look for good-quality wool crepes, wool with Lycra blends, and imported cottons and knits.

Length

Decide the desired length for your T-shirt. If you plan to wear it with the slim pants, make the T-shirt crotch length or longer. If you're unsure about the length, measure the length of a favorite T-shirt from the base of the neck to the hem. Note the neckline's position at center back. This is important because the neckline of my T-shirt for the Rodale Designer Collection is 2 inches (5 cm) below the base of the neck at center back. (If your T-shirt starts right at the base of the neck, but the length is the same as this pattern, your T-shirt is actually 2 inches, or 5 cm, shorter than the pattern.) Compare your desired length with the finished length of my T-shirt in the Rodale Designer Collection, which you can find in "Finished Lengths and Hem Widths" on page 208.

Draw a new hemline at the bottom of the T-shirt patterns. If necessary, tape on extra tissue paper to extend the patterns, or cut some tissue off to shorten them.

Cut Out the T-Shirt Pattern Pieces

15 MINUTES

The T-shirt has only three pattern pieces—and these can be cut out quickly if you use pattern weights instead of pins. If you have ever used a rotary cutter, you know that this is a great timesaver as well. How you place your patterns on the fabric varies, depending on the fabric's width.

1 Straighten the crosswise grain on both ends of your fabric. To do this, pull a thread close to each edge. If it breaks, just pull on the thread next to it. The idea is to draw the thread until the fabric puckers. If you have a knit fabric or a woven one on which it's hard to find a cross-grain thread, see the Quick Class "When the Going Gets Tough" on this page.

2 Now cut the fabric along this pucker. Make the cutting line as straight as possible so that you have a straight edge that is on-grain.

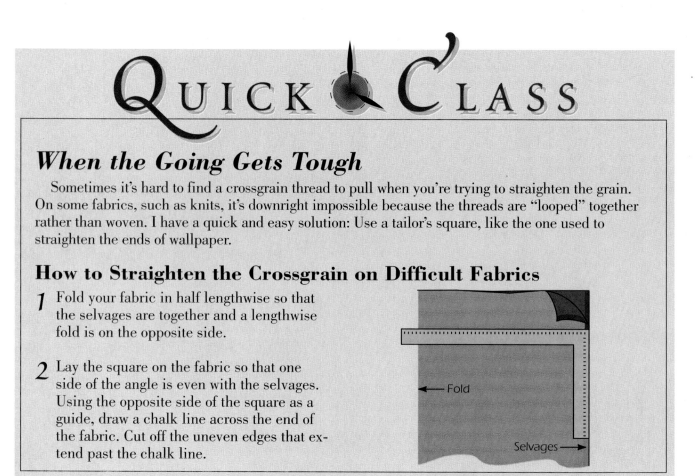

QUICK CLASS

When the Going Gets Tough

Sometimes it's hard to find a crossgrain thread to pull when you're trying to straighten the grain. On some fabrics, such as knits, it's downright impossible because the threads are "looped" together rather than woven. I have a quick and easy solution: Use a tailor's square, like the one used to straighten the ends of wallpaper.

How to Straighten the Crossgrain on Difficult Fabrics

1 Fold your fabric in half lengthwise so that the selvages are together and a lengthwise fold is on the opposite side.

2 Lay the square on the fabric so that one side of the angle is even with the selvages. Using the opposite side of the square as a guide, draw a chalk line across the end of the fabric. Cut off the uneven edges that extend past the chalk line.

Fold

Selvages

3 Place the pattern tissues on the fabric according to the layout for your size and fabric width. Pin or place weights on patterns on the fabric with the pattern foldlines even with the folds on the fabric.

4 Cut out the front and back pattern pieces. If necessary for the sleeve, refold the remaining fabric as indicated in the layout for your fabric width and body size. Lay the sleeve pattern on the fabric with the grainline on the pattern parallel to the selvages. To accomplish this quickly, pin one end of the pattern's grainline arrow to the fabric. Measure the distance between the pinned end of

the arrow and the selvages. Now pivot the pattern on the fabric until the opposite end of the arrow is the same distance from the selvage. Cut out two sleeve pattern pieces.

DOUBLE UP You're going to love this T-shirt so much that I bet you'll make more. So, next time, cut your T-shirt pattern from several fabrics in one session. You'll be surprised at the amount of time that you save.

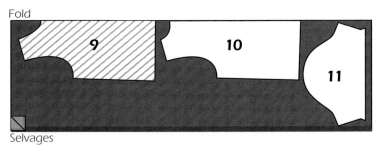

45-inch (115-cm)-wide fabric, with/without nap, small and medium

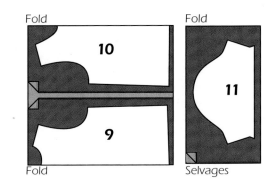

60-inch (150-cm)-wide fabric, with/without nap, all sizes

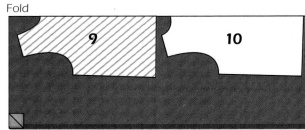

45-inch (115-cm)-wide fabric, with/without nap, large

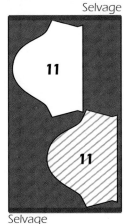

45-inch (115-cm)-wide fabric, with/without nap, large

PATTERN LAYOUT KEY		T-SHIRT	
Right side of fabric		Name	Number
Wrong side of fabric		Front	9
Right side of tissue		Back	10
Wrong side of tissue		Sleeve	11

Construct Your T-Shirt

2 ¹/₄ HOURS

I love this T-shirt because the construction process is fast and flawless. The front and back pattern pieces fit together so perfectly! The garment has set-in sleeves, but don't let that scare you. I offer plenty of tips that will help you through the process.

Sew the Shoulder Seam

1 All the seam allowances are ⁵/₈ inch (1.5 cm) wide and the stitch length is medium (10 to 12 stitches per inch or 2.5 on a 0-to-4 stitch length setting), unless otherwise indicated. For knits or fabrics with "give," like georgette or rayon crepe, use a narrow zigzag set at 10 to 12 stitches per inch or 2.5 on a 0-to-4 stitch length setting. If you're sewing a knit, use woolly nylon thread on the bobbin. Remember to hand wrap it on the bobbin so the thread doesn't lose its stretch.

2 Sew the front and back pattern pieces together at only one of the shoulder seams. The manner that you use to join them is determined by the type of seam finish that you want for your garment.

If you're using wool jersey or rayon challis, sew your pattern pieces with right sides together, and serge the seam allowances.

Alternately, you can use a flat fell seam. See the Quick Class "I Fell for This Technique" on the opposite page. The "mock" version, however, is more appropriate for knit fabrics like acetate slinky knit and velour. Follow the directions in the Quick Class "The Fastest Mock Flat Fell Seam" on page 39.

French seams are best for fine fabrics. See the Quick Class "A 'Seamless' Finish" on page 26.

Prepare the Neckline

1 Since the neckline is a single thickness of fabric and is probably going to stretch, it's a good idea to stabilize the neckline with twill tape or a narrow piece of self-fabric cut from the selvage. Cut the twill tape the same length as the exact distance around the neckline, as measured ³/₄ inch (2 cm) from the cut edge of the neck. Place the twill tape on the wrong side of the fabric so that one edge is ³/₄ inch (2 cm) from the cut edge of the neckline. The tape extends into the seam allowance. If you use self-fabric, put the unfinished lengthwise edge of the strip closest to the cut edge of the neck.

2 Pin the tape to the neckline so that the neckline matches the length of the twill tape. Using a ⁵/₈-inch (1.5-cm) seam allowance, sew the twill tape to the neckline. Place the fabric closest to the feed dogs to ease the slightly larger neck to fit the tape. Press the seam flat.

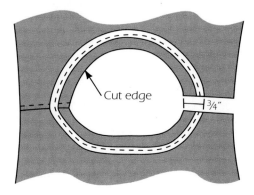

Cut edge

3/4"

QUICK CLASS

I Fell for This Technique

A flat fell seam is the perfect finish if you want the inside of a garment to look as good as the outside. This is especially important if you plan to make your T-shirt, or the tuxedo shirt in the following chapter, from a heavier fabric. In this book I also teach you how to make a mock flat fell seam for knits. On wovens, use a traditional flat fell seam to enclose the cut edges of the seam allowances so they don't ravel. Wool and rayon challis, for example, need a traditional flat fell treatment.

The traditional flat fell seam is created by wrapping the wider seam allowance over the narrower one on the right side of the garment. I'm recommending you work from the wrong side of the garment, however, because the seams are less visible. In addition, your wrapping is more forgiving because exact amounts aren't seen from the outside.

How to Make a Flat Fell Seam

1 The first few times that you make a flat fell seam, it's best to do it on a straight seam. Start with the right sides of your fabric pattern pieces together and the cut edges matching. Sew your seam using a 5/8-inch (1.5-cm) seam allowance. Press the seam allowances open.

2 Trim the seam allowance that's closest to the front (if the seam is vertical) or hem (if the seam is horizontal). To make the shoulder seam on the T-shirt, for example, trim the front seam allowance. The amount that you trim depends on the fabric. For most, you trim to 1/8 inch (3 mm). The seam allowance should be slightly wider if you're making your garment with medium- to heavy-weight fabric. In this case, it's best to trim to 1/4 inch (5 mm).

3 Turn under 1/4 inch (5 mm) on the cut edge of the remaining seam allowance. This is the seam allowance that you didn't trim in Step 2. On the T-shirt shoulder seam, you're turning under 1/4 inch (5 mm) on the cut edge of the back seam allowance.

4 Wrap the wider (back) seam allowance over the trimmed (front) seam allowance. Pin it in place securely through all layers. Change to a stitch length that's slightly longer than regular stitching and topstitch through all layers, close to the fold that you just made. Press the shoulder seam flat from the right side.

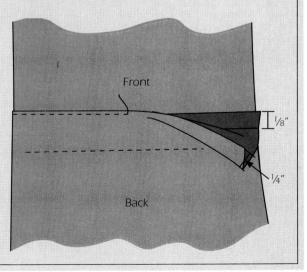

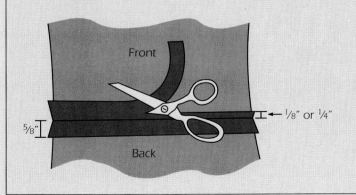

3 Trim off the neckline seam allowance ⅛ inch (3 mm) from the staystitching. Don't remove the staystitching or the twill tape.

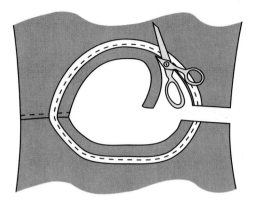

4 The neckline is trimmed with bias tape. You can use packaged bias tape or make your own with a bias-tape maker. If you make your own, start with 2-inch (5-cm)-wide bias-cut strips of self-fabric, lightweight linen, or satin. (For instructions on how to make bias tape, see the Quick Class "Bound to Succeed" on page 58.)

5 To help the bias conform to the neckline, shape it with an iron. Cut a length of bias tape that's long enough to go around the neckline. Slightly stretch the open side of the bias (the side with two folded edges), and steam it.

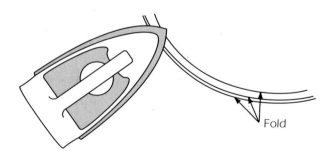

Fold

SHAPE WITH SPRAY STARCH Use a little spray starch when shaping your bias tape. This makes it easier to topstitch the bias tape to the neckline and eliminates ripples.

Finish the Neckline

1 With the right side of the T-shirt up, enclose the cut edge of the neckline inside the bias tape. The cut edge of the neckline butts against the inside fold of the bias. The slightly narrower side of the bias tape is on the right side of the T-shirt. Pin the bias tape in position from the narrower side.

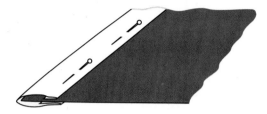

2 Topstitch the bias tape to the neckline. The best position for the topstitching is close to the outer fold, which you previously shaped. The topstitching will catch all layers of the bias tape, since the slightly narrower side of the bias tape is on top.

3 With cut edges even, sew together the remaining shoulder seam. If the front and back aren't exactly the same length at the shoulder, you don't need to cut off any fabric. When you sew the seam, place the longer of the two shoulders closest to the feed dogs on the sewing machine bed. These feed dogs move fabric slightly faster than the presser foot so they'll ease the longer side to fit. If you made a French seam, hand tack the seam allowance flat toward the front.

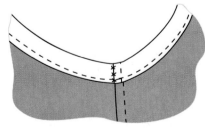

I'M BIASED I like taking short-cuts, even when I cut bias strips. Once you find the true bias on your fabric, don't unfold the fabric. Since the fabric is double, you can cut two strips at a time. (Be sure to cut on the fold first.)

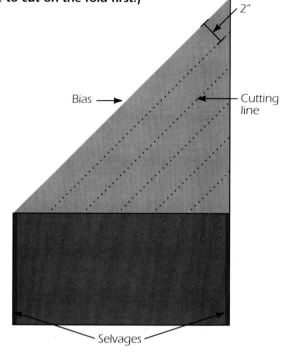

2"

Bias →

← Cutting line

Selvages

Put in the Sleeves

1 Run a row of easestitching around the sleeve cap. (See the Quick Class "Take It Easy" on page 84.) Position the sleeve cap on a tailor's ham and shape it with steam.

---

thread TALES

Through the years, I have developed a way to figure out what types of garments I'll love to make *and* wear. There's a series of questions that I ask when I'm evaluating my wardrobe. The next time you think about overhauling your wardrobe or are about to make something new, try answering these questions.

1 Why do you like your favorite garments so much? Look carefully in your closet and pull out five or six items that you love. Examine these pieces carefully.

2 What sleeve style and length do your favorite T-shirts have?

3 What collar and pocket styles do you prefer?

4 What kind of waistbands do your skirts and pants have?

5 What length and width are your favorite pants? Note this measurement, and apply it to all future pants that you make.

6 What style is your favorite skirt? Is it straight, gored, circular, or A-line? What's the circumference? I like short straight skirts with long jackets or long sweaters. Gored skirts are my favorite in warm weather, and I combine them with a tank top or close-fitting sweater. The fabric that I use for these gored skirts is always drapey and often wrinkle-resistant.

Sandra

QUICK CLASS

Take It Easy

A sleeve cap is made slightly larger than the armhole so that it conforms to the shape of the arm. To make it fit smoothly, you must run an easeline between the front and back notches on the sleeve. This is a row of stitching placed near the seamline but within the seam allowance. The stitch length and pressure on the fabric is determined by the fabric's weight. A heavy fabric requires a long stitch and heavy pressure against the back of the presser foot. Conversely, a fabric as lightweight as silk needs very little pressure and a medium-length stitch.

How to Ease and Shape a Sleeve Cap in 3 Minutes

1 Slide the sleeve cap under the presser foot at the front or back notch. Position your finger behind the presser foot on top of the fabric. In the next step, you'll sew the ease-stitching with your finger applying medium pressure against the presser foot. This prevents the fabric from coming out as fast as it would like to by pushing it against the back of the presser foot.

2 Sew a row of easestitching approximately ½ inch (1 cm) away from the cut edge . Your stitching line doesn't need to be this exact distance from the edge; just make sure it's within the seam allowance so that it doesn't show on the right side of the garment after the sleeve is sewn into the armhole.

3 The fabric bunches up behind the presser foot as you easestitch. Keep pushing at the back of the presser foot with your finger. After 3 to 4 inches (7.5 to 10 cm) of easestitching, remove your finger and let the bunched fabric relax. Your easestitching slightly drew up the fabric. Reposition your finger and continue to sew until you reach the notch on the other side of the sleeve cap.

4 Pin the sleeve into the armhole, matching the notches. If the sleeve is too big, unpin it and add another row of easestitching next to the first. The rows can overlap.

If the sleeve is too small for the armhole, unpin and gently tug the fabric to snap a thread. This will release some of the fullness.

5 Unpin and press the ease in the sleeve cap over a tailor's ham or pressing mitt. Pressing helps shrink in the sleeve cap and set the ease. Press only within the seam allowances, using a press-and-lift motion, so that the ease is only flattened for stitching, not removed.

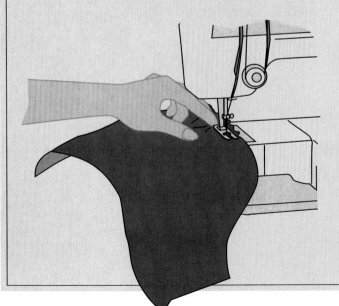

2 Pin the sleeve into the armhole, matching the notches. Place the pins on the sleeve side. Use the same seam finish at the armhole and shoulder seams. If you're sewing French seams, pin the sleeve into the armhole with wrong sides together. For flat fell seams, start with right sides together and remember to trim the armhole seam allowance on the T-shirt body so that the sleeve cap seam allowance can fold around it.

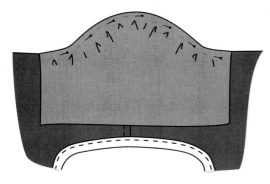

3 At the sewing machine, place the sleeve side up and the T-shirt body's armhole against the feed dogs. Sew the seam. If you get a pucker or pleat in the sleeve, remove the stitches for 1/2 inch (1 cm) on both sides of the pleat. Clip the seam allowance in the T-shirt's armhole. With the sleeve closest to the sewing machine, insert the garment under the needle, pull the seam taut, and sew it again. Clipping the body's seam allowance gives you a little extra room to ease out the pleat. Ease and shape the remaining sleeve, and sew it into the T-shirt body in the same manner.

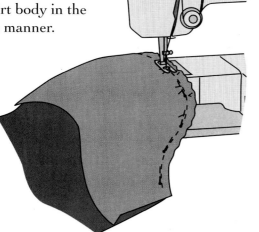

PRESS NOW To save time, press the armhole seam allowances toward the sleeve from the finished side of the T-shirt before you sew the side seams. After the side seam is sewn, the armhole is more difficult to press.

4 Sew the side seam and the underarm seam in the sleeve of the T-shirt in one continuous seam, starting at the hem and ending at the bottom of the sleeve. Finish the seam with the seam finish that you prefer. (See Step 2 of "Sew the Shoulder Seam" on page 80.) Join the remaining sleeve and side seam the same way.

Machine Hem Your T-Shirt

1 Finish the bottom cut edge of the T-shirt and sleeves with a row of serging. If the fabric is lightweight, fold under 1/4 inch (5 mm) instead. You can also finish the sleeve hems with strips of bias-cut fabric or purchased bias tape that matches the neckline trim. The fabric or tape is applied in the same manner that the trim was applied to the vest armholes. (See "Apply the

Extended Wear

My T-shirt pattern for the Rodale Designer Collection can be extended by 20 to 24 inches (50 to 60 cm) and worn as a dress. Follow the same procedure as for the T-shirt. The only difference is that the garment is longer. You can use these same instructions to extend any top that has straight side seams.

How to Make a Dress with Your T-Shirt Pattern

1 Note the circumference of the T-shirt at the hem, as listed in "Finished Lengths and Hem Widths" on page 208.

2 Measure the distance around your hips at the widest part. This is usually about 9 inches (22.5 cm) below the waist.

3 Compare the measurements taken in Steps 1 and 2. The pattern needs to be at least 4 inches (10 cm) larger than your hip measurement. If it is, you can proceed to Step 4. If not, you'll need to alter the bottom so that it's big enough, while maintaining a nice fit around the bust. See "Large Hips or Protruding Seat" on page 77.

4 To determine exactly how much length to add to the T-shirt pattern, take a measurement on your body 2½ inches (5 cm) below the position of a jewel neckline at center back down to the desired finished length for your dress.

5 Measure the length of your T-shirt pattern at center back.

6 Subtract the T-shirt pattern length from the desired dress length, and tape a piece of butcher's paper (or tissue paper) equal to this amount to the hem of the front and back patterns.

7 Referring to "Fit Your T-Shirt Pattern" on page 76, alter the T-shirt pattern to fit any other parts of your body.

8 Use the table below as a general guide for the amount of fabric that you should buy. It will be sufficient if you're adding 27 inches (68 cm) or less to the T-shirt pattern.

9 Cut out your pattern pieces and sew them together, following the general instructions in this chapter.

Fabric Yardage for T-Shirt Dress*

Fabric width	Small	Medium	Large
45 inches (115 cm)	3¾ yards (3.4 m)	3¾ yards (3.4 m)	3¾ yards (3.4 m)
60 inches (150 cm)	5 yards (4.5 m)	5 yards (4.5 m)	5 yards (4.5 m)
Contrasting fabric for trim†			
All widths	½ yard (0.4 m)	½ yard (0.4 m)	½ yard (0.4 m)

* *To determine how much to add to the T-shirt pattern, take a measurement on your body 2 inches (5 cm) below the jewel neckline at center back to your desired finished length. This yardage is calculated for an addition of 27 inches (68 cm) in length.*

† *For the neckline, if you don't use purchased bias tape*

Trim" on page 59.) If the fabric is a knit, no edge finish is necessary because knit won't fray. You can proceed to Step 2.

Serged

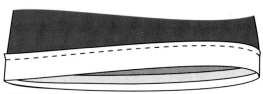

Wide bias tape

Folded under ¼"

2 At the bottom of the T-shirt and sleeves, fold a 1-inch (2.5-cm) hem to the wrong side. Place the pins on the outside of the T-shirt.

3 Insert a double needle in your sewing machine. Hemming by machine is fast, easy, and professional looking if you use a double needle.

Two rows of parallel stitching are created simultaneously on the right side. The rows are joined by a single bobbin thread with a zigzag stitch on the wrong side.

4 If your T-shirt fabric is a knit, the topstitching needs to stretch a little to prevent snapped stitches. I suggest you switch to woolly nylon thread in the bobbin. It's a bit curly and is often used on a serger. It works well on a conventional machine and gives a seamline additional stretch. For tips and instructions on sewing with a double needle, see "Hem Your Pants" on page 43.

5 Topstitch the hem in place. It's best to do this with the double needle positioned close to the top of the hem. If your machine has a free arm, use it to simplify sewing the hem on the sleeve. A free arm is narrow so that the sleeve slips right over it and rests smoothly on the bed of the sewing machine.

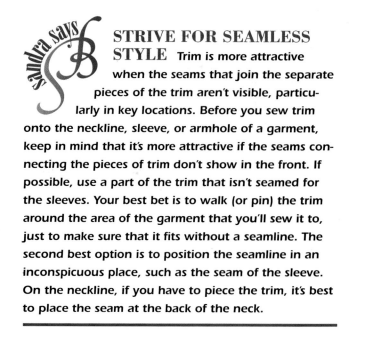

STRIVE FOR SEAMLESS STYLE Trim is more attractive when the seams that join the separate pieces of the trim aren't visible, particularly in key locations. Before you sew trim onto the neckline, sleeve, or armhole of a garment, keep in mind that it's more attractive if the seams connecting the pieces of trim don't show in the front. If possible, use a part of the trim that isn't seamed for the sleeves. Your best bet is to walk (or pin) the trim around the area of the garment that you'll sew it to, just to make sure that it fits without a seamline. The second best option is to position the seamline in an inconspicuous place, such as the seam of the sleeve. On the neckline, if you have to piece the trim, it's best to place the seam at the back of the neck.

THE NEXT STEP

Sheer Delight T-Shirt

3 HOURS

You only need to make a couple of these T-shirts to realize how comfortable, versatile, and flattering they are. Once you're familiar with the assembly procedure, the next step is to consider making one in chiffon. It looks great worn over a sleeveless leotard or a tank top.

With the tips in this section, you'll be working on chiffon as easily as you sew with cotton. The only "trick" you need to know is that you should use French seams. (See the Quick Class "A 'Seamless' Finish" on page 26.)

Add to Your Shopping List

- ✂ Tissue paper or butcher's paper
- ✂ Fine machine embroidery thread or good-quality cotton or polyester thread (cotton-covered polyester is too heavy)
- ✂ Sharp pins
- ✂ Fine sewing machine needle: 8/60H, 9/65H, or a 10/70 H-J

Appropriate Fabric

As I already mentioned, chiffon is a great choice. But any other sheer, like organza or georgette, will also work well.

GET A GRIP Chiffon slips and slides all over the cutting table, making it difficult to pin or cut. You can prevent the fabric from slip-sliding away by covering your cutting table with a double layer of tissue paper. Pin a double layer of chiffon to the tissue paper, along the selvages at 10-inch (25-cm) intervals. Also pin the crosswise cut edges to the tissue paper. Cut through all layers when cutting out the patterns.

Size Your Pattern

Garments cut in sheer fabrics are flattering when they're loose. So cut your T-shirt pattern one size larger at the side seams from the bottom of the armhole to the hem on both the front and the back and one size larger at the underarm on the sleeve.

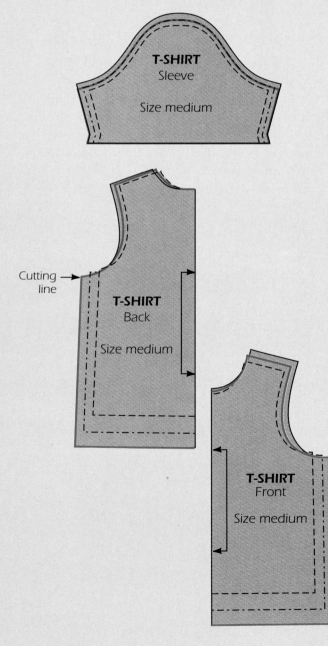

T-SHIRT
Sleeve

Size medium

Cutting → line

T-SHIRT
Back

Size medium

T-SHIRT
Front

Size medium

TAPE WORKS To prevent the sewing machine needle from pushing lightweight fabric down into the bobbin thread slot, shift your needle position to the far left so that there is space in the bobbin thread hole only on the right side.

If you can't change the needle position, use a small piece of transparent tape to cover the hole where the bobbin thread comes out. Don't let the tape cover the feed dogs. When the needle punctures the tape in order to make the first stitch, it creates a bobbin thread slot that's much smaller than the original.

Cut Out the Patterns and Construct Your T-Shirt

1 Using new sharp pins, pin the patterns to the chiffon and the tissue paper. (See "Get a Grip" on the opposite page.) Keep the pins within the seam allowances of the patterns to avoid snagging the fabric in the garment pattern pieces.

2 If you don't own a pair of sharp, top-quality scissors, this will become immediately apparent when you try to cut chiffon. Dull scissors chew at the fabric rather than make a clean cut. For accurate cutting on chiffon, cut through the pattern, fabric, and the tissue paper. After cutting, throw away the tissue paper.

3 Using French seams throughout, sew a shoulder seam, add the trim, sew the remaining shoulder seam, insert the sleeves, and then sew the side and armhole seams, as explained in "Construct Your T-Shirt," starting on page 80. For chiffon, I prefer a 8/60H or 9/65H needle. My second choice is a 10/70 H-J needle and a good-quality cotton or polyester thread.

Hem Your Chiffon T-Shirt

Hand hemming gives a high-quality look to a chiffon garment. Hand stitching isn't that time-consuming and can usually be done while you're doing something else, like watching TV or talking on the phone.

1 To make the hand-hemming process more manageable, run a line of machine stay-stitching through a single layer of fabric, ½ inch (1 cm) away from the cut edge of the hem.

2 Cut off the bottom of the hem close to the staystitching; about ⅛ inch (3 mm) away is sufficient.

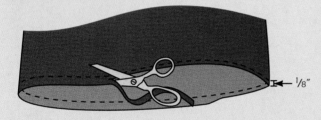

3 Press ¼ inch (5 mm) to the wrong side of the chiffon. Your staystitching line will guide you, and it'll prevent the hem edge from stretching during pressing.

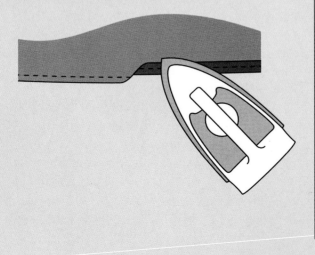

4 Sit in a comfortable chair with good lighting. Roll under another ¼ inch (5 mm) of chiffon at the hem. This encloses the cut edge and the staystitching. Pin the rolled hem in place.

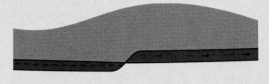

5 Using a single thread, hide the knot at the end of the thread by tucking it under the roll, then slide your hand sewing needle along the fold for ½ inch (1 cm). Bring the needle out of the fabric. Take a stitch in the hem fold and then in the T-shirt. Slide the needle back into the fold, progressing ½ inch (1 cm) farther. Continue around the hem in this manner.

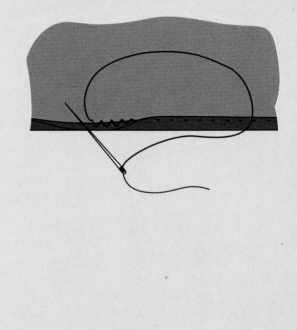

Decorative Neckline

5 MINUTES

What a neat little project! It's a super variation on the basic T-shirt. A decorative stitch, like the machine feather stitch, is an attractive replacement for topstitching at the neckline. Combined with decorative threads, you can create some very special effects.

1 Assemble your T-shirt, following the general instructions up to Step 2 of "Finish the Neckline" on page 82.

2 Using a decorative stitch, sew the bias tape to the neckline close to the outer fold, which you previously stretched. The stitching will catch both layers of bias tape, since the slightly narrower side of the bias tape is on top.

3 Switch back to the straight or narrow zigzag stitch, depending on the type of fabric that you're sewing, and finish the T-shirt, following the general instructions.

SEW EASY If you can't change the needle position on your sewing machine, simply sew a little farther away from the edge of the fabric. This prevents the needle from pushing fine fabric like chiffon down into the hole through which the bobbin thread feeds.

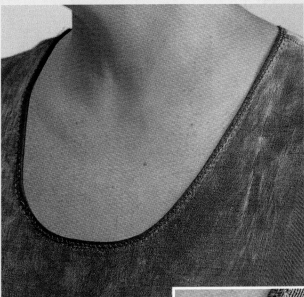

I make good use of the feather stitch on my machine. It's nice in places where you'd like to create a little more interest without being fussy. This stitch is one of several that you might consider using on the neckline of your T-shirt.

Tuxedo
SHIRT

Goof-Proof and Versatile

Ten years ago, while vacationing in Florence, Italy, I fell in love with a shirt like this one. I couldn't resist buying it, and I'm glad I did because I still love it. It's the most flattering shirt I've ever owned because the cut is great. It hangs nicely and skims the hips in a manner that flatters without accentuating them.

When I designed my patterns for the Rodale Designer Collection, I looked to my favorite shirt for inspiration. The result is a cut that I think you'll find incredible. It fits well in the shoulders yet has enough fabric to slide over high hips. Plus, this shirt is very slimming because the lines are clean and the front hem is shaped to curve up across the hip area. This tuxedo shirt functions as a "big shirt" with the ability to camouflage a multitude of sins, while avoiding the "bigness" that destroys the look of most overblouses. We all want people to notice us and our pulled-together look, not the voluminous top that we're wearing.

My tuxedo shirt works well with both slim and full pants in addition to skirts. Your choice is to decide if you're going to wear it tucked in, hanging loose as an overblouse, or over a shell so that the tuxedo shirt acts as a jacket.

After you make the basic shirt, you may want to expand your wardrobe by stitching another tuxedo shirt in a sheer or very lightweight fabric.

Most sewers find it difficult to get a professional-looking neckband at the front neck opening. My technique is simple because it eliminates the pressing and trimming steps, and the results are first class. Both sides of the collar are interfaced to keep them crisp and even during the collar application process.

What You Need

There are many ways that you can express your creativity with this shirt. Your fabric choices will greatly influence the final look of the garment, making it suitable for formal wear if made from chiffon or for casual wear if made of viyella or Guatemalan cotton.

"You can wear the tuxedo shirt buttoned or open with a shell or T-shirt underneath. If you use it as a lightweight jacket, remember to use an attractive finish on the seams."

Fabric Yardage for Tuxedo Shirt

Fabric width	Small	Medium	Large
45 inches (115 cm)	2⅝ yards (2.4 m)	2⅝ yards (2.4 m)	3⅜ yards (3 m)
60 inches (150 cm)	2¼ yards (2 m)	2¼ yards (2 m)	2⅜ yards (2.1 m)
Interfacing*			
Front and hem facings	⅝ yard (0.5 m)	⅝ yard (0.5 m)	⅝ yard (0.5 m)
Collar	⅛ yard (0.1 m)	⅛ yard (0.1 m)	⅛ yard (0.1 m)

* Medium-weight interfacing is suitable for most of the recommended fabrics. If your fabric won't tolerate fusing without becoming too stiff, use a double layer of Stacy's Shape-Flex on the collar. For silk or velvet, use silk organza interfacing on the front and hem facings and a double layer of heavier-weight interfacing, like Stacy's Woven Sew-In, in the collar.

Appropriate Fabric

The shirt that inspired my pattern is made of black rayon faille.

Good fabric choices for my shirt include sand-washed silk, 2- or 3-ply silk crepe de chine, medium-weight linen, lightweight corduroy, velveteen, wool crepe, rayon crepe, rayon velvet, lightweight flannel, viyella, and medium-weight cotton. To be honest, it's difficult to make a mistake in fabric choice with this shirt. Almost anything works. A fabric with some body will show off the shirt's flattering silhouette.

For a sheer shirt or one made from very light-weight fabric, refer to "Add to Your Shopping List" on page 112.

If your shirt fabric is heavy, you may want to cut the shirt facings from a lighter-weight fabric. In this case, you'll need 5/8 yard (0.5 m) of the lighter fabric.

Both sides of the collar and the facings need interfacing. Interfacing gives the collar additional shaping, and heavier interfacing in the front self-facings helps the front of the shirt support buttons and buttonholes.

Since the shirt has a stand-up collar, you need medium-weight interfacing for the collar. In fact, you may want to double the interfacing or for more body, use double layers of interfacing on both of the collar pattern pieces. To determine the suitability of fusible interfacing for your fabric, fuse a piece of interfacing to a scrap of it. If the fabric becomes crisp but doesn't bubble or turn boardlike, then the fusible interfacing is suitable.

Fusible interfacing ruins silk. For such fine fabrics, your best choice for the collar and the front facings is Stacy's Woven Sew-In or silk organza to which you fuse a heavier-weight interfacing.

Notions

- ✂ Matching thread
- ✂ A package of matching or coordinating Wright's wide or double-fold bias tape (optional; used to finish the armhole seam allowance only on medium- to heavy-weight fabric)
- ✂ About seven buttons (the number that you use will depend on the button diameter and your personal taste)
- ✂ Miscellaneous supplies, as listed in "The Sewing Basket" on page ix

Sandra says

CUT CORNERS It takes a lot of time and energy to make your own bias tape just to provide a clean finish for the armholes on your tuxedo shirt. I use purchased bias tape, and I don't worry if it perfectly matches the fabric color. In fact, I often use black or off-white since the tape goes on the inside of the garment. I always keep black and off-white in my supply drawer so that I don't have to make another trip to the store if I run out just before I finish my garment.

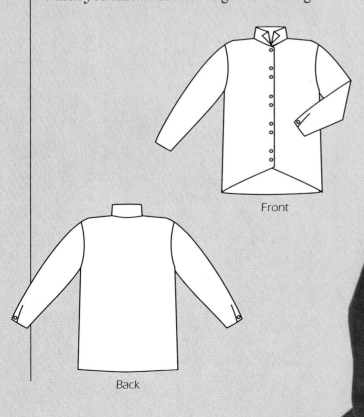

Front

Back

Fit Your Tuxedo Shirt Pattern

All of the patterns in this book are multisized so you can use different sizes for different parts of your body. Since this pattern doesn't have any shaping at the waist, you can ignore this area. This means you only need to adjust the patterns for your bust and hips. It couldn't be easier!

Get Started

Choose the size from the size table on page 208 that best fits your bust. In other areas, use the cutting lines that suit your body measurements. When transitioning between sizes, aim for gradual changes so that the seams are flat.

Cutting line →

Broad Back and/or Narrow Upper Chest

With these sorts of figure problems, you may need to experiment a little to get the perfect size combination. If you have the time, make a mock-up front, back, and one sleeve in scrap fabric. You can refine your needs here, and then cut perfect pattern pieces out of the fashion fabric.

For all of the alterations in this section, the shoulder seams on the front and back are no longer the same length. When the shirt is sewn together, I'll show you a trick to make the length of these two pattern pieces match. Don't add a dart unless the back is more than 1/2 inch wider than the front. (To make a dart, see "Full Back" on page 52 and "Join the Vest Fronts and Back" on page 57.)

Many women have a broad back but are narrow across the upper front chest, which is the area between the armholes just below the collar bone at the base of the neck. You know you have this problem if a ready-to-wear shirt feels comfortable across the back but there are vertical wrinkles across the upper front, since the shoulder seam is not positioned correctly. Also, the armhole seam falls onto the upper arm.

If this sounds like you, use the cutting line for your bust size at the upper back on the back pattern, and follow a smaller size in the upper front chest, from armhole to shoulder only.

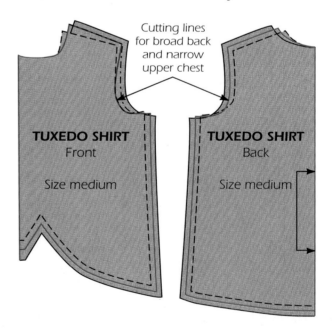

Cutting lines for broad back and narrow upper chest

TUXEDO SHIRT Front
Size medium

TUXEDO SHIRT Back
Size medium

It's possible to have only a broad back or a narrow upper chest. If the backs of your ready-to-wear garments feel tight, you have a broad back.

To adjust your pattern to fit, use a larger size from the armhole to the shoulder on the back pattern. If you have a narrow upper chest without a broad back, use a size or two smaller in the area from armhole to shoulder.

Large Hips or Protruding Seat

You have this figure variation if ready-to-wear shirts don't hang smoothly over your hips and seat.

Measure your hips around the widest part. Based on this measurement, choose the size that you want to use for the hip area of your shirt from the size table on page 208.

If your hip measurement is larger than the largest size, you need to add the number of inches necessary to match your personal measurement. Simply subtract the size large hip measurement from the size table on page 208 from your personal measurement. This number needs to be added to the shirt's hips. Divide the number by four. Add this to the hip area at each side seam on the front and back patterns. Redraw your side seam, starting at the armhole, and at the cutting line for the size that matches your bust. Draw a new, straight cutting line to the size you selected for the hem.

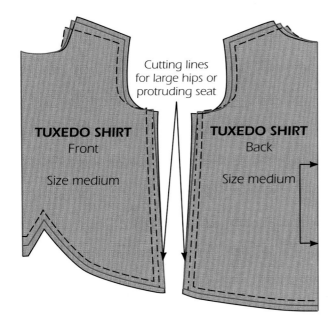

Cutting lines for large hips or protruding seat

TUXEDO SHIRT
Front

Size medium

TUXEDO SHIRT
Back

Size medium

Long or Short Torso

I doubt that you'll need to adjust the length because it looks great on all sizes. If you want to make a change, do so at the lengthen/shorten line on the front and back patterns.

To make the shirt longer, cut along the lengthen/shorten line on the back pattern, and tape a piece of paper along the cut edge. Measure up from the pattern's cut edge the amount that you want to add. Draw a line on the paper at this distance. Tape the other part of the pattern to the line that you just drew. Repeat the same procedure to lengthen the torso on the front pattern.

To shorten your shirt, fold up half the extra length required along the lengthen/shorten line, and tape the fold in place.

Long or Short Arms

Put an arm at your side and bend your hand at the wrist. This bend is where your sleeve should end. Measure your arm from the top of the shoulder down to your bent wrist. Now compare this length to the table "Finished Lengths and Hem Widths" on page 208. Chances are great that you can use the cutting lines for one of the sizes on the pattern. If you're not that lucky, then you can make your sleeve pattern longer or shorter by following the directions in "Long or Short Torso" above. I don't bother altering the sleeve length on my patterns because I usually wear my sleeves rolled or pushed up.

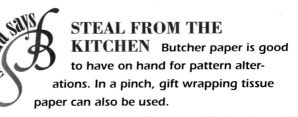

STEAL FROM THE KITCHEN Butcher paper is good to have on hand for pattern alterations. In a pinch, gift wrapping tissue paper can also be used.

Cut Out Your Shirt Pattern Pieces

30 MINUTES

*When I create a pattern, I make the shapes as user-friendly as possible.
For example, I don't add unnecessary notches. Like most of you, I don't like
cutting out patterns so I try to make the process as easy as possible. And,
when I do cut patterns, I make an evening of it and do several at a time.*

Get Ready

1 Straighten the cut ends of your fabric by
pulling a thread close to each edge. If it breaks,
just pull on the thread next to it. The idea is to
draw the thread until the fabric puckers. Cut the
fabric along this pucker, so that you have a straight
edge that is on-grain. If your fabric is difficult to
straighten, see the Quick Class "When the Going
Gets Tough" on page 78.

2 Lay the fabric flat. Place the pattern tissues
on the fabric according to the layout for your
body size and fabric width on the opposite page.
(You may need to cut out all of the patterns except the sleeve, then cut the sleeves from a single
layer of the remaining fabric.) If your fabric has a
nap or one-way design, refer to "Layout for
Napped or One-Way-Design Fabrics" on this
page. Pin the patterns to the fabric by placing
pins in all the corners and along the gaps. As you
cut, use smooth, long motions whenever possible,
holding the pattern flat against the fabric with
your opposite hand. If your shirt fabric is heavy,
you may want to cut your hem facings from a
lighter-weight fabric.

3 Before taking the pattern tissue off the fabric
pattern piece, transfer all notches to the fabric
with tailor's tacks, dressmaker's tracing paper, or a
water- or air-erasable marking pen. (See the Quick
Class "A Tailor-Made Solution" on page 55.)

A MARK IN TIME . . . You'll
save "nine" in the long run if you carefully transfer all the notches on your
patterns to the fabric pattern pieces.
These pattern markings are important and
must be clearly visible on the fabric. They help you
quickly find your matchpoints and ensure that you're
joining the correct pattern pieces together. After all,
no one likes ripping out a sleeve after sewing it into
the wrong armhole.

Layout for Napped or One-Way-Design Fabrics

1 If you're using a fabric with a nap, like velvet,
or a fabric with a design that has a top and
bottom, be sure to cut all of the pattern pieces with
the bottoms pointed in the same direction. The nap
should be smooth when you run your hand from
the top to the bottom, and the top of the design on
a one-way print should be at the top of the pattern.

2 Position the pattern grainlines parallel to the
selvages so that they're on the fabric. (The selvages are the tightly woven edges that run along
both lengthwise edges of your fabric.) Cut out the
pattern pieces.

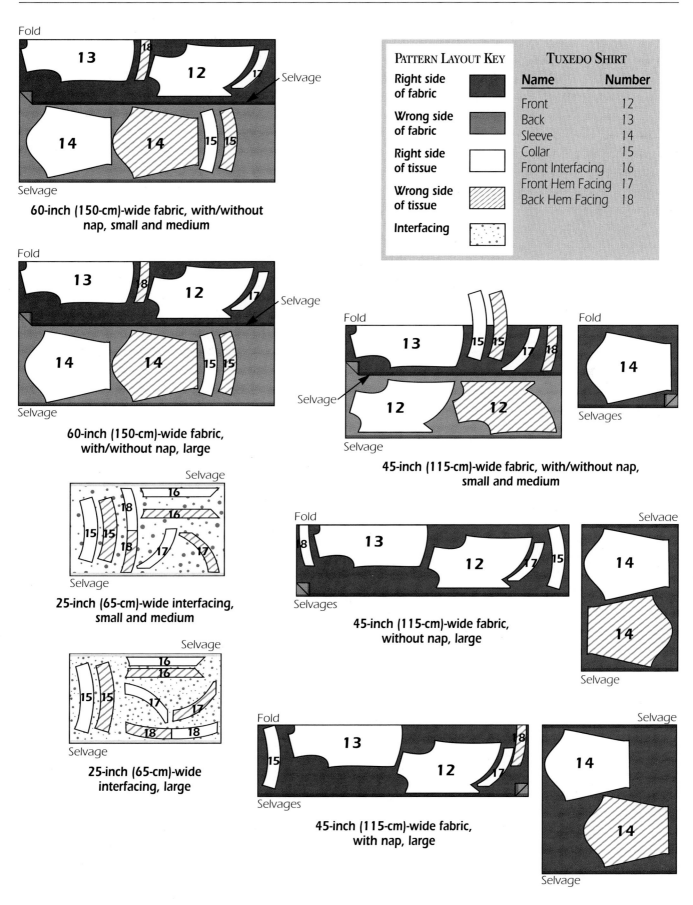

PATTERN LAYOUT KEY

Right side of fabric	
Wrong side of fabric	
Right side of tissue	
Wrong side of tissue	
Interfacing	

TUXEDO SHIRT

Name	Number
Front	12
Back	13
Sleeve	14
Collar	15
Front Interfacing	16
Front Hem Facing	17
Back Hem Facing	18

60-inch (150-cm)-wide fabric, with/without nap, small and medium

60-inch (150-cm)-wide fabric, with/without nap, large

25-inch (65-cm)-wide interfacing, small and medium

25-inch (65-cm)-wide interfacing, large

45-inch (115-cm)-wide fabric, with/without nap, small and medium

45-inch (115-cm)-wide fabric, without nap, large

45-inch (115-cm)-wide fabric, with nap, large

Make the Tuxedo Shirt Self-Facing

20 MINUTES

To save you time, I designed the shirt with a self-facing. In other words, you don't have to cut or sew on a separate placket. Creating the self-facing is a simple process, but the steps vary according to the type of interfacing and the weight of the fabric that you're using.

1 The collar and hem are interfaced. From the interfacing, cut two collars, two front hem facings, and one back hem facing, as shown on page 99. Set these pattern pieces aside.

2 This shirt has a self-facing, which means that the front pattern extends past center front by a few inches. During construction this extension is folded to the wrong side to act as a facing. There is a separate pattern for the interfacing that is applied to the self-facing, which is called the front interfacing. Cut two front interfacing pattern pieces.

3 Before making the self-facing on your tuxedo shirt, the lengthwise cut edge closest to center front must be finished. The procedure for applying interfacing to the self-facing and finishing the edge varies according to the weight of your shirt fabric.

Do a Trial Run

To decide if you like the way a garment fits, test it first in scrap fabric. Trust me, this trial run will take no more than 30 minutes. After you refine the fit, you can powerhouse through the real thing.

How to Transfer Fitting Changes to Your Pattern

1 Cut the fronts and back from an old sheet, and baste them together.

2 Try on the garment. Pinch and pin the fabric until you're happy with the way it looks. Too tight? Then take out the basting and repin.

3 Take off the garment. Rub chalk over the pins. Measure the distance between the chalk marks and take away that amount from the patterns. For example, if you pinched 2 inches (5 cm) out of the hip area, then you need to take this off the side seams of your front and back patterns. Divide 2 inches (5 cm) by 4, since there are four "parts" to your side seams. Now take away ½ inch (1 cm) at the hips on every side seam.

Interface a Lightweight Fabric

1 On the wrong side of the fabric, position the interfacing along the foldline on the front pattern piece. The front interfacing is narrower than the self-facing (the part extending past the foldline, which will be inside of the shirt when the garment is completed). This prevents bulk on the front edge of the facing. Fuse or baste the interfacing to the front.

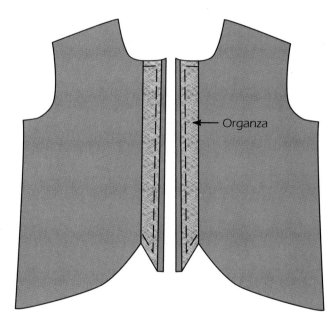

Organza

2 Press under ¼ inch (5 mm) on the self-facing edge of the front. Machine stitch it in place using a medium stitch length (10 to 12 stitches per inch or 2.5 on a 0-to-4 stitch length setting).

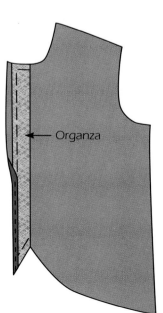

Organza

3 Repeat Steps 1 and 2 for the remaining front pattern piece. In the same manner, apply interfacing to both collar pattern pieces and the front and back hem facings. Don't turn under any of the cut edges on the fabric pattern pieces.

Interface a Medium- to Heavy-Weight Fabric

1 Fuse or hand sew your interfacing to the wrong side of both of the collar pattern pieces and the front and back hem facings.

2 Serge or zigzag the long edge of the self-facing. This is the long vertical edge of the front that extends a few inches past the foldline. Repeat these steps for the remaining front pattern piece.

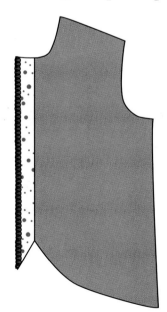

FUSE IT FAST I'm a fan of the Elnapress. This is a miniature home version of the "clamshell" press that dry cleaners use. It's really a timesaver because it fuses a much larger surface than your iron can each time you position it on the fabric.

Construct Your Tuxedo Shirt

2 HOURS

To reduce the time you spend at your sewing machine, I designed this shirt with some fast construction techniques in mind. For example, the sleeve is sewn to the body before the side seam is sewn. This results in one long seam that starts at the bottom of the sleeve and ends at the hem.

Join the Shoulders

1 All the seam allowances are ⅝ inch (1.5 cm) wide, and the stitch length is medium (10 to 12 stitches per inch or 2.5 on a 0-to-4 stitch length setting), unless otherwise indicated.

2 With right sides together, join the front and back at the shoulders. If you altered the upper chest or back pattern, the width of the front and back shoulders is different. In this case, match the cut edges at the start of the seam, and sew them together with the back shoulder against the feed dogs and the front shoulder closest to the presser foot. The feed dogs will ease, or shorten, the longer back shoulder so that, at the end of the seam, it's the same length as the front shoulder.

3 Finish the shoulder with a flat fell seam. This is a wonderful way to finish your seams so I urge you to give it a try. The technique is a lot easier than you might think. (See the Quick Class "I Fell for This Technique" on page 81.)

Prepare the Neckline

1 The front self-facings are open. The next step is to staystitch the neckline of the shirt ½ inch (1 cm) from the cut edge.

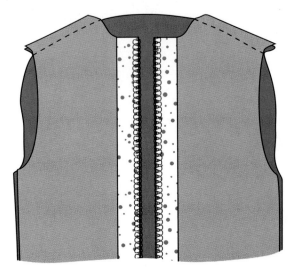

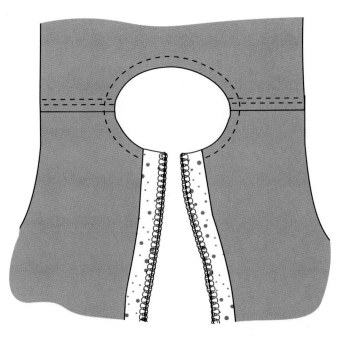

2 With the right sides together, fold one front self-facing back onto the shirt. With small machine stitches and starting at the facing fold, sew a ³/₄-inch (2-cm)-long line with a ⁵/₈-inch (1.5-cm) seam allowance at the neck edge. Make sure that the stitching stops before the end of the facing.

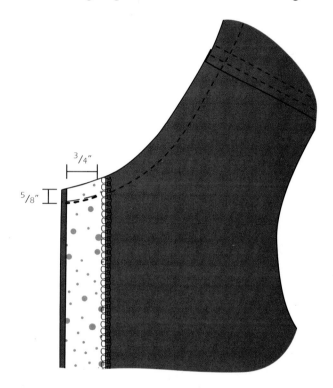

3 At the end of the stitching that's nearest to the finished edge of the self-facing, make a clip into the seam allowances from the neckline almost to the stitching. Stop the clip ¹/₁₆ inch (1.5 mm) away from the stitching line. Trim off the corner of the facing edge.

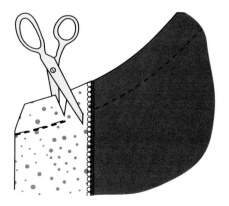

4 Turn the facing right-side-out. It's a lot easier to do this if you use a point turner to push out the corner. Be careful not to overwork it.

5 Press the self-facing to the wrong side. To prevent the finished edge of the self-facing from imprinting on the front, you can press with an envelope between the edge and the front. Repeat Steps 1 through 5 for the remaining self-facing.

Apply the Neckband and Collar

1 At the front neck edge of the shirt, pin the right side of one collar pattern piece against the wrong side of the front. (This collar pattern piece will now be referred to as the under collar.) The notches on the collar are matched to the shoulder seams. Both ends of the collar extend beyond the neck seam allowance by ⁵/₈ inch (1.5 cm). The unsewn top end of the facing is included with the neckline of the shirt. Clip into the neckline of the shirt at 1-inch

(2.5-cm) intervals so that the collar and neck-line fit smoothly. Pin, and then sew the under collar to the shirt's neckline, using a ⅝-inch (1.5-cm) seam allowance.

2 With right sides together, pin the matching shape of the upper collar against the under collar along the short sides and long un-stitched edge.

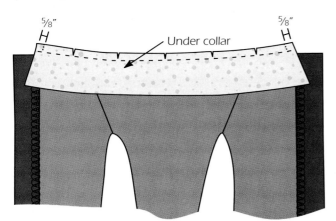

Under collar

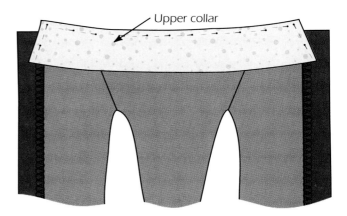

Upper collar

QUICK CLASS

A Classy Collar Trick

Now here's a trick for sewing the ends of your collar. It's used extensively in the garment in-dustry for ready-to-wear clothes because it improves the finished appearance. I like it because it's easy to master and it's fast.

How to Sew a Nice Collar Quickly

1 Fold or roll up the end of the neck on the front, making it as small as you can.

2 With the neck end of the shirt sandwiched in between the ends of the upper collar and the under collar, sew the two collars together with ⅝-inch (1.5-cm) seam al-lowances. Start sewing the seam at the center of the straight side where the collar is not attached to the neck.

3 Continue around the short collar ends and into the neckline seam where the under collar and the shirt neckline are already joined. Remember to hand walk the cor-ners. (See the Quick Class "Let Your

Fingers Do the Walking" on page 191.) Continue this seam into the neck for 2 inches (5 cm). Be careful not to catch the shirt in with the stitching as you sew this seam. Repeat Steps 1 through 3 on the other side of the collar.

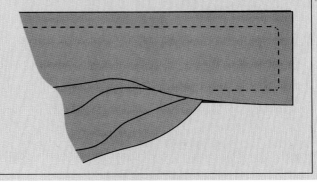

3 Sew the front neck ends. A very fast method is explained in the Quick Class "A Classy Collar Trick" on the opposite page.

4 Trim off the corners on the collar, and trim all the sewn seam allowances in the collar and neckline to ¼ inch (5 mm). Turn the collar right side out. Use a point turner, not scissors, to push out the points.

5 Along the neck edge between the under collar and the shirt, fold under ⅝-inch (1.5-cm) seam allowances on the upper collar. Topstitch the opening closed. Continue topstitching all around the collar, sewing very close to the collar edges in order to flatten them.

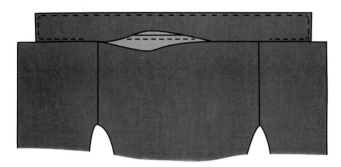

6 Press and pound the collar flat with a tailor's clapper. Fold the collar points down diagonally. The amount that you fold the points down is up to you. Press the points. On the underside, take a few discreet stitches to hand tack the points so they won't flip up.

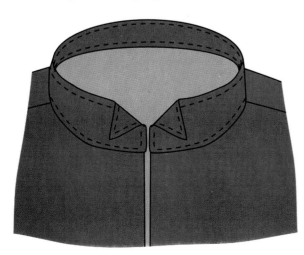

USE ZIGZAG STITCHES
If your fabric is a knit or another material that you think will relax after it's sewn (like wool jersey or rayon crepe), sew your seams with a tiny zigzag stitch rather than a straight stitch. This will put a slight stretch in the seam, preventing seams from looking drawn up after the fabric relaxes.

Set In the Sleeves

1 An armhole is usually 1½ to 2 inches (3.5 to 5 cm) smaller than a sleeve cap. This additional fabric in the sleeve is called ease, and it's necessary for wearing comfort as well as fit because the top of the sleeve has to go over the top of the arm. To make the sleeve fit the armhole, easestitch and shape it. This technique is explained in the Quick Class "Take It Easy" on page 84.

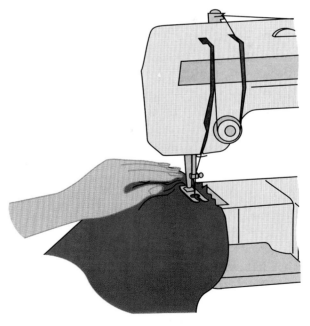

2 Don't sew the sleeve side seams yet. Pin the sleeve into the armhole, matching the notches and placing the pins on the sleeve side.

Sew the sleeve into the armhole from the side seam, around the cap, to the remaining side seam. Flatten out the ease as you sew by pulling the fabric flat with your fingers positioned on either side of the presser foot. Ease and shape the remaining sleeve, and sew it into the shirt body in the same manner.

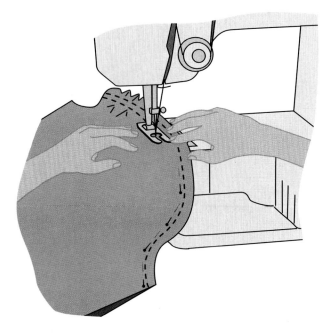

Finish the Armhole Seams

You can choose one of several methods to finish your armhole seam allowances.

Because you may want to use the shirt occasionally as a jacket, you will enjoy it more if all seams are finished. Decide on a treatment that suits the tuxedo shirt fabric, and also take into consideration the amount of time that you have to make the garment.

The fastest method is serging, but you can also use a flat fell seam or wrap the cut edges with bias tape. A flat fell seam is a good finish for lightweight fabrics. For heavier fabrics, a bias-trimmed armhole is the best option because this gives a clean finish. A flat fell seam tends to be too bulky for heavy fabrics because there are several layers of fabric at the seamline.

Serge the Seams

1 After the sleeve is put in the armhole, serge the armhole and the sleeve seam allowances together on the wrong side of the garment.

2 Press the seam allowances toward the sleeve. Now repeat this entire procedure for the remaining sleeve.

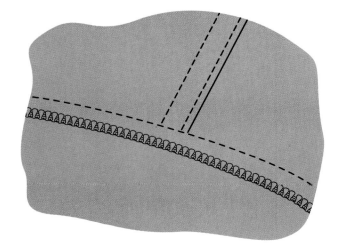

Use Flat Fell Seams

1 Press the armhole seam allowances open. Trim the shirt seam allowance to a skimpy 1/4 inch (5 mm) wide.

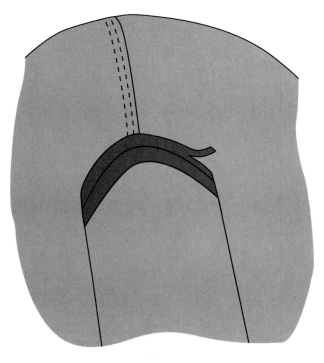

2 Now press the sleeve seam allowance over the previously trimmed shirt seam allowance. Wrap the sleeve seam allowance around the trimmed seam allowance, enclosing the cut edge. Pin in position.

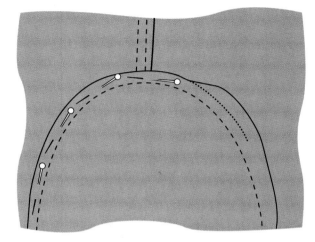

3 Topstitch the seam allowances from the wrong side of the garment. Position the top-stitching on the body side, not the sleeve side, of the finished garment. Repeat this procedure for the remaining sleeve.

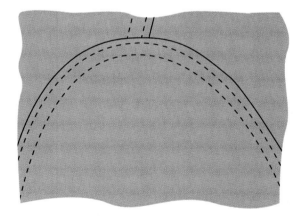

"PREFAB" IS FAB If you can track down a package of Wright's double-fold bias tape, you can save some time by skipping a few steps. The tape, which is readily available in fabric stores, is already pressed and ready to use.

thread
TALES

How many times have you had the nagging feeling while making a garment that you'll never wear it? You're having too much fun to stop sewing but you're starting to feel guilty about the amount of money you spent on the fabric.

This happened to me. I sacrificed a length of white 3-ply silk crepe de chine for an unwearable tuxedo shirt.

A little while ago the fashion "hotshots" were predicting (once again) that the white shirt would be a pivotal piece in a woman's wardrobe.

I don't own a white shirt. But I like to dress fashionably so I decided to make one with a double front so people wouldn't be able to see through it. Since this shirt was to be such an important part of my wardrobe, I bought an expensive piece of fabric. After all, I planned to wear it two or three times a month.

With my precious fabric tucked under my arm, I immediately rushed to my sewing studio. About two hours into the project, I began to question why I hadn't made a white shirt before.

An hour or so later I completed the blouse and headed for the mirror. Then I discovered why I had such doubts while I was sewing: I don't look good in white. I never have.

A few days later I started the same process all over again, this time with black fabric.

Sandra

Wrap the Seam Allowances with Bias Tape

1 Open a package of Wright's wide bias tape. Press the tape in half lengthwise, making one side ⅛ inch (3 mm) wider than the other.

2 Enclose the cut edges of the armhole seam allowances inside the bias tape with the wider side against the sleeve seam allowance and the narrower side against the body seam allowance. Place the pins on the body seam allowance side. Topstitch the bias tape in place through all layers of the fabric.

3 Press the bias-encased armhole seam allowances toward the sleeve. Finish the remaining sleeve's seam allowances in the same manner.

IT'S NOT A "BASTE" OF TIME Since fit is so important, get in the habit of machine basting your side seams for the first fitting. The basting stitches are much easier to remove if you remember to slip in a bobbin in a contrasting color thread before you start.

Join the Fronts to the Back

1 With right sides facing, pin together the front and back along the side seam. The sleeve seams face out toward the sleeve. Unless your seams are flat-felled, the armhole seam allowances are pressed toward the sleeve. Match the sleeve exactly at the armhole underarm seam. Put a pin across the seam to keep it from moving.

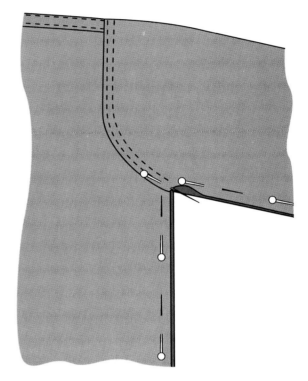

2 Sew the side and sleeve in one continuous seam, starting at the bottom of the sleeve and ending at the shirt hem. As you sew, hand walk the machine stitching over the armhole underarm seam to prevent breaking the needle. (See the Quick Class "Let Your Fingers Do the Walking" on page 191.) Sew together the remaining side and sleeve in the same manner.

3 Do a flat fell finish on the side/sleeve seams or wrap them with bias tape. (See "Use Flat Fell Seams" on page 106 and "Wrap the Seam Allowances with Bias Tape" on this page.)

Finish Your Tuxedo Shirt

1 HOUR

The front of this shirt is curved, so shaped facings are used to finish the front and the back of the garment. Such facings are easier to apply and faster than hemming. If your tuxedo shirt fabric is heavy, you may want to cut the facings from a lighter-weight fabric.

Hem the Sleeves

You can serge the hem, apply bias tape, or turn up a narrow hem. If you want to apply bias tape, follow the steps in "Wrap the Seam Allowances with Bias Tape" on the opposite page and proceed to Step 2. A narrow hem, which is explained in the following steps, is suitable for lightweight fabrics.

1 Serge the cut edge of the sleeve, or turn it under 1/4 inch (5 mm), if you would rather make a narrow hem.

2 To complete the narrow hem, turn under 3/4 inch (2 cm). If the edge was serged or if you attached bias tape, turn under 1 inch (2.5 cm). Press on the foldline. Pin near the hem's upper edge.

3 Topstitch the sleeve hem in place from the wrong side of the sleeve. This is easiest if you have a free-arm sewing machine.

The way that I place a button at a sleeve hem makes it both functional and attractive because you can position the buttonhole for a snug or loose fit. It's a great technique for eliminating a cuff and is much faster than the fussier "tailored" method.

4 Slip the sleeve, right side out, over a sleeve roll, a rolled-up magazine, or a towel, and press it.

5 Fold the sleeve in half lengthwise so that the seam is on one side. Starting at the hem, press a 6-inch (15-cm)-long crease in the opposite side. This is important because the crease is the start of

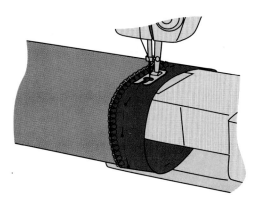

creating an overlap for the button and buttonhole closure that you're making for the bottom of both of the sleeves.

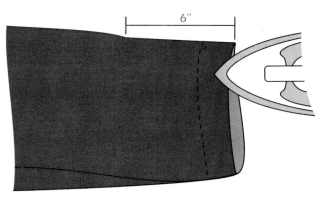

Add Hem Facings

1 With right sides together, sew a front hem facing to each side of the back hem facing. Press the seam allowances open, and trim them to ¼ inch (5 mm).

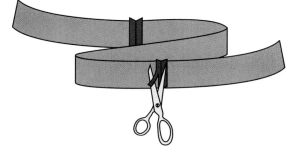

6 Place the shirt on a table so that the front of the shirt is facing up. On the side of the sleeve with the crease, and with the sleeve still folded, mark and then make a buttonhole through all the layers of the fabric. Position it parallel to the topstitching and ½ inch (1 cm) away from the fold. Repeat Steps 1 through 6 for the remaining sleeve.

7 Try on the shirt to determine the position of the button at the sleeve hems. At the buttonhole on one sleeve, fold the front of the sleeve over the back until the sleeve has the desired circumference. Insert a pin through the buttonhole to mark the position for the button. Take off the shirt, and sew on the button.

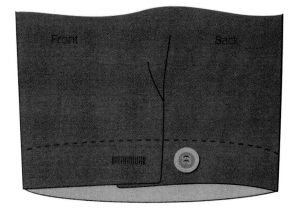

2 Finish the inside curve of the hem facing by serging, enclosing it with wide bias tape, or pressing it under ¼ inch (5 mm).

Wide bias tape

¼" pressed under

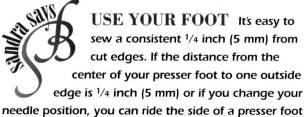

Serged

USE YOUR FOOT It's easy to sew a consistent ¼ inch (5 mm) from cut edges. If the distance from the center of your presser foot to one outside edge is ¼ inch (5 mm) or if you change your needle position, you can ride the side of a presser foot along the cut edge of the fabric.

3 Fold the front self-facings to the right sides of the front along the foldlines. Pin in place with the cut edges of the hems even. With right sides together, place the hem facing on the shirt with the lower cut edges even. The hem facing will be on top of part of the self-facings. Make sure that the side seams match. The hem facing won't go all the way to the foldline for the self-facing. Baste, then sew it to the shirt front.

4 Snip through the seam allowances almost up to the stitching line along the curves for the length of the hem facings. The snips should be spaced about ¹/₂ inch (1 cm) apart.

5 Turn the hem facing and self-facings to the wrong side of the shirt along the seamline. Press. Pin the hem facing to the wrong side of the shirt along the inside, curved edge. Top-stitch it in place. Continue topstitching up the front of the shirt, close to the folded edge, through the front and the self-facing. Remove the basting stitches.

MY FAVORITE NOTION I'm always on the lookout for terrific buttons. My favorite sources are craft fairs, junk shops, and estate sales. Also, I never buy buttons for an outfit without first checking my "stash" to see if I already own something that will work. I may not have the exact number of buttons the pattern calls for but if I'm only one short, I eliminate one buttonhole and reposition the rest.

Make Buttonholes

1 Try on the shirt. Decide where you would like to position your buttons, and place pins on these spots. Personally, I like one buttonhole in the middle of my bust area and another buttonhole at the neck.

2 Sew your buttonholes on your right front and your buttons on the left front at the corresponding locations. The diameter of your button determines the position of both your buttons and buttonholes on the front. To figure out the positions, see "Add a Closure to Your Vest" on page 61.

Insert Shoulder Pads

It's perfectly acceptable to attach a pair of shoulder pads with Velcro. In fact, you can use the same set for several garments if they all have Velcro strips sewn on the shoulder seams. For instructions on attaching shoulder pads with Velcro strips, see the Quick Class "To Pad or Not to Pad" on page 203.

THE NEXT STEP

Sheer Tuxedo Shirt

4 HOURS

I love to dress up, particularly in a classic garment like a sheer shirt. But I don't like my undergarments and the front facings to be visible to the whole world. My technique for eliminating "show through" is rather simple and works for light-colored as well as for sheer fabrics.

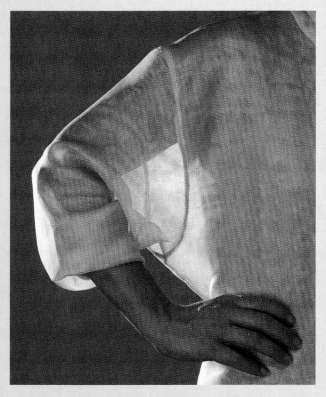

A sheer tuxedo shirt can be stylish and modest if you use a double-layer front. That is, it's constructed with four front pattern pieces instead of two. Instead of cutting two fronts with self-facings, I eliminate the self-facing on the front pattern, add a seam allowance to the front edge, and cut four front pattern pieces from the fashion fabric. This is an excellent technique for working with chiffon, georgette, and other semitransparent fabrics.

Add to Your Shopping List

Whatever your size or fabric width, to determine the amount of material that you need, refer to the yardage table on page 94. This table lists the yardage needs for a shirt made from fabric that isn't sheer. Since you cut only two front pattern pieces, you'll need a bit more fabric for a tuxedo shirt made from sheer fabric.

Of course, cutting two additional front pattern pieces takes a little more fabric. But I find that if I buy an additional ¾ yard (0.7 m) of fabric, no matter what the fabric width, I'll have enough material for the additional fronts.

Appropriate Fabric

Organza, chiffon, lightweight linen, white or pastel crepe de chine, and any other fabric that's normally a bit too sheer is suitable for the sheer tuxedo shirt. Lightweight fabrics are the most appropriate choice for this shirt. And you may want to use organza for interfacing. If more body is desired, you can apply interfacing to the organza.

Alter Your Pattern

1 Cut off the self-facing along the foldline on the front. If desired, you can fold the self-facing out of the way rather than cut it off.

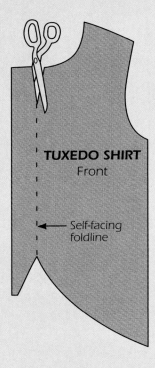

TUXEDO SHIRT
Front

← Self-facing
foldline

2 Mark an X on the pattern near the foldline to remind you to add a ⅝-inch (1.5-cm) seam allowance along this edge.

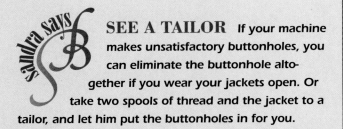

SEE A TAILOR If your machine makes unsatisfactory buttonholes, you can eliminate the buttonhole altogether if you wear your jackets open. Or take two spools of thread and the jacket to a tailor, and let him put the buttonholes in for you.

TAKE TIME OFF Finding time to sew can be a problem. I avoid this frustrating problem by scheduling an entire day of sewing every month. I stay in my pajamas from dawn to dusk, don't cook any meals, and avoid the phone.

Cut Out the Shirt Pattern Pieces

1 Straighten the grainline on your fabric, and lay out your patterns. Don't cut out the front hem facings, and remember to cut four fronts, each with the added ⅝-inch (1.5-cm) seam allowance along the former self-facing foldline.

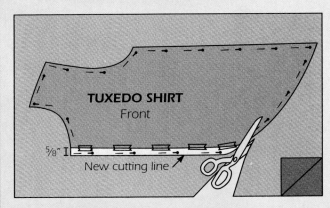

TUXEDO SHIRT
Front

⅝" |←

New cutting line ↗

2 Add a ⅝-inch (1.5-cm) seam allowance to one long edge of the front interfacing pattern. Cut out the interfacing pattern pieces—two collars and two front interfacings—from lightweight organza or self-fabric.

Construct the Sheer Tuxedo Shirt

1 Set aside a right and a left front. Interface the remaining two fronts, a right and a left, which I'll now call the shirt front linings.

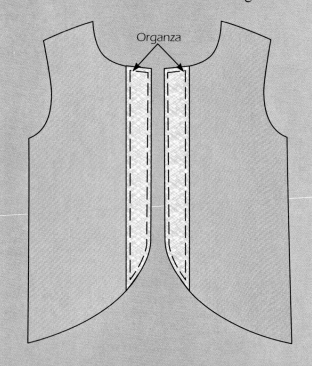

Organza

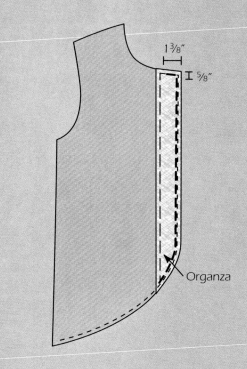

1³⁄₈"

⁵⁄₈"

Organza

2 Place the right side of a front against the right side of a matching front lining (the one with the interfacing on it). Sew a seam at the neckline, starting 1³⁄₈ inches (3.4 cm) in from the front edge and ⁵⁄₈ inch (1.5 cm) down from the cut edge of the neckline. Make the seam follow the neckline, sewing toward the front edge of the shirt. The seam is ³⁄₄ inch (2 cm) long. At the corner, pivot and sew down the front of the shirt, ⁵⁄₈ inch (1.5 cm) in from the cut front edges. Continue down the front, around the curve, and onto the bottom of the shirt to the side seam.

3 Press back the seam allowance on the front lining pattern piece. Trim the front and lower edge seam allowances to ¹⁄₄ inch (5 mm). Cut off the point at the neckline and the lower edge to eliminate bulk.

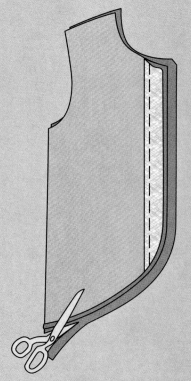

4 Turn the front and front lining right side out. With wrong sides together and remaining cut edges matching, hand baste around all the edges, including the side seam, the armhole, and the shoulder. As you stitch the front edge, roll the seam slightly toward the lining side.

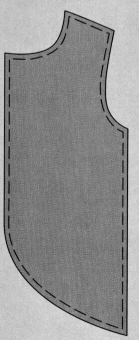

5 Press the seamed edges, and pound them flat with a tailor's clapper. Join the remaining front and front lining in the same manner.

Tailor's clapper

6 Continue constructing the shirt, following the steps under "Construct Your Tuxedo Shirt" on page 102 up to sewing the side and sleeve seams. Use French seams to construct the garment. (See the Quick Class "A 'Seamless' Finish" on page 26.) As you work through the instructions, handle the front and front lining as a single pattern piece and eliminate the front hem facings. They aren't necessary because you already finished the front hem when you sewed the front and front lining together.

7 The back is ⅝ inch (1.5 cm) longer than the front. Sew the side and sleeve seams as explained in the general instructions, but let the excess ⅝ inch (1.5 cm) at the back hem extend past the bottom of the front.

8 Finish the back hem by using the excess ⅝ inch (1.5 cm) for making a narrow hem, for attaching bias tape, or for sewing on the back hem facing.

Shawl Collar
JACKET

A Simply Great Garment

My closet was the first place I looked for inspiration when I decided to include a jacket in my designs for the Rodale Designer Collection.
I pulled out the jacket that I wear the most and asked myself why it was my favorite. The reasons were pretty obvious. It goes with almost everything, it's comfortable and flattering, and it can be dressed up or down. I feel great when I wear it.

Now you'll own a jacket like this. My jacket pattern creates the perfect piece for almost everything you own. You can wear it with pants, skirts, and dresses. It's much like my favorite but it's "tweaked" to look and feel even better.

I also designed it so that you can make it quickly. Construction is easy and fast because it has cut-on rather than set-in sleeves.

If you really want to make a classy-looking jacket, use contrasting fabric to pipe the collar, or make an inside pocket with a flap. These additional treatments are featured in "The Next Step," which begins on page 134.

You can also attach a unique patch pocket that has two openings. This paper bag pocket, which is also featured in "The Next Step" on page 138, is made much like a conventional patch pocket–but it's funkier looking.

The inside of an unlined jacket doesn't have to look ugly. I'll show you how to finish the center back seam allowances by wrapping them with bias tape.

What You Need

You don't have to spend hours figuring out what fabric, notions, and interfacing you need for this jacket. The list of supplies isn't extensive or complicated. Also, a wide range of materials are suitable, and you may already have a nice piece in your fabric collection that's just perfect for a contrasting collar.

"Because this jacket has cut-on sleeves (they're part of the body pattern rather than sewn on), many of your normal fitting concerns will disappear. Extra ease is part of this garment's style so you don't need to make many adjustments."

Fabric Yardage for Jacket

Fabric width	Small	Medium	Large
45 inches* (115 cm)	3½ yards (3.1 m)	3½ yards (3.1 m)	3½ yards (3.1 m)
60 inches* (150 cm)	2⅜ yards (2.1 m)	2⅜ yards (2.1 m)	2⅜ yards (2.1 m)
Additional fabric			
Contrasting fabric for collar (optional)	1⅛ yard (1 m)	1⅛ yard (1 m)	1⅛ yard (1 m)
Lining fabric for shoulder pads (optional)	¼ yard (0.2 m)	¼ yard (0.2 m)	¼ yard (0.2 m)
Underlining, 45 inches (115 cm) wide (optional)	3½ yards (3.1 cm)	3½ yards (3.1 m)	3½ yards (3.1 m)
Fusible knit interfacing for front (optional), sleeve and back hems, and collar	2 yards (1.8 m)	2 yards (1.8 m)	2 yards (1.8 m)

This yardage includes enough fabric to cut four collar pattern pieces. Don't reduce this yardage if you want to cut two of the collar pieces in contrasting fabric.

Appropriate Fabric

Since I travel a lot, I look for fabrics that resist wrinkles. I strongly suggest that you also choose a jacket fabric that doesn't look crumpled by the end of the day. Several fabrics qualify: wool crepe, wool flannel, wool gabardine, wool and Lycra blends, medium-weight linen, denim, velvet, and silk tweed. Steer away from wool gabardine if you're new to sewing because it's hard to get professional-looking results from this challenging fabric. You may also want to try making the jacket in silk crepe de chine.

Another option that you should consider is using a different fabric for two of the four collar pieces. This fabric should coordinate with the jacket fabric since it will show when the collar and lapels turn back.

Note: Before buying your interfacing, take a small piece home and try fusing it to your fabric to make sure you like the result.

SHOP AT HOME If you're the kind of person who buys a lot of fabric but rarely makes anything with it, now is the time to do a little shopping in your closet. Bring out five or six pieces of fabric that might be suitable for this jacket. Take these fabrics to your mirror and then to your closet to see if any of them suit your hair color and wardrobe.

Next place a few of the fabrics in a basket where you'll see them frequently. If you see them a lot, chances are, you'll be able to decide if they'll make a nice garment, or you'll think of another use for them. Even if none of your selected fabrics work for this project, you might find a home for them, either in your wardrobe or someone else's.

Notions

- Matching thread
- Two packages of wide bias tape or a serger
- Beeswax
- Button, 1½-inch (3.5-cm) diameter or larger
- Raglan-style shoulder pads
- Miscellaneous supplies, as listed in "The Sewing Basket" on page ix

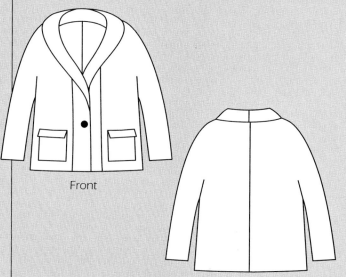

Front

Back

Fit Your Jacket Pattern

With my pattern, you don't need to make adjustments for a broad or narrow back or a narrow upper chest. The cut of this jacket will fit without these alterations. I fitted the garment on many different body shapes to ensure that it works for all figures.

Get Started

What you need to be concerned about is using the right size for certain areas of your body. Select your pattern size by choosing a size from the size table on page 208 that corresponds to your bust measurement. Don't cut out the patterns yet. You'll personalize the fit at different points of your body by moving to different cutting lines where appropriate. For example, a pear-shaped figure may require a size small in the upper chest (the area from the armhole to the neck) and a size medium or large in the hips. Your actual measurements determine the size that you need in each area.

Each section that follows explains how to determine if you have a particular problem and how to adjust your pattern to accommodate your body shape.

of the jacket in the the table "Finished Lengths and Hem Widths" on page 208. Instructions to lengthen or shorten your jacket follow. It's very important that you add or subtract the same amount on the front, back, and collar patterns.

Lengthen Your Pattern

Cut through the pattern along the lengthen/shorten line. Place a piece of tissue paper under the pattern, and spread the pattern the amount desired. Tape the pattern to the tissue paper along the cut edges. On the new tissue, draw the cutting lines for the sides of the pattern.

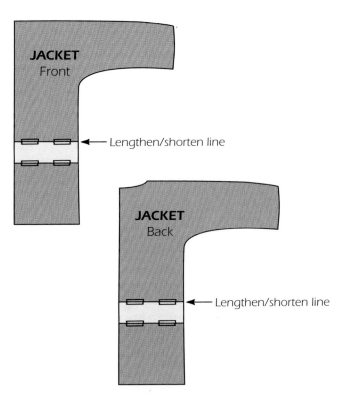

Long or Short Torso

The jacket length is your choice. Go to your closet and pick a jacket that has a length that you like. Measure it at center back from the neck to the hem.

Compare this number to the finished length

Measure from neck to hem

Shorten Your Pattern

Make a fold along the lengthen/shorten line. The width of the fold should be half the amount that you want to subtract from the length of the jacket. Straighten the cutting lines, as above.

Long or Short Arms

This jacket has cut-on sleeves, so you measure from the nape of your neck, over your shoulder, to the bottom of your wrist bone.

Compare this measurement to the finished sleeve length for my jacket pattern, which is listed in "Finished Lengths and Hem Widths" on page 208. Alter your sleeve at the sleeve lengthen/shorten line, following the same procedure explained in "Long or Short Torso" on the opposite page.

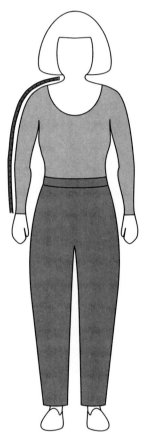

Large or Small Tummy or Hips

If you have trouble buttoning up your jackets, you might need to adjust the hip or the tummy area. But don't make changes on your patterns without carefully looking at the measurements in the size table on page 208 because the fit of this jacket is very forgiving.

Also, if you find that jackets are usually too loose through your hips (lucky you), I don't think that you should take in this jacket pattern. I designed this garment so that it has plenty of

ease. It's meant to be boxy looking.

Measure your hips and then measure your tummy. The best place for taking a tummy measurement is about 2½ inches (6 cm) down from your waist. The larger of these two measurements (the hips or the tummy) determines which cutting lines you'll use for your front and back patterns from the underarm to the hem. Choose the corresponding size from the size table on page 208.

Put an X on the new cutting line for the hips at the lengthen/shorten line on the body of your pattern.

At the underarm, draw a new line from the cutting line that you selected for your bust out to the cutting line for the size that you're using at the hips. This line should move out smoothly and gradually.

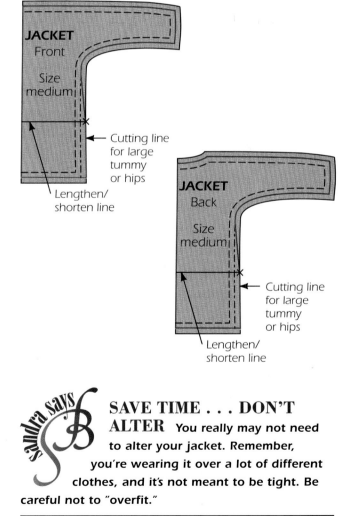

Cut Out Your Jacket Pattern Pieces

25 MINUTES

This garment only has three patterns since the sleeves are included with the body of the jacket. Without a separate sleeve pattern, you don't have to worry about matching strips, plaids, or prints at the top of the armhole when you're cutting out the pattern pieces.

1 Pretreat your fabric. Place your fabric on the cutting surface so that it's only one layer thick. Don't fold it in half lengthwise.

2 If your collar will be made in a contrasting fabric, cut two collar pattern pieces from your contrasting fabric. You need a "right" and a "left" collar, so cut one from the fabric with the tissue right side up and cut the second with the tissue right side down. Cut two more collars from your fashion fabric for the under collar. Place the patterns on the fabric with the grainline parallel to the selvages, following the pattern layout on the opposite page that corresponds to your size and fabric width.

3 Place pins in all the corners and spaced along the gaps. As you cut, use smooth, long motions, holding the pattern flat.

Cut Out the Interfacing

1 All four collar pattern pieces and the back hems are interfaced. To reduce bulk, the hems on the front pieces aren't interfaced. The back isn't interfaced, but you may interface the front, if you wish. Fold under the bottom 2 inches (5 cm) of the front pattern so that you don't cut interfacing for the hem.

2 The sleeve hems on the front pattern aren't interfaced. Fold under 1½ inches (3.5 cm) at the bottom of the sleeve if you will be interfacing the front pattern pieces.

3 Fold the interfacing in half lengthwise, and lay the front pattern on it so that the grainline is on a diagonal, which is the bias. Pin, then cut out the fronts through both layers of interfacing to obtain two fronts. The interfacing pieces for the fronts are 2 inches (5 cm) shorter than the jacket length, and the sleeves are 1½ inches (3.5 cm) shorter than sleeve length on the pattern.

4 Position your collar patterns on the interfacing so that the grainline is on the bias. Cut four collars from the interfacing.

JACKET
Front

1½"

2"

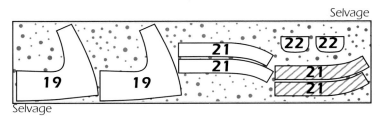

28-inch (71-cm) -wide interfacing (interfacing is optional for jacket front), all sizes

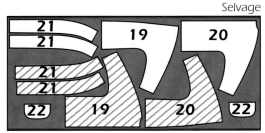
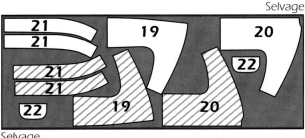

45-inch (115-cm)-wide fabric, with/without nap, small and medium

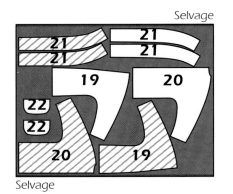

60-inch (150-cm)-wide fabric, with/without nap, small and medium

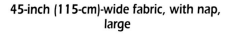

45-inch (115-cm)-wide fabric, with nap, large

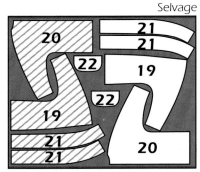
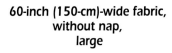

60-inch (150-cm)-wide fabric, without nap, large

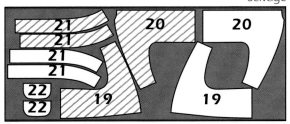

45-inch (115-cm)-wide fabric, without nap, large

PATTERN LAYOUT KEY	JACKET	
Right side of fabric	**Name**	**Number**
Right side of tissue	Front	19
	Back	20
Wrong side of tissue	Collar	21
	Pocket Flap*	22

The pocket flap (pattern 22) is optional. Only cut it out if you plan to include a pocket flap on the jacket, as featured in "Inside Pocket with a Flap" on page 140.

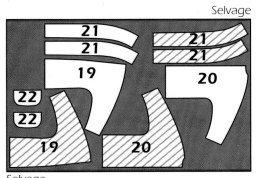

60-inch (150-cm)-wide fabric, with nap, large

Prepare the Jacket Pattern Pieces

20 MINUTES

Trust me, fusing is the most time-consuming part of making this jacket because the sewing is so simple. Before constructing the jacket, optional interfacing is added to the front pattern piece, and reinforcing strips, also of interfacing, are applied to the hems on the back and the sleeves.

Test Your Interfacing

1 Experiment with a scrap of fusible interfacing and a scrap of the jacket fabric to make sure that the interfacing completely bonds to the fabric. Apply a bit of the interfacing to the back of the fabric scrap, as shown in the Quick Class "Fast and Easy Fusibles" on page 56.

2 Fusing onto the wrong side of the pattern pieces may not be advisable for finer fabrics. In this case, use a sew-in interfacing or add an underlining. See the Quick Class "Underline Your Style" on the opposite page. If you choose to underline, you'll find that the jacket will wrinkle less.

Press the Hems

1 To help the back hem maintain its shape, cut two 2-inch (5-cm)-wide bias-cut strips of either fusible or sew-in interfacing, each one as long as each back pattern piece at the hem. Cut two more strips, each 1¹/₂ inches (3.5 cm) wide, for the sleeve hems.

2 Fold the 1¹/₂-inch (3.5-cm) hem to the wrong side on both of the sleeves and a 2-inch (5-cm) hem on the back pattern pieces. Press along the folds, then open out the hems.

3 Fuse or baste the interfacing strips to the hem areas above the hem crease on the jacket backs and sleeves. Don't interface the hem allowance, which is the area that is folded to the wrong side. This is to eliminate bulk.

4 Press up 2-inch (5-cm) hem allowances on the bottom of the fronts and backs.

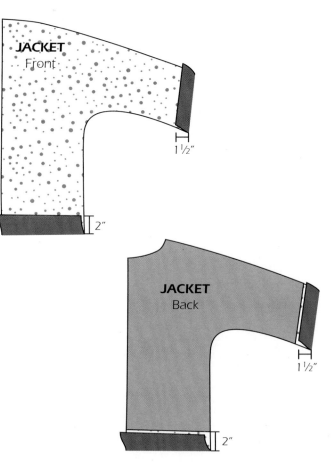

QUICK CLASS

Underline Your Style

If the test you conducted in "Test Your Interfacing" on the opposite page made your fabric boardlike or bubbly, don't fuse interfacing directly onto the wrong side of the pattern pieces. Instead, use a sew-in interfacing if your fashion fabric is medium weight, or else underline the garment and apply interfacing to the underlining if your fabric is lightweight.

Underlining gives lightweight fabric more substance so you can use it to make garments for which the material wouldn't ordinarily be suitable. Essentially, underlining is adding another piece of material to the back of a lightweight fabric.

To underline, you merely cut all of the patterns from both your fashion and underlining fabrics. So, you need the same amount of underlining as you do fashion fabric. Common fabrics used for underlining are cotton batiste, voile, prewashed silk organza, or even an old sheet. I often use flannelette to underline silk. Make sure that the care instructions for your underlining are the same as your fashion fabric. If you use flannelette, preshrink it in hot water and a hot dryer.

How to Make Underlining

1 Select an underlining fabric. Remember to preshrink the underlining in the washer and dryer.

2 Cut your pattern pieces from the underlining. For the jacket, use the interfacing patterns as your guides, and cut out two fronts and four collars. Like the interfacing pattern pieces, the body hems are 2 inches (5 cm) shorter than the jacket pattern pieces cut from the fashion fabric, and the sleeve hems are 1 1/2 inches (3.5 cm) shorter.

3 If you plan to interface, fuse the interfacing to the underlining. Since underlining is hidden inside the jacket, it doesn't have a right or wrong side. Just make sure that you fuse interfacing to a left side and a right side.

4 Hand baste the underlining pattern pieces to the wrong side of the matching fashion fabric pattern pieces. If you interfaced the underlining, the underlining layer is positioned with the underlining closest to the wrong side of the fashion

fabric because interfacing is stiffer. If you're underlining with flannelette, place the fuzzy side against the wrong side of the fashion fabric.

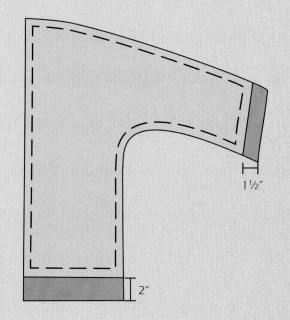

5 Construct your garment following the general instructions. At every step, you treat each underlining/fashion fabric pattern piece as though it's a single layer.

QUICK CLASS

Wrapping It Up

One method of clean finishing the cut edges of your seam allowances is called a Hong Kong finish. It's an attractive way to cover exposed cut edges on unlined garments. Traditionally, this edge finish is created by sewing strips of bias-cut fabric to the seam allowances. You can take a short cut by using packaged bias tape or make your own with a bias-tape maker. To make your own, start with 1¾-inch (4.5-cm)-wide bias-cut strips of lightweight fabric, either handkerchief linen, silk crepe de chine, or silk charmeuse, and see the Quick Class "Bound to Succeed" on page 58.

How to Wrap a Seam Allowance with Bias Tape

1 Fold and press the bias tape so that one half is slightly wider than the other. About ⅛ inch (3 mm) is sufficient for an extension on your bias tape. If this is the first time you've tried this, you should practice on a small piece of scrap fabric first.

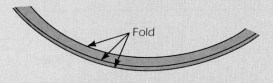

Fold

3 Since both seam allowance edges are separately enclosed, attach the bias tape to one seam allowance, then repeat the process for the remaining seam allowance. With the right side of the seam allowance up, enclose the cut edge of the seam allowance inside the bias tape. The cut edge of the seam allowance butts against the inside fold of the bias. The slightly narrower side of the bias tape is on the right side of the seam allowance. Pin the bias tape in position from the narrower side of the bias tape.

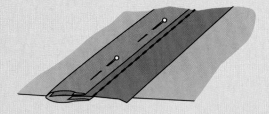

2 If your seam allowance is curved, shape your bias so that it conforms to the curve. Cut a length of bias tape that's long enough to extend past both ends of the seam allowance. Unfold it, slightly stretch one side, and steam it with an iron.

Fold

4 Topstitch the bias tape to the seam allowance through all layers, catching the bias tape on the back of the seam allowance in the stitching.

Mark the Pattern Pieces

1 Pin the patterns back onto the fronts. Transfer the pattern marks to the pattern pieces after fusing is completed. Otherwise, the interfacing covers up the pattern markings and you have to make the marks all over again.

2 Using dressmaker's tracing paper or a water- or air-erasable marking pen, mark the pocket placement and front edges on the front pattern pieces.

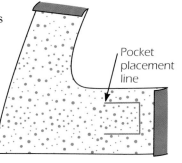

Pocket placement line

Finish the Hem Edges

1 Unfold the pressed hem on all of your fabric pattern pieces: the fronts, backs, and sleeves. Now finish the cut bottom edge of the hems with serging or sew-on bias tape. If you're using bias tape, see the Quick Class "Wrapping It Up" on the opposite page.

2 Again fold up the hem on the fronts and on the sleeves. Don't fold up the hem on the backs. They need to be open so that you can sew the backs together along the center back during the next part of the construction process.

Construct Your Jacket

3 HOURS

Now for the fun part. Because the sleeves are cut-on rather than cut separately and sewn to the body later, many construction steps are eliminated. You sew the shoulder seams and the sides seams, and you're ready for the collar! You can put this jacket together on a Saturday afternoon!

Join the Backs to the Fronts

1 When you're at your machine, remember that all the seam allowances are ⅝ inch (1.5 cm) wide and the stitch length is medium (10 to 12 stitches per inch or 2.5 on a 0-to-4 stitch length setting), unless otherwise indicated. Staystitch the neck on the backs ½ inch (1 cm) from the cut edge.

2 With the right sides of the backs together and the cut edges even, sew the center back seam, including the unfolded hem.

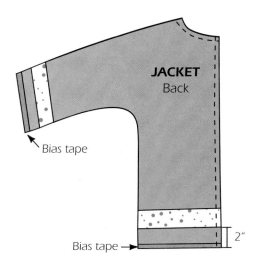

JACKET Back

Bias tape

Bias tape →

2″

3 With right sides together, pin the fronts to the back at the shoulders. When you sew the shoulder seams, you're also making the tops of the sleeves.

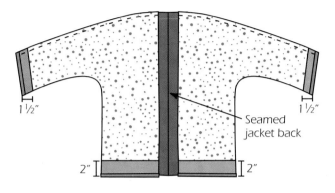

1½"

2"

2"

1½"

Seamed jacket back

Attach the Under Collar

1 If you're making part of the collar in a contrasting fabric, use the contrasting fabric pattern pieces for the upper collar. To make the under collar, sew a right and a left collar piece together at center back with the right sides together, then press the seam allowances open. Join the remaining collar pattern pieces together in the same manner to make the upper collar. Set aside the upper collar.

2 With right sides together, match the center back seam on the jacket back to the center back seam of the under collar. Match the collar notches to the shoulder seams. Pin the rest of the collar to the neckline of the jacket. The bottom of the collar will extend past the jacket hem on both sides. Don't unfold the front hems. Sew in one continuous seam. Fold out the under collar so that the front and under collar are both right side up. Finger press.

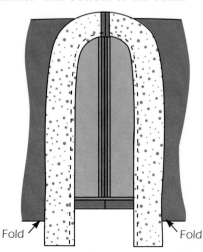

Fold

Fold

Join the Jacket at the Underarm Seams

1 Fold down the hem allowance at the bottom of the front and back side seams and the sleeves. Slip a bobbin with thread in a contrasting color into the sewing machine. With right sides together and cut edges even, machine baste both of the underarm seams, making each seam one continuous row of stitching. Start at the bottom of the jacket and end at the bottom of the sleeve.

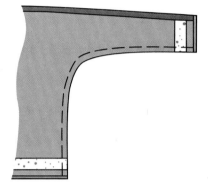

2 Try on the jacket over a T-shirt or a blouse. Slip in a pair of shoulder pads. Play with the collar to determine a flattering roll line. Lap the right front over the left front. How does the jacket fit? Do you need to take in or let out the side seams? If you never wear a jacket closed, don't overlap the fronts. Analyze the fit again. Feel free to raise the underarm seam an inch or so. Keep in mind that the jacket can be worn over a larger variety of sleeve styles if the armhole isn't too high. Place a pin on the left front where you want to sew on a button.

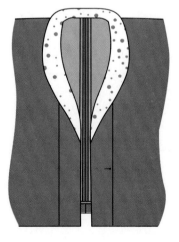

3 When you're comfortable with the fit through the underarm and the shape of the collar, the next step is to join the fronts to the back by sewing the side seams on your jacket. Sew, then clip the curved portion of the underarm seam allowances at $1/2$-inch (1-cm) intervals. Each clip stops $1/8$ inch (3 mm) from the seamline. The seam allowances must be well clipped or else the jacket will wrinkle at the underarm. After clipping them, you should be able to extend the seam into a straight line.

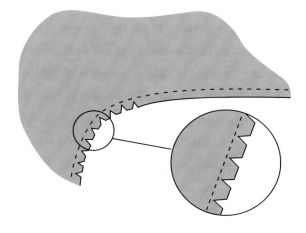

QUICK CLASS

The Straight and Narrow

Try this three-step pressing process to give you the nicest-looking seams. Pressing over a curved surface eliminates seam imprints on the right side of the fabric.

How to Create a Puckerless Seam

1 Sew your seam, then press it as it was stitched, with the seam allowances together and closed.

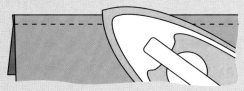

2 Now turn the seam wrong side up, and place it on top of a sleeve roll. Press the seam allowances open. Never put more than the weight of the iron when you're pressing on the wrong side.

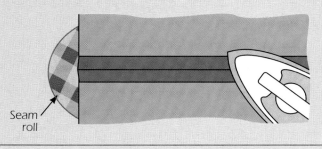

Seam roll

3 Turn the seam over so that the seam allowances are against the ironing surface and the right side of the seam is up. Depending on the type of seam you're making, your fabric may or may not be right side up. Cover the seam with a press cloth and press. You can use more pressure when the right side of the fabric is up.

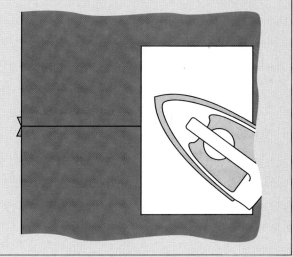

4 Extend one of the side seams in a straight line so that you have one hand at each end of the seam. With the seam extended, pull it quickly. This is called cracking. The stitches may pop in a few places.

5 Sew the underarm seam again, close to the first seamline. If stitches popped anywhere else in the seam, sew another line of stitching in those areas. Cracking and reinforcing the seam prevents popped stitches when the garment is worn. Press the underarm seam allowances open. Crack the remaining underarm seam.

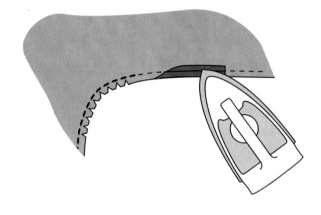

6 Finish the side seam allowances with a serger, a flat fell seam, or bias tape. (See the Quick Classes "The Fastest Mock Flat Fell Seam" on page 39, "I Fell for This Technique" on page 81, or "Wrapping It Up" on page 126.) If the underarm seam is clean finished with bias tape, wrap both of the seam allowances together, not separately, in a single piece of bias tape.

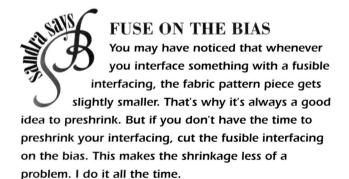

FUSE ON THE BIAS
You may have noticed that whenever you interface something with a fusible interfacing, the fabric pattern piece gets slightly smaller. That's why it's always a good idea to preshrink. But if you don't have the time to preshrink your interfacing, cut the fusible interfacing on the bias. This makes the shrinkage less of a problem. I do it all the time.

Apply the Upper Collar

1 With the right sides of the upper collar and under collar together and the cut edges even, sew the outer edges of the collar together. At the bottom, sew across the collar with a seamline that's an extension of the hem crease. Remember to hand walk the corners. (See the Quick Class "Let Your Fingers Do the Walking" on page 191.)

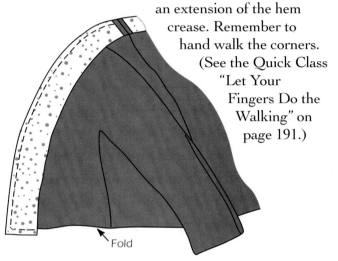
Fold

2 Press one of the seam allowances open as far as you can, then slip the seam onto a tailor's ham or a rolled-up towel to press it open.

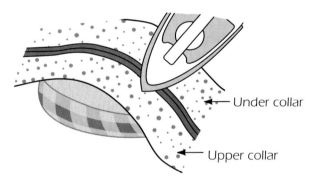
Under collar

Upper collar

3 Trim the collar and neck edge seam allowances to ¼ inch (5 mm). At the bottom of the collar, trim the corners on an angle, and cut off the excess collar hem allowance below the seam. Turn the collar right side out. Use a point turner to push out the sharp points at the lower edge.

4 Hand baste the outside collar edge. On the lower front portion of the jacket, roll the seamline so that it's just inside the jacket. At the point where you want the collar to start rolling out, shift the seamline so that it's on the under collar side.

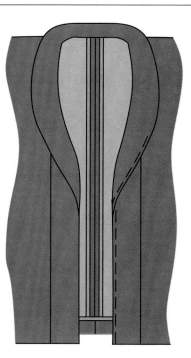

5 Press and pound the outside edge of the collar with a tailor's clapper. Remove the hand basting.

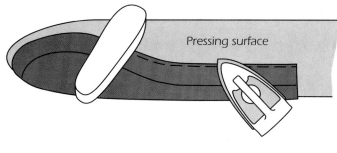

Pressing surface

Make the Buttonhole

If you had a bad experience with machine buttonholes and want to avoid them altogether, now—before the collar is finished—is the time to put in an alternate closure. Consider making a buttonhole window or just eliminate the closure altogether.

If you prefer a machine-made buttonhole, don't make it until after you sew down the loose edge of the upper collar. (See "Sew Down the Jacket Collar" on this page.) For machine-sewn buttonholes, follow the instructions that are included in your sewing machine manual.

Buttonhole Window

1 This treatment is explained in detail in "Add a Buttonhole Window" on page 68. Make a buttonhole window on both the upper collar and the under collar. The wrong sides of the buttonhole windows will face each other. You'll end up with what almost looks like bound buttonholes on both sides.

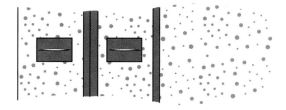

2 After the collar is complete, slipstitch the inner edges of both of the windows together so that the two openings will act as one when you button up your jacket.

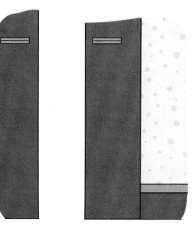

Sew Down the Jacket Collar

This is one of the few times during the construction process where you need to do some hand stitching. If you don't like handwork, why not do this while watching a favorite TV program?

1 One long edge of the collar is still free. Along this edge, fold under about ⅝ inch (1.5 cm) or however much is needed so that the fold can be matched to the seamline that joins the under collar to the jacket. Clip the seam allowances to allow the collar to curve gently around the neck.

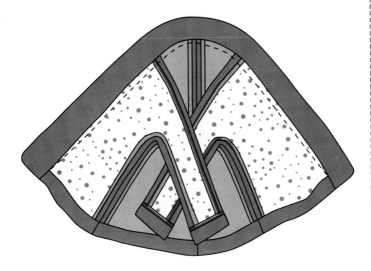

2 It's most attractive when the fold covers the seamline, so slipstitch the fold to the seamline. See the Quick Class "Slipsliding Away" on page 193.

Finish Your Jacket

30 MINUTES

All that you need to do now is sew the hems, attach the button, and cover and insert the shoulder pads. If you've ever tried covering shoulder pads with fabric, you know that it can be a bit tricky. So I'm going to give you my step-by-step instructions, which will make the process so much simpler.

Hem the Jacket

1 Hand sew both the jacket and sleeve hems using a blind hem stitch. (See Step 6 on page 178 for instructions.) To make the hem stitching completely invisible on the outside of the jacket, take your stitches only through the interfacing.

2 If you used sew-in interfacing for the back and sleeve hems, remove the basting stitches that held the strips in place during the construction process.

Attach the Button

1 Run a length of thread through beeswax and then press it. This will strengthen the thread and prevent the thread from knotting frequently.

2 Sew on the button using doubled thread. If the button is heavy, sew a smaller button on the inside of the garment.

Cover the Shoulder Pads

1 If you have narrow shoulders and the shoulder pads seem too long, trim off some of the fabric on the skinny ends of both pads.

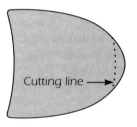

Cutting line →

2 Flatten a shoulder pad on lining fabric, and trace the outline. Add a 2-inch (5-cm) seam allowance, and cut out. Cut three more lining pieces. Place a piece of lining, right side out, on both sides of the pad. You may have to put a dart in the lining on the top, rounded part of the shoulder pad.

3 Pin the lining pieces together with the shoulder pad inside. Don't pin so tightly that you flatten the pad.

4 Overlock the edges around both pads. If you don't have a serger, sew the lining edges together, then pink the seam allowances.

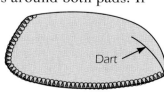

Dart →

5 Try on the jacket. Position the pads along the shoulder seamline. The fat part of the shoulder pad is toward the sleeve. Fold it in half, and pin it into your jacket from the outside. Repeat for the remaining pad.

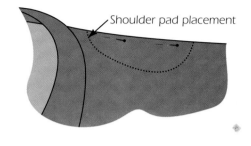

Shoulder pad placement

6 Take off the jacket. On the inside of the garment, hand sew the top of each pad to a shoulder seam with double thread that is strengthened with beeswax. If you prefer to attach your shoulder pads with Velcro, see the Quick Class "To Pad or Not to Pad" on page 203.

The Final Touch

1 Set your iron on medium-high with steam in order to press the neckline, center front edges, armholes, and side seams.

2 Place a press cloth over the area and spray it lightly with water. Apply the iron using a press-and-lift motion. Remove the iron, and cover the area that you just pressed with a tailor's clapper. This forces moisture into the cloth, allowing it to flatten to professional standards.

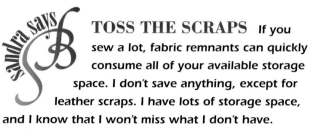

TOSS THE SCRAPS If you sew a lot, fabric remnants can quickly consume all of your available storage space. I don't save anything, except for leather scraps. I have lots of storage space, and I know that I won't miss what I don't have.

THE NEXT STEP

Piped Collar

30 MINUTES

Placing piping along the outside edge of the collar adds both interest and pizzazz. You can purchase piping or you can make your own. If you choose to make your own, you'll find complete instructions in this section.

Adding piping to a seam is easy, and the results are dynamic. All you need to do is sew cable cord into a bias-cut fabric strip, and sandwich the piping between the collar pattern pieces when you sew the seam.

Add to Your Shopping List

✂ 1½ yards (1.3 m) of piping
   or
✂ ¾ yard (0.7 m) of fabric
✂ ¾ yard (0.7 m) of lining fabric, if your piping fabric is very lightweight
✂ 1½ yards (1.3 m) of ¼-inch (5-mm)-diameter cable or rattail cord

Appropriate Fabric

Look for an interesting fabric if you're going to make your own piping, but don't choose a fabric that's too heavy. Silk charmeuse, silk crepe de chine, handkerchief linen, and wool jersey all make nice piping.

Piping looks super when it's in a color or texture that acts as a counterpoint to the fashion fabric used for the rest of the garment. Fabric that has a narrow stripe or some sheen, for example, offers excellent contrast to a tweed.

If the fabric you choose for the piping on your shawl collar jacket is very lightweight, the ridges from the cable cord may show through on the outside of the covered piping. If this is the case, just use two layers of fabric to cover the cable cord. If your piping fabric is expensive, then the inside fabric layer could be a lining scrap.

Make the Piping

1 Cut a 2½-inch (6-cm)-wide, 72-inch (183-cm)-long strip of fabric. If the fabric is woven, the strips for the piping must be cut on the bias.

Woven

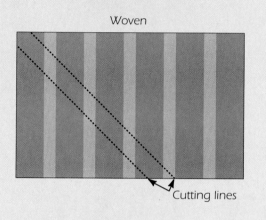

Cutting lines

If the fabric is a knit, the strips can be cut on the crosswise grain.

Knit

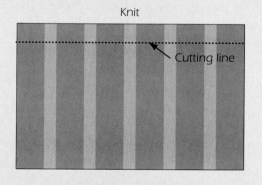

Cutting line

You can piece short strips to obtain the specified length, but try not to use strips that are shorter than 36 inches (91 cm), or the seams joining the pieces will be visible on your collar.

2 To cut and join your crosswise grain or bias fabric strips, see the Quick Class "Bound to Succeed" on page 58. If your fabric is striped, you need to match stripes when piecing the bias-cut strips. See the Quick Class "Easy Pieces" on page 136.

3 If your piping is very lightweight and the ridges from the cable cord show, cut another slightly narrower strip of lining fabric or purchased bias tape. Center the narrower strip on the wrong side of the piping fabric strip, and treat the two layers as a single unit in the following instructions.

4 Center the cable cord on the wrong side of the piping fabric. Wrap the piping fabric around the cord.

5 Switch to a zipper foot on your sewing machine. Anchor the cord within the wrapped fabric by sewing close to the cord through all layers. Trim the seam allowances so that the distance between the sewing line to the cut edges is ⅝ inch (1.5 cm).

Attach the Piping

1 Cut out and assemble your jacket following the general instructions. Stop before the section "Apply the Upper Collar" on page 130.

HASTE MAKES WASTE

If you baste the piping on by machine, the job will get done fast, but you'll be furious with the results. While machine basting is faster, hand basting prevents a piped seam from shortening.

2 Before you attach the upper collar to the under collar, hand baste the piping to the outside edge of the right side of the upper collar with the cut edges of the piping and the collar even.

Hide any seam made in the piping when it was pieced by positioning the piping seam at center back. Try to scrunch a little extra length of piping into the seam so that there's extra fabric to help the piping lie smooth on the finished jacket. If your piping is too short, the collar won't lie flat.

QUICK CLASS

Easy Pieces

As I said earlier, striped fabric makes super piping. The design is most attractive when you cut the strips on the bias. If you need to piece the strips to come up with a longer length, you have to know how to join the ends so that the striped design isn't interrupted.

How to Piece Striped Fabric Strips

1 Cut the ends of your bias-cut fabric strips parallel to the stripe in the fabric's design.

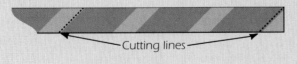

Cutting lines

2 Fold under ½ inch (1 cm) on one end of a strip. Finger press the fold so that a crease would be visible if you opened the fold.

3 Position this fold on the next strip so that stripes are continuous from one to the next. Make snips on the second, unfolded strip where the fold from the first strip is positioned.

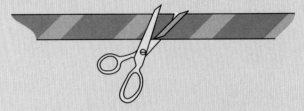

4 Open the fold on the first strip, and place the two strips together, matching the foldline to the snips. Sew your seam by following along the foldline you created in Step 2. Press the seam allowances open, and trim them to ¼ inch (5 mm).

3 With the right sides of the upper collar and under collar together and the cut edges even, pin the outer edges together. Place the pins on the upper collar side, where hand basting is visible.

4 Sew the upper and under collars together using the zipper foot and positioning the seam a threadline deeper than the hand basting that attached the piping to your upper collar. Sewing a bit closer to the cord results in a tight fit around the piping. If your fabric layers are heavy, then you should lengthen your machine stitches to maintain a uniform stitch length without shortening the seam.

5 To reduce bulk at the hem of both ends of your collar, pull 2¼ inches (5.5 cm) of the cable cord out of the piping's fabric cover at one end. The piping fabric will scrunch up. Cut off the cord, and allow the piping fabric to relax. Repeat at the hem at the other end of the collar. There won't be any cable cord in the final 2¼ inches (5.5 cm) of both ends of the collar, which eliminates bulk in the hem.

2¼"

6 With the right sides of the upper collar and the under collar together and cut edges even, sew across the bottom. The seamline should be at the same position as the hem crease on the jacket front. Remember to hand walk the corners. (See the Quick Class "Let Your Fingers Do the Walking" on page 191.) Continue constructing your jacket, starting with Step 2 in "Apply the Upper Collar" on page 130.

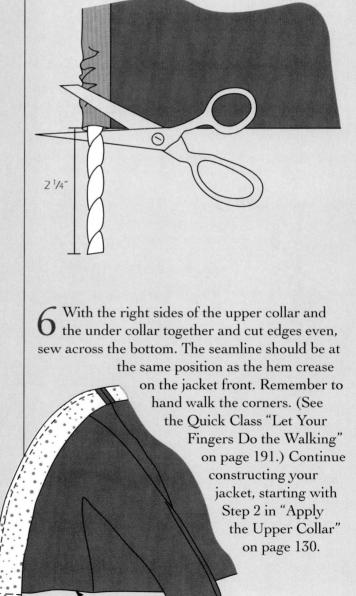

Sew collars together at bottom

Fold

Paper Bag Pocket

45 MINUTES

This is actually two pockets in one. You make a "bag" from fashion fabric, then join the top to another "bag" of lining fabric. Next, the lining is tucked inside the fashion fabric bag. Then the pocket is pressed and sewn to the jacket in almost the same manner as a patch pocket.

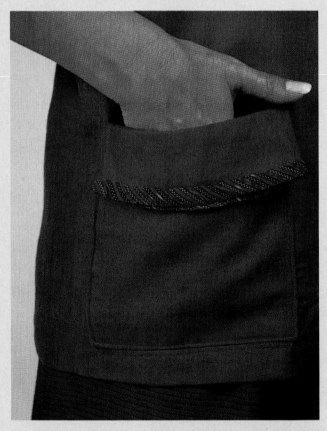

To make the pocket extra special, cut the contrasting lining 2 inches (5 cm) longer than recommended in Step 1. When you turn the bag right-side-out, the lining wil show on the outside of the pocket.

Add to Your Shopping List

- ✂ ¼ yard (.2 m) of fashion fabric
- ✂ ¼ yard (.2 m) of contrasting lining fabric

Cut and Construct the Pocket

1 Cut a 7 × 18-inch (17. × 5 45-cm) piece of fabric out of the garment's fashion fabric and another out of a contrasting lining. Fold each piece of fabric in half with right sides together so that the dimensions are now 7 × 9 inches (17.5 × 22.5 cm).

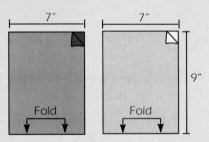

2 With the fold at the bottom, sew both long sides of the fashion fabric and one long side of the lining, using ¼-inch (5-mm) seam allowances. Sew the remaining open long side of the lining rectangle, but leave a 2-inch (5-cm) opening in the middle of the seam to turn the pocket right side out.

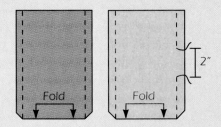

3 Trim the corners diagonally at the bottom near the fold. Press one seam allowance back. Each piece now resembles a little bag.

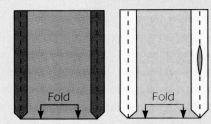

4 Turn the lining bag right side out. Slip the lining bag inside the fashion fabric bag, with the right sides together.

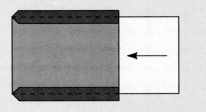

5 Pin the tops of the bags together to form a circle, and join them with a ¼-inch (5-mm) seam allowance.

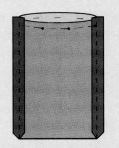

6 Pull the lining out of the fashion fabric bag. Press the seam allowances open. Turn the joined bags right-side-out through the opening.

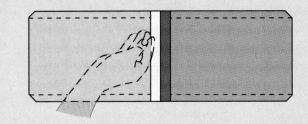

7 Push the lining inside the fashion fabric bag. Press and pound all the edges flat. Position and pin the pocket on the garment, using the pocket placement line for guidance. Topstitch the pocket to the garment, starting and ending the seam 2 inches (5 cm) below the top edge of the pocket. Use small stitches (18 to 20 stitches per inch or 1.5 on a 0-to-4 stitch length setting) to reinforce the first and last ½ inch (1 cm) of the seam.

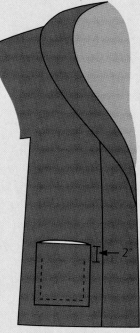

Front

8 Fold down the top of the pocket that wasn't sewn to the jacket. This is the loose 2 inches (5 cm) at the top, which will now form a flap.

Inside Pocket with a Flap

1 HOUR

This detail is found on many quality jackets. While it takes slightly longer to construct than a patch pocket, the results are worth it. If you're an inexperienced sewer, save this pocket variation for a time when your skills are more developed.

In ready-to-wear garments, flap pockets are a signpost of a quality garment. Lucky us, we can easily add them to any jacket that we care to make. Since the raw edges of the flap are visible on the "back side" of this pocket, it should only be applied to a jacket that you plan to line.

Add to Your Shopping List

✂ ¼ yard (0.2 m) of fashion fabric
✂ ¼ yard (0.2 m) of lining fabric
✂ ¼ yard (0.2 m) of fusible knit interfacing

Get Started

1 Follow the general instructions for preparing your jacket, and stop before "Construct Your Jacket" on page 127.

2 On the wrong side of both front patterns, draw a horizontal line joining the pocket placement marks. Mark the new line for the pocket flap placement on the front pattern pieces.

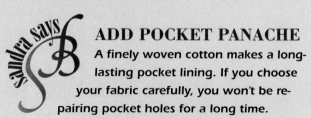

ADD POCKET PANACHE
A finely woven cotton makes a long-lasting pocket lining. If you choose your fabric carefully, you won't be repairing pocket holes for a long time.

Make the Flap

1 Cut two pocket flaps on the grain from the fashion fabric and two on the bias from the lining and interfacing. Set aside one fashion fabric and one lining fabric pocket flap pattern piece.

2 Trim a scant ⅛ inch (3 mm) off all of the edges, except for the top, of one lining flap. Fuse the interfacing pattern piece to the wrong side of the pocket flap.

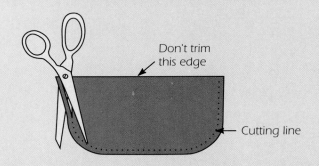

Don't trim this edge

Cutting line

3 Place a lining flap and a fabric flap together with right sides facing and the cut edges matching. This won't be difficult because the lining pocket flap will stretch. Pin the pattern pieces together, placing your pins on the lining side. The pinned flaps won't lie perfectly flat because one side is slightly larger than the other.

4 With the flap cut from the fashion fabric against the feed dogs, sew the flap pattern pieces together using ¼-inch (5-mm) seam allowances. Don't sew the long straight edge at the top of the flap.

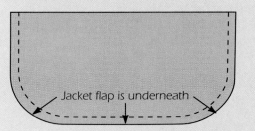

Jacket flap is underneath

5 Turn the flap right side out. Topstitch it close to the edge of the flap, or press and pound the flap with a tailor's clapper.

6 Position the flap on one of the fronts with the cut edges at the pocket placement line, the finished edge of the flap pointing to the shoulder, and right sides facing. Pin the flap to the front with the pins positioned 1 inch (2.5 cm) from the lower cut edge of the flap. Make another pocket flap for the remaining front.

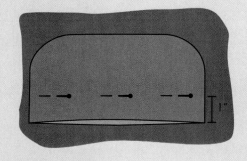

1"

Make the Pocket Bag

1 Cut two 7 × 11-inch (17.5 × 27.5-cm) pieces of lining to make two pocket bags. Set one lining piece aside.

2 Fold a lining in half to make a 7 × 5½-inch (17.5 × 13.5-cm) rectangle, and make small snips on both sides of the fold.

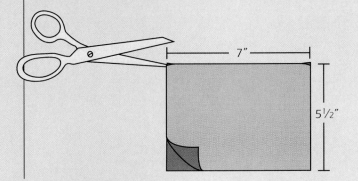

7"

5½"

3 Open the pocket bag. Center it over the flap so that the snips are aligned with the cut edges of the flap. Pin the pocket bag to the shawl collar jacket.

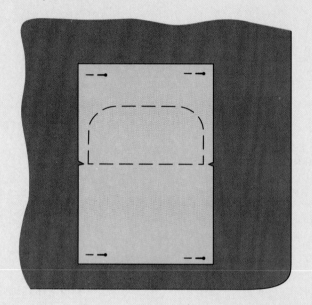

4 Turn the front wrong side up so that you can see your markings for the pocket placement. Sew the pocket bag and the flap to the jacket using small stitches (18 to 20 stitches per inch or 1.5 on a 0-to-4 stitch length setting), positioning the stitching line ¼ inch (5 mm) above the placement line. If the outside edge of the right toe of your presser foot is ¼ inch (5 mm) from the needle, you can use it as a guide when you sew. Insert the front under the presser foot with the lower edge of the jacket to the right. Let the edge of the presser foot ride along the pocket placement line as you sew. Stop the stitching line exactly at the end of the flap. You can feel the bulk decrease. Don't backstitch. Instead, use small machine stitches to reinforce the beginning and the end of the stitching line.

5 Sew another row of stitches parallel to the first exactly ¼ inch (5 mm) below the pocket placement line. You aren't sewing on the flap. This time the stitching line should be ¼ inch (5 mm) shorter at both ends. This determines the success of the pocket, so be precise.

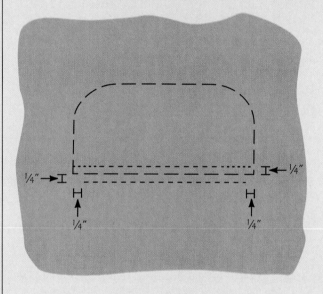

6 Cut an opening along the pocket placement line through the front fabric only (not the flap). Cut diagonally into each corner to within three garment threads of the stitching, leaving long fabric triangles at each end.

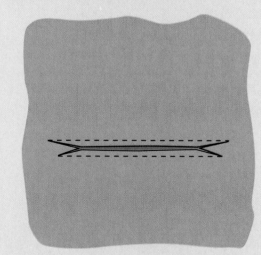

7 Turn the pocket bag to the inside of the jacket through the opening. The flap now folds down to cover the opening. The fabric triangles made in Step 6 should be on the wrong side of the jacket.

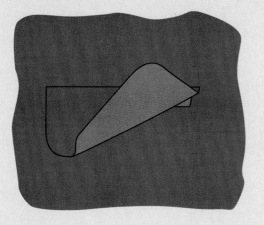

8 Form the pocket bag by sewing up the sides of the pocket. The sides will be unequal at the bottom so let the lining relax in the down position, then pin and sew it. Round the corners slightly at the bottom. Trim off excess lining at the bottom of the pocket.

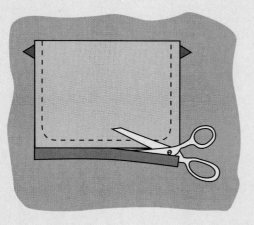

9 Sew the fabric triangles to the top of the pocket bag near the opening. Don't sew through the jacket. These triangles are pointing upward at a slight angle. Don't attempt to straighten them; merely stitch them to the pocket bag.

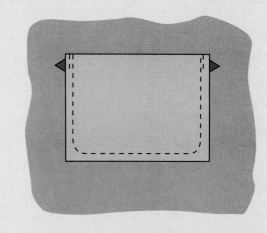

10 Cover the pocket with a press cloth, spray it lightly with water, and steam press it. Then pound it flat with a tailor's clapper. Using the pocket and lining that you set aside in Step 1, make a second pocket, and sew it and another flap to the remaining front in the same manner.

11 Finish sewing your jacket together, following the general instructions in "Construct Your Jacket" on page 127.

SKIP THE FIT If you're like me, there are occasions when you don't have time to pretest the fit of your commercial pattern by making the garment out of a scrap fabric. In this situation cut out your pattern pieces with 1-inch (2.5-cm)-wide seam allowances. Given the inconsistency of fit among the pattern companies, wider seam allowances will usually give you enough leeway to rescue many garments that don't fit when they're sewn up.

Gored
SKIRT

The Perfect Pattern

The perfect gored skirt—with emphasis on the word *perfect*—is the most versatile skirt you'll ever own. Because the grainline is in the center of each panel, the fullness is evenly distributed, which is very flattering. The skirt has an elasticized waistband for comfort and a side zipper, so that you don't have excess fabric bulk at the tummy or the waistband. If the skirt didn't have a zipper, you would need much more fabric gathered in at the waistband so that you could stretch it wide enough to pull over your hips.

To stretch your sewing skills, you'll learn a waistband trick that helps the skirt fall gracefully over the high hip and tummy, thus camouflaging these fuller areas. I'll also introduce a type of waistband that adjusts to fit you even when your weight fluctuates.

This pattern is one of my all-time favorites because it's so simple, yet a few variations, like changing the fabric, can make the finished garment look very different. My gored skirt for the Rodale Designer Collection can be made in cotton knit or even satin. By switching to a stretchy fabric, like wool jersey, and following the instructions in "The Next Step," you can make a pull-on version without a zipper.

Also in "The Next Step," you'll learn how to make a flowing skirt from my basic 6-gore pattern. See "12-Gore Georgette Skirt" on page 161.

The elasticized waistband on this skirt is constructed with an easy assembly method very similar to that used for the full pants (page 15) and the slim pants (page 41). After the waistband is sewn to the skirt, it's wrapped around an elastic circle and then topstitched in place. In this chapter I'll also explain how to insert a zipper quickly and accurately.

What You Need

If you're reluctant to splurge on a fabric you love, I urge you to set aside your reservations. This might just be the perfect pattern for that fabric since only a little is needed. If you have some elastic and a zipper on hand, you may already have everything you need to get started.

"To make this skirt, I used 12 gores rather than 6. This was easy to do because, since the waistband is elasticized, I didn't even need to adjust the pattern at the waist. However, I did use French seams so that raw edges wouldn't be visible through the sheer fabric. I thought that you'd like to try making a skirt like this, so I included instructions for it in "The Next Step" on page 161."

Fabric Yardage for Skirt

Fabric width	Small	Medium	Large
45 inches (115 cm)	3⅛ yards (2.8 m)	3½ yards (3.1 m)	3⅝ yards (3.3 m)
60 inches (150 cm), with nap	3⅛ yards (2.8 m)	3½ yards (3.1 m)	3⅝ yards (3.3 m)
60 inches (150 cm), without nap	2⅛ yards (1.9 m)	2⅜ yards (2.1 m)	2½ yards (2.25 m)

Appropriate Fabric

The most flattering gored skirt is made in a drapey fabric like imported cotton knit, lamb suede, rayon crepe, rayon velvet, silk charmeuse, velour, wool challis, or wool crepe. You should avoid stiff fabrics because the skirt you end up with won't be very slimming. Fabrics that aren't suitable are linen, pig suede, wool flannel, and wool gabardine.

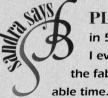

PLAN AHEAD I buy elastic in 5-yard (4.5-m) lengths. Sometimes I even buy more. This saves a trip to the fabric store, which saves me valuable time.

Notions

- ✂ Matching thread
- ✂ 1/2-inch × 10-inch (1-cm × 25-cm) piece of lightweight fusible interfacing for the zipper area
- ✂ 9-inch (22.5-cm) zipper
- ✂ Transparent tape
- ✂ 1-inch (2.5-cm)-wide nonroll monofilament elastic, such as Ban-rol Stretch Elastic
- ✂ Snap or flat hook and eye
- ✂ Miscellaneous supplies, as listed in "The Sewing Basket" on page ix

ZIP IT UP If your hips are more than 12 inches (30 cm) larger than your waist, you will have to insert a zipper in your skirt. But if your fabric has some stretch and the difference between your hips and waist is not so great, a zipper may not be necessary. See the Quick Class "The Acid Test" on page 151.

Front

Back

Fit Your Skirt Pattern

I doubt that you'll spend more than 30 minutes on alterations for your skirt. After all, there's only one pattern piece. In fact, I suspect that very few of you will need to make any alterations since the skirt is cut generously and the waistband is elasticized.

Get Started

All my patterns in the Rodale Designer Collection are multisized so you can cut different sizes to fit different parts of your body. Very few people are perfectly proportioned, so I'm going to guide you through adjusting the skirt pattern to fit your waist and hips and then personalizing the skirt length. The sections below show how to make the necessary changes to your pattern.

Small or Large Hips

When deciding if you have small or large hips, you're merely looking at your waist-to-hip ratio. If your hips are 12 inches (30 cm) or more larger than your waist, you have large hips. If the difference between your waist and hips is 7 inches (17.5 cm) or less, you have small hips.

TRY MY TUMMY TIP If you have a protruding tummy, it's better camouflaged by using a larger waist size. Measure the pattern width 3 inches (7.5 cm) from the waist. Subtract 1¼ inches (3 cm) for the seam allowances. Multiply by six because there are six gores. This flat pattern measurement should equal your personal tummy measurement plus 2½ inches (6 cm) for ease.

Mark Your Hipline

Mark your hipline on the skirt pattern. The hipline is marked on commercial patterns, but it's doubtful that the widest part of your hips (called the full hip) matches that line. To personalize your pattern, measure your hips in two or three locations to determine the widest part, which is your full hip. If your hips are small and you have a tummy, your full hip location may be as high as 2½ to 3 inches (6 to 7.5 cm) from your waist. Insert a pin though your clothes at the widest point. Now measure down from your waist to this pin. Measure and mark the same distance on your skirt pattern from the waistline down at the side seams, and draw a line joining the marks.

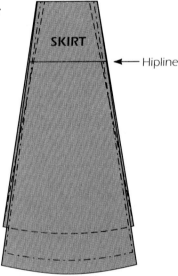

Alter the Skirt Pattern for Your Hips

Compare your full hip measurement to the size table on page 208. Select the size into which your measurement falls, and use the cutting lines for this size from the hipline to the hem.

Thick or Small Waist

Unless you're perfectly proportioned, which is rare, the cutting line for your waist will be a different size than your hips. Most women who have a small or thick waist know it. A woman with a small waist is always getting compliments, but if her garments fit at the hips, the waist is too big. If a woman has a thick waist, her purchased garments fit at the hips but the waist is much too small.

Select your waist size by matching your measurements to the size table on page 208. Use the cutting lines for your waist size (either small, medium, or large) at the waist, transitioning smoothly out to your hip size about 3 inches (7.5 cm) above the hipline. (See "Mark Your Hipline" on the opposite page.)

Skirt Length

Measure your favorite skirt at the side seam from the waistline to the hem. Compare this number to the finished length of the pattern, which is listed in "Finished Lengths and Hem Widths" on page 208.

Measure from waistline to hem

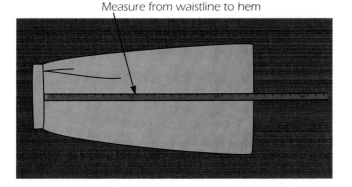

Alter the length on the skirt pattern before you cut out the fabric pattern pieces. If you cut fabric off the bottom after the skirt is constructed, you'll ruin the silhouette because you'll cut off much of the style's fullness.

The best way to lengthen or shorten the skirt pattern is to work within the body of it, just as you did when you adjusted the length of your slim pants on page 35.

If you need to lengthen or shorten the skirt pattern by more than 2 inches (5 cm), alter the pattern in several places. The best way to do this is to divide the total amount that you need to add or take away into several even increments and alter the pattern in several spots. After the alterations, remember to connect the cutting lines along the sides with a ruler.

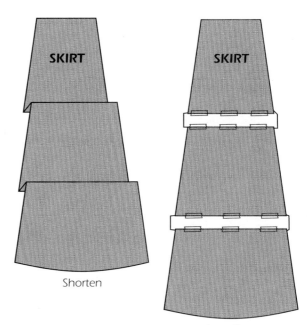

Shorten

Lengthen

SHOP FAST, SHOP SMART
Start shopping for fabric with a purpose, never hurry, and buy only items that are on your list. Unless you have unlimited funds, your wardrobe will transition slowly, but over time you will see that the "I have nothing to wear" syndrome comes to mind less and less and the fabric and garments that you do make will still be favorites five years from now. Making the items from this book and carefully shopping for accessories will make you feel very put together. Watch out, you may just start feeling really good about yourself! If this book accomplishes that, I will personally feel that it's a great success.

Cut Out Your Skirt

15 MINUTES

***W**hy not prepare your fabric and pattern pieces on a weeknight, so that you can get right to the good stuff—the sewing—at your first opportunity? Because I want you to be happy with the fit of your skirt, I'm giving you instructions on how to make a customized waistband later in this chapter.*

1 Cut six pattern pieces from your fashion fabric. Position your skirt pattern as indicated on the layout below, according to your size as well as the fabric width. Remember to leave enough room to cut the skirt pattern three times from the double layer of fabric, or six times from a single layer of fabric. In the following instructions, I'll call each skirt pattern piece a gore.

2 Along the lengthwise grain, measure a piece of fabric that is 43 inches (109 cm) long and 4 inches (10 cm) wide. This will be used to cut your waistband later. Set it aside for now.

3 If you don't want to use flat fell seams, serge or pink all of the cut edges on each of the gores for the skirt.

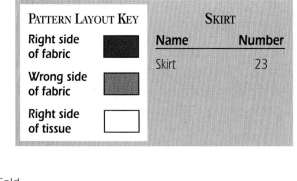

PATTERN LAYOUT KEY		SKIRT	
Right side of fabric	⬛	**Name**	**Number**
Wrong side of fabric	⬛	Skirt	23
Right side of tissue	⬜		

Fold

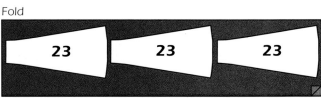

Selvages

60-inch (150-cm)-wide fabric, with nap, all sizes

Fold

23   **23**   **22**

Selvages

45-inch (115-cm)-wide fabric, with/without nap, all sizes

Selvage

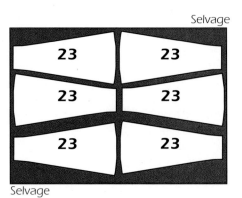

Selvage

60-inch (150-cm)-wide fabric, without nap, all sizes

Construct Your Skirt

2 HOURS

Since one pattern determines the shape for all of the skirt pattern pieces, construction is super easy. Once you've determined if you need a zipper, all that's left to do is insert the zipper, join the gores, attach the waistband, insert the elastic, and make the hem.

Prepare to Insert the Zipper

1 You might be able to get away with omitting the zipper if you have either narrow hips or a thick waist (in other words, if the difference between your hip and waist measurements is minimal). See the Quick Class "The Acid Test" below for a simple way to determine if a zipper is necessary. All the seam allowances are ⁵⁄₈ inch (1.5 cm) wide, and the stitch length is medium (10 to 12 stitches per inch or 2.5 on a 0-to-4 stitch length setting), unless otherwise indicated.

2 All of the skirt pattern pieces are identical so the zipper can go in any seam. This seam will then become a side seam. With right sides facing, sew together two gores, starting at the hem and stopping 8 inches (20.5 cm) from the waistline. Backstitch but don't break the threads.

The Acid Test

The acid test for whether you need a zipper is if you can step into your skirt when all of the seams joined together. You have a better chance of being able to do this if your waist isn't too much smaller than your hips and if the fabric has some stretch.

How to Determine if You Need a Zipper in Your Skirt

1 Baste together the side seams of your gores to make a circle.

2 Step into your skirt and slide it up to your waist. If you can do so without straining the side seam, a zipper may not be necessary (lucky you).

3 To make a skirt without a zipper, remove the basting stitches that were used to join the gores. Even though you may be using a woven fabric, assemble the skirt following the instructions in "Make a Pull-On Skirt with Stretchy Fabric," starting with "Construct Your Pull-On Skirt" on page 160.

3 At this point, lengthen the stitch so that you're machine basting the remainder of the seam. Make sure that you sew a full ⅝-inch (1.5-cm) seam allowance. The width of the seam allowance is important for the proper installation of the zipper. Press the seam allowances open.

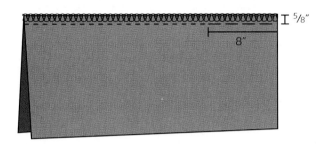

4 Adding strips of interfacing to the seam allowances in the zipper area prevents the zipper from being wavy and the ends from poking out at the base. Cut two strips of light-weight fusible interfacing ½ inch (1 cm) wide and 10 inches (25 cm) long.

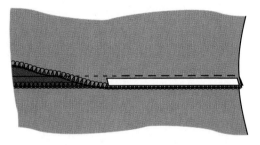

5 Place your joined gores on a pressing surface wrong side up. Slide the interfacing strips, fusible side up, behind each side of the open seam allowances in the zipper area. (The glue is on the fusible side, which will be either bumpy or shiny.) The strips extend below your machine basting.

6 Cover the zipper area with a press cloth. Spray it lightly with water. With an iron on the medium-high temperature setting, fuse the interfacing strips to the seam allowances. Use an up-and-down motion, allowing the iron to stay in each place approximately ten seconds.

Sandra says

QUICK BASTE WITH TAPE It isn't necessary to insert endless pins into your zipper tape before you sew it to your garment. In fact, this could be one of the reasons that your zippers turn out lumpy. I simply tape the zipper to the skirt across the seam. Three pieces of transparent tape will be enough to hold the zipper in position as you sew.

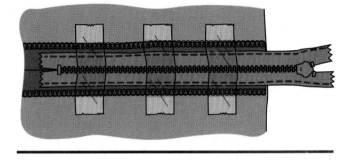

Insert the Centered Zipper

1 Position the teeth of the zipper, right side down, against the open seam allowances. The top of the zipper tabs and the slider should be above the cut edge of the skirt. The metal "tab" at the bottom of the zipper is at the beginning of the basting in the seamline. Secure the zipper with transparent tape.

2 Replace your standard presser foot with a zipper foot that allows the needle to sew close to the zipper teeth without riding on the teeth. Position the zipper foot so that the needle is on the left side of the foot.

3 Place the skirt under the presser foot with the wrong side up, and the top of the taped zipper under the needle. Most of the zipper is to the left. Position the right half of the zipper tape so that the needle is sewing directly on the prominent thread line that the manufacturer wove into the zipper tape.

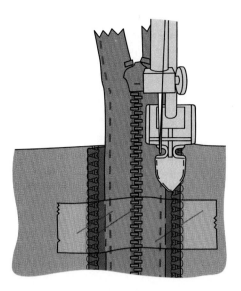

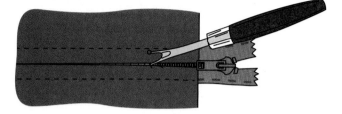

6 Take the transparent tape off the zipper. Turn the skirt right side out. Remove the machine basting from the zipper area with a seam ripper. Pull out any leftover threads. Don't trim off the excess zipper tape until after the waistband is sewn onto your skirt.

4 Sew down the right side of the zipper, going ⅛ inch (3 mm) past the metal zipper stop at the bottom of the teeth. Stop sewing. Leaving your needle down in the fabric, raise the presser foot, and turn the fabric so that your next few stitches will make a corner. Lower the presser foot, and sew across the bottom of the zipper to the prominent thread line on the other side of the zipper tape. Stop sewing.

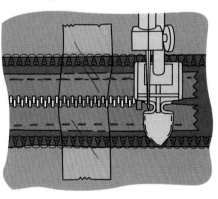

Join the Gores

With right sides facing and cut edges even, sew the remaining gores together along the long, lengthwise edges. Bumpy seams are caused when the fabric stretches as you're sewing. To prevent this, sew from the hem up to the waist.

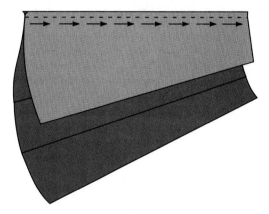

5 Again, leaving your needle down, raise the presser foot and turn the corner. Drop the presser foot, and sew up the other side of the zipper. Sew until you reach the top of the skirt.

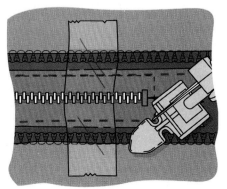

Sandra says **WHEN I FELL** It should take only 20 minutes more to construct this skirt with flat fell seams. But don't decide to use this finish just based on the amount of time you have to make it. The type of fabric and the desired appearance of your garment are also important. Flat fell seams are suitable for any weight of woven fabric. Don't use this treatment on knits because the seams will be bumpy.

Make and Prepare the Waistband

1 Measure your waist. Add 5 inches (12.5 cm) to this number. This allows some extra length for the overlap at the zipper as well as for fitting ease. Cut a waistband that is this length and 3½ inches (8.5 cm) wide from the piece of fashion fabric that you set aside earlier.

2 Don't stabilize the waistband with interfacing; the elastic is sufficient. Fold one long side up ⅝ inch (1.5 cm), and press the fold.

3 On the unfolded long side, make a clip into the seam allowance of the waistband exactly ⅝ inch (1.5 cm) from one short end. Also make a second clip into the waistband seam allowance 1⅝ inch (4 cm) from the other end.

This will help you match the waistband to the skirt's waist and ensure that you leave enough fabric extending past the zipper opening so that you can make an extension after you have sewn the waistband to the skirt.

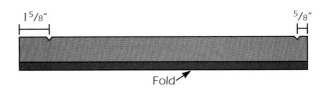

1⅝" ⅝"

Fold

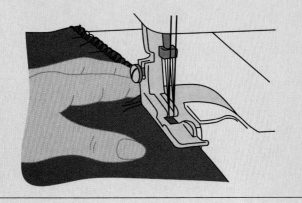

QUICK CLASS

Crowd Your Stitches

The easing technique, which can be done on a conventional sewing machine or a serger, not only prevents stretching but also actually draws up the edge slightly. This is a good thing because the edge needs to be pulled in a bit so that it can lie flat, without tiny folds, when it's folded to the inside of the skirt.

How to Ease and Stabilize an Edge

1 Hold your left index finger behind the presser foot as you sew. This prevents the fabric from coming out of the machine as fast as it wants to because the fabric bunches up.

2 After sewing about 10 inches (25 cm) (or more if your fabric is thin), lift up your finger to release the fabric that has bunched up behind the presser foot.

3 Reposition your finger behind the presser foot again, and continue in the same manner. You do this as many times as necessary until the edge of your fabric pattern piece is eased.

4 Don't backstitch and don't "tug" your fabric after you remove it from the machine. Almost everyone who tries crowding immediately tugs the fabric the first time they take it off the machine. Resist the urge!

Attach the Waistband

1 Measure the skirt's waist. This measurement should be larger than your honest personal waist measurement; how much larger depends on your body shape. The skirt should be 4½ inches (11 cm) larger if you have a tummy and a full high hip; 3½ to 4½ inches (8.5 to 11 cm) larger if you have a slight tummy and slight fullness in the high hip; or 3 inches (7.5 cm) larger if you have a flat tummy and gradual hip curve.

2 If your skirt's waist measurement doesn't fit within the ranges listed in Step 1 based on your figure type, then you need to adjust the skirt. If the skirt's waist isn't big enough, let out the seams slightly at the waist.

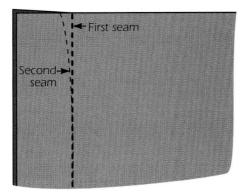

If the skirt's waist is too large, take in the side seams. To do this, use larger seam allowances. Put on the skirt and, at each seam, pin in part of the amount that you need to add. Now re-sew each of the side seams, using the pins as guides for making larger seam allowances.

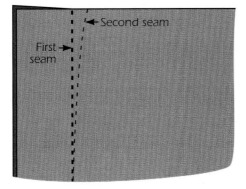

3 Make smooth transitions between the old and the new seams when you're stitching the new seamlines. A good starting place for your alterations is at the fullest part of the hip, tapering gradually to the waist. Remove the old stitching lines. Press all the skirt seam allowances open.

4 Run an ease line (a row of medium-length stitches on the seamline) around the skirt at the waist. You may want to crowd the stitches, as explained in the Quick Class "Crowd Your Stitches" on the opposite page.

5 Place the right side of the unfinished long edge of the waistband against the wrong side of the skirt, positioning the clips so that the one that's 1⅝ inches (4 cm) from the end is on the right side of the zipper as you look at the skirt from the outside. The clip that is ⅝ inch (1.5 cm) from the end is on the left side. The waistband and the skirt go together quite naturally since they were based on the same waist measurement.

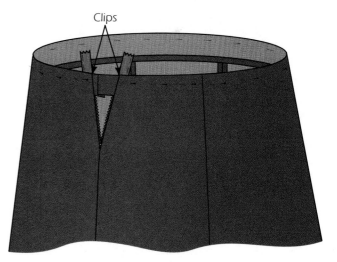

6 Sew the waistband to the skirt, using a ⅝-inch (1.5-cm) seam allowance. If the skirt is a little larger than the waistband, place the skirt closest to the feed dogs. The "teeth" ease in the excess fabric so the lengths match. Sew slowly at the zipper tape and turn the flywheel to manually walk the needle through the teeth of the zipper.

7 Press the waistband and seam allowances up. Close the zipper to make sure that the seamline at the waist matches at the top of the zipper. If not, re-sew to make both sides the same.

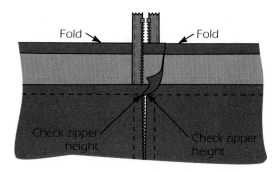

Fold ← → Fold

Check zipper height

Check zipper height

Insert the Elastic

1 Measure your waist, and subtract ³⁄₄ inch (2 cm) from the number. Cut a length of elastic to this measurement.

2 Place a pin ⁵⁄₈ inch (1.5 cm) from the end of the elastic, and put another pin 1⁵⁄₈ inches (4 cm) from the other end of the elastic. Fold the elastic in half with the pins matching. Place a third pin at the fold, which is midway between the end marks.

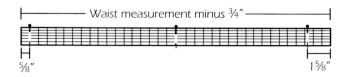

— Waist measurement minus ¾" —

⁵⁄₈"   1⁵⁄₈"

3 On the skirt, place a pin in the center of the gore directly across from the zipper. This will make it easier for you to sew in the elastic.

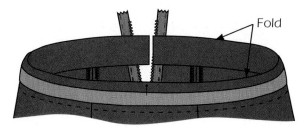

Fold

4 Position the elastic on the wrong side of the waistband, between the waistband and the seam allowances, matching the pins.

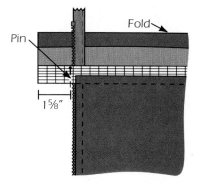

Pin

Fold

1⁵⁄₈"

5 The ends of the elastic extend into the ends of the waistband and one long edge of the elastic is as close as possible to the seam that joins the waistband to the skirt. Stretch the elastic slightly so that it fits the waistband. Pin the elastic to the seam allowances to hold the elastic in place.

6 Sew the elastic to the waistband through the seam allowances, using a long zigzag stitch and stretching the elastic to fit as you sew.

7 Fold the waistband in half lengthwise with right sides together so that the long folded edge of the waistband extends just below the seamline. Using a ⁵⁄₈-inch (1.5-cm) seam allowance, sew vertically through all thicknesses at the end of the 1⁵⁄₈-inch (4-cm) extension. The elastic is included in the seam. The narrow hem folded under on the ⁵⁄₈-inch (1.5-cm) extension in the waistband remains folded up when you sew the ends.

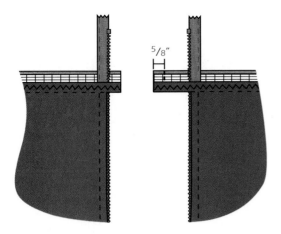

8 Sew the remaining end of the waistband, which has the ⅝-inch (1.5-cm) extension, using a ½-inch (1-cm) seam allowance.

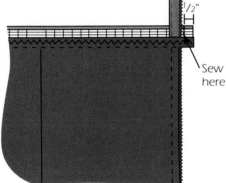

9 One end of the waistband is longer than the other. Trim the corners at both ends of the waistband diagonally, and trim the seam allowances to ¼ inch (5 mm). Trim off the excess zipper tapes that extend into the waistband.

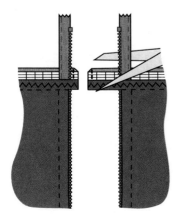

thread
TALES

A dressmaker made most of the garments shown in this book, but I do the majority of my own sewing. Years ago, when I opened a sewing school, I promised that if I ever became so busy that I couldn't find time to make my clothes, I'd quit. After all, it was a love of sewing that drew me into this field.

As you can imagine, with my television show, books, and videos, I am very busy these days. And I'm away from home a lot because every spring and fall, I travel for two months.

But I'm still sewing because I've developed timesaving tricks and techniques, which I'm sharing with you in this book.

Fortunately, I also need less sleep than I did years ago.

When I sit down at my sewing machine, I always place a stack of index cards beside me. I jot down any problems I encounter while sewing, and add the solution as I solve the problem. Some of these ideas turn into sewing columns or tips for my lectures.

I love working with oddball or "challenging" fabrics so I can learn to "tame" the fabric. I explore solutions for preventing ripply hems and puckered seams and for making alternate interfacings. I also like to develop techniques for styling details I see on ready-to-wear clothes. Many of these "solutions" are now part of the garments in this collection.

Sandra

Finish the Waistband

1 Turn the ends of the waistband right side out, and wrap the rest of the waistband around the elastic to the right side of the skirt so that the folded edge extends slightly past the seamline. Pin the waistband from the outside of the skirt.

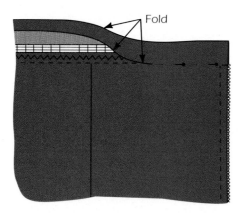

Fold

2 Sewing from the outside of the skirt, complete the waistband by topstitching it through all thicknesses, close to the edge of the waistband. Don't catch the elastic in the topstitching.

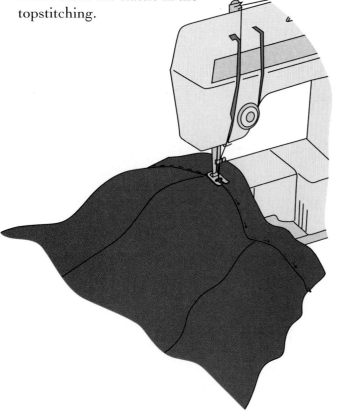

3 The elastic will pull in the excess fabric at the waistband, thus preventing the waistband from lying perfectly smooth until you're wearing the skirt. The band will be comfortable and will conform to your shape. Attach a snap or a flat hook and eye to the waistband extension and the other side of the waistband.

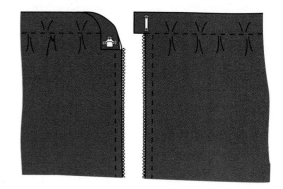

Hem the Skirt

1 Because you determined the finished skirt length before you cut out the skirt gores, you shouldn't need to adjust the hem. Serge or zigzag the bottom edge of the skirt. Since your skirt fabric may be stretchy and the hem is wider than the rest of your skirt, you should use the technique explained in the Quick Class "Crowd Your Stitches" on page 154 to prevent the hem from stretching as you finish the edge.

2 Press up a 1-inch (2.5-cm) hem. Pin the hem to the skirt from the outside of the skirt. Secure the hem with two rows of topstitching, made from the right side of the skirt, 3/4 inch (2 cm) from the hem's fold. You can do this very quickly with a double needle. (See the Quick Class "Two Spools in One" and "Do Double Time" on page 44.) If your machine can't accommodate a double needle, sew two rows of stitching about 1/4 inch (5 mm) apart. Don't forget to use woolly nylon thread on the bobbin. This will result in two rows of stitching that have more "give" than regular straight stitches, so the stitches won't be as likely to break.

Pull-On Skirt with Stretchy Fabric

1 1/2 HOURS

This is a fast, fun-to-make garment because you don't insert a zipper. And working with a stretchy fabric is a breeze. You don't need a special stretch stitch, and you don't have to worry about snapped stitches when you pull on the finished garment if you use my trick.

A skirt made from wool jersey, as shown here, will look much different than one constructed from lamb suede or stretch velour. If you choose a stretchy fabric such as wool jersey or stretch velour, you won't need a zipper regardless of your hip and waist measurements. And you don't need to use a fancy stretch stitch when you sew the gores together.

Add to Your Shopping List

I always use woolly nylon in the bobbin so that the seams have more stretch. (Remember to hand wind woolly nylon thread onto the bobbin, otherwise it loses its flexibility.)

	Fabric Yardage for Pull-On Skirt		
Fabric width	**Small**	**Medium**	**Large**
45 inches (115 cm)	3 1/8 yards (2.8 m)	3 1/2 yards (3.1 m)	3 5/8 yards (3.3 m)
60 inches (150 cm), with nap	3 1/8 yards (2.8 m)	3 1/2 yards (3.1 m)	3 5/8 yards (3.3 m)
60 inches (150 cm), without nap	2 1/8 yards (1.9 m)	2 3/8 yards (2.1 m)	2 1/2 yards (2.25 m)

Appropriate Fabric

I suggest that you use wool jersey or stretch velour. Alter your pattern, and preshrink your fabric, if necessary.

Cut Out the Pattern Pieces

1 Alter your pattern and preshrink your fabric, if necessary.

2 If you have large hips, make this skirt slightly wider than the pattern so that it pulls easily over your hips. The best way to do this is by cutting out the six skirt patterns ¾ inch (2 cm) outside the cutting lines for your size for the lengthwise seams. You'll still sew with ⅝-inch (1.5 cm) seam allowances.

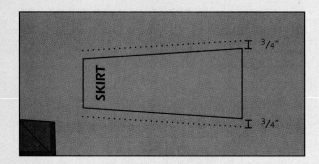

3 To create a custom waistband, subtract 4 inches (10 cm) from your hip measurement. This is the length of your waistband.

4 On the crosswise grain, where the fabric has maximum stretch, cut a 4-inch (10-cm)-wide strip of fabric to the length that you just determined. Cut one waistband.

Construct Your Pull-On Skirt

1 Join the six skirt gores, using ⅝-inch (1.5-cm) seam allowances and tiny zigzag stitches. Serge or zigzag the seam allowances together.

2 Place a pin or chalk mark in the middle of one of the gores. Mark the center of the gore directly opposite in the same manner. These pins indicate center back and center front on your skirt.

3 Measure your waist and subtract 4 inches (10 cm). Cut a piece of elastic to this length. If your fabric is slightly heavy, like velvet or velour, cut the elastic 5 inches (12.5 cm) smaller than your honest waist measurement.

4 Finish one long edge of the waistband by serging or pinking. This edge will be used on the inside of the skirt.

5 Join the waistband to the skirt as described in "Full Pull-On Pants," following the instructions in "Apply the Waistband" on page 15, "Join and Insert the Elastic" on page 16, and "Complete the Waistband" on page 17.

6 Hem the skirt, as explained in "Hem the Skirt" on page 158.

12-Gore Georgette Skirt

3 HOURS

I'm going to show you how to make a fuller skirt with 12 gores. Each of the gores is cut exactly the same size as the original skirt pattern—you'll just use more of them. Therefore, you need almost double the amount of fabric. I recommend that you use georgette, which is delightful to wear.

Because georgette is somewhat sheer, the skirt must be considerably fuller to keep it from being skimpy and revealing. That's why I recommend making a full skirt with georgette. I also think that you should use French seams to join the gores together.

Add to Your Shopping List

Like the skirt in the general instructions, this one also has a zipper. So you can follow the notions list on page 147, adding only liquid seam sealer and 40 inches (1 m) of string to your shopping list.

	Fabric Yardage for 12-Gore Skirt		
Fabric width	**Small**	**Medium**	**Large**
All fabric widths	6 yards (5.4 m)	6½ yards (5.8 m)	6¾ yards (6.1 m)

Note: Refer to this yardage table when determining the amount of fabric that you need. Don't use the table in the general instructions.

Appropriate Fabric

Georgette is the absolutely best fabric to use to create this sheer, full skirt. It "floats" rather than clings to your body. However, that doesn't mean that you can't use this pattern for a skirt that follows your figure a bit closer. Just about any fabric will sew up nicely.

Cut Out and Construct Your Georgette Skirt

1 Select your pattern size by matching your waist and hip measurements to the size table on page 208. Following the general instructions starting on page 150, prepare your fabric, and cut out your pattern pieces. Don't bother altering the pattern because this skirt is so full that it isn't necessary. Remember that you need to cut out 12 gores.

2 Stabilize the seam allowances for the zipper, and insert the centered zipper, following the directions in "Construct Your Skirt" starting on page 151.

3 Join the gores, following the directions in "Join the Gores" on page 153. Use French seams to join them since georgette tends to fray. (See the Quick Class "A 'Seamless' Finish" on page 26.)

The French seam shown above is a super way to finish many types of fabrics. It's ideal if your seam allowances fray and you don't own a serger. It's also great when you have a sheer fabric, where the inside of garment could be visible from the outside. That's why I chose French seams for my favorite georgette skirt, shown here.

Sandra says

SEW FRENCH For the highest-quality look, use French seams on skirts made of georgette or chiffon. (See the Quick Class "A 'Seamless' Finish" on page 26.) To eliminate any pucker in the seams, use a 10/70H needle with regular thread or a 8/60H or 9/65H needle with fine machine embroidery thread.

4 A custom waistband is easy to make. Cut a waistband that's 5 inches (12.5 cm) larger than your waist measurement and $3\frac{1}{2}$ inches (8.5 cm) wide on the crosswise grain.

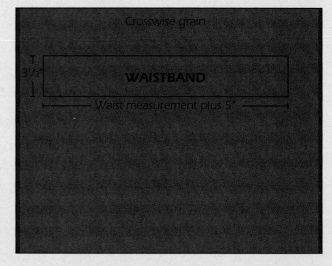

Crosswise grain

$3\frac{1}{2}$"

WAISTBAND

Waist measurement plus 5"

5 Fold $\frac{5}{8}$ inch (1.5 cm) of one long edge to the wrong side. Place the fabric on a table wrong side up. On the other long edge, which is unfolded, snip into the fabric $1\frac{5}{8}$ inches (4 cm) away from the short end on your left. Place another snip $\frac{5}{8}$ inch (1.5 cm) from the short end on your right.

6 At the waist of the skirt, zigzag a row of long, wide stitches over a length of string that's positioned ¹/₂ inch (1 cm) from the edge of the waist. Keep the string centered so that it isn't caught in any of the stitches. Pull the string to gather the skirt so that it fits the waistband. An ease line isn't necessary on a gathered skirt.

7 Sew the waistband onto the waist of the skirt, as explained in Steps 5 through 7 of "Attach the Waistband" on page 155, and in "Insert the Elastic" on page 156. Pull out the string and sew down the waistband, as explained in "Finish the Waistband" on page 158.

Hem Your Georgette Skirt

1 To prevent georgette from stretching as you sew the hem on your machine, first press ¹/₂ inch (1 cm) to the wrong side of the skirt.

PINLESS IS PAINLESS
To save time, don't pin the pattern to the fabric every few inches. Instead place your pins in all the corners, with others spaced along the gaps. Or, don't use pins at all. Instead place pattern weights in the center and corners of your pattern. As you cut, use smooth, long motions whenever possible, and hold the pattern flat against the fabric with your opposite hand.

2 Using a narrow zigzag stitch, sew over the fold. The stitches go on and off the fold. If the fabric is stretching as you sew, use your finger to hold the fabric behind the presser foot. See the Quick Class "Crowd Your Stitches" on page 154. Experiment with the stitch length and width before sewing on your fabric.

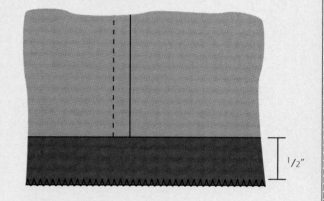

¹/₂"

3 Trim off the ¹/₂-inch (1-cm) hem allowance close to the stitching. If you don't see any threads poking out of your zigzag stitching, your hem is complete. But some georgette ravels, so you need to seal the edge with a liquid seam sealant, or turn the hem under again and sew it in place with a line of straight stitches. Press your hem flat. If you turn the hem under a second time, crowd the second row of stitching again to prevent the hem edge from stretching.

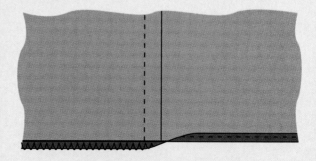

Raglan-Sleeve DRESS

A Dress Code You'll Love

By the time you finish making my dress in the Rodale Designer Collection, you'll think of the raglan sleeve as your best friend. If you have shoulders that are narrow, sloping, square, or broad, you'll discover that the raglan sleeve is the most flattering and forgiving. The gentle shape of this sleeve conforms to the body's natural curves. Plus, you don't need to worry about sleeve "ease," which is often difficult to work with in sleeve caps.

This dress is also easy to make because it doesn't have a zipper. It has enough ease that when you want to put it on, you simply pull it over your head.

With this garment, I offer you several style choices. The neckline can be bias bound, or you can sew on a fabric or hand-knitted cowl. There are also a couple of lengths. The tunic and the lounge robe that the other models on the opposite page are wearing are made from the same pattern and instructions—I just changed the length. See the Quick Class "The Long and Short of It" on page 171.

The most challenging part of the dress is the neckline, and I'm offering you several choices. One option is attaching a fabric cowl. This takes a bit longer because the neckline is first stabilized with twill tape.

What You Need

Everyone should be able to decide what length and design options they want, which is why I offer so many construction choices for my garments. With my mid-calf dress pattern, for example, you can also make a tunic or lounge robe by using the alternate cutoff lines.

"The fabric for this dress was hand-woven by a weaver named Bianculli, using chenille, cotton, linen, and metallic yarns. The fabric makes such a statement that accessories are unnecessary. As you can see, the lines of this dress are quite simple, which makes the pattern suitable for loose-weave fabrics as well as for material that has a lot of personality. Instructions to make the fabric collar on this dress are on page 182."

Fabric Yardage for Dress

Fabric width	Small	Medium	Large
45 inches* (115 cm)	3⅓ yards (3 m)	3⅓ yards (3 m)	3½ yards (3.1)
60 inches (150 cm)	2⅜ yards (2.1 m)	2⅜ yards (2.1 m)	2⅜ yards (2.1 m)
Additional fabric for neckline trim	**Small**	**Medium**	**Large**
All widths	½ yard (0.4 m)	½ yard (0.4 m)	½ yard (0.4 m)

Don't use 45-inch (115-cm)-wide napped fabric.

Fabric Yardage for Tunic

Fabric width	Small	Medium	Large
45 inches* (115 cm)	2⅞ yards (2.6 m)	2⅞ yards (2.6 m)	2⅞ yards (2.6 m)
60 inches (150 cm)	2 yards (1.8 m)	2 yards (1.8 m)	2 yards (1.8 m)

Don't use 45-inch (115-cm)-wide napped fabric.

Fabric Yardage for Lounge Robe

Fabric width	Small	Medium	Large
45 inches* (115 cm)	3 yards (2.7 m)	3 yards (2.7 m)	3½ yards (3.1 m)
60 inches (150 cm)	2¾ yards (2.5 m)	2¾ yards (2.5 m)	2¾ yards (2.5 m)

Don't use 45-inch (115-cm)-wide napped fabric.

Appropriate Fabric

Use any medium-weight woven such as linen, raw silk, sandwashed rayon, wool crepe, or wool jersey. A lighter-weight fabric such as 2-ply silk crepe de chine is too flimsy, unless it's underlined in cotton batiste or flannelette. (See the Quick Class "Underline Your Style" on page 125.) Cotton knit, stretch velour, and wool jersey make attractive neckline trim.

Front

Back

BE PREPARED How much time have you wasted because you purchased fabric that didn't coordinate as you intended . . . and all because you didn't bring along a fabric swatch? Always carry small fabric swatches of your current sewing projects and clothes in your wardrobe. Not only is this a great help when buying accessories, but companion fabrics also can be purchased without guesswork.

Notions

- ✂ Matching thread
- ✂ Package of ¼-inch (5-mm)-wide twill tape
- ✂ Package of ½-inch (1-cm)-wide Seams Great
- ✂ Miscellaneous supplies, as listed in "The Sewing Basket" on page ix

Fit Your Dress Pattern

So you don't have a perfect figure. Hardly anyone does. As a sewer you're probably resigned to the fact that you have to alter your patterns, even though it isn't much fun. Well, guess what? The lines in this dress are so simple that altering the patterns will be painless.

Get Started

Since this pattern is multisized, you can cut one size in one area and transition to another size as needed to fit your body shape. If you're unsure what size you should use at different parts of your body, refer to the size table on page 208. Start with the size that best fits your dominant feature, probably your bust or your hips, for this garment.

Broad Back and Narrow Upper Chest

Having both a broad back and a narrow upper chest is pretty common.

If you have this problem, your dresses feel comfortable across the back but there are vertical wrinkles in your clothes across the front between the armholes as well as another set of wrinkles just below the collar bone at the base of the neck. Also, the armhole seam falls on to the upper arm.

If you have this figure variation, cut the upper back of the back pattern a larger size and the upper front chest of the front in the smaller size. Remember to cut the respective parts of the sleeve to match their corresponding cutting lines on the dress. To simplify cutting and construction, stick to one size at the neck on both the front and back patterns.

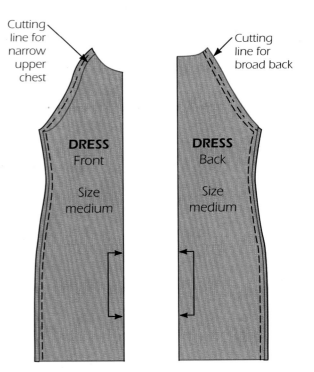

Cutting line for narrow upper chest

Cutting line for broad back

DRESS Front Size medium

DRESS Back Size medium

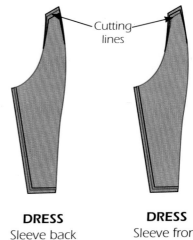

Cutting lines

DRESS Sleeve back Size medium

DRESS Sleeve front Size medium

Protruding Tummy

You have a protruding tummy if pleats pop open on the front of your pants. You'll also notice that your pants and skirts are difficult to zip up. A one-piece dress gets "hung up" on your tummy. This is the area where a snug fit is the most unflattering.

Measure the front and back patterns from side seam to the center foldline about 2½ to 3 inches (6 to 7.5 cm) down from the waistline. Add these two numbers together and multiply by 2. (Since the patterns are cut on the fold, the pattern tissues are half the width of the fabric pattern piece after it's cut out.) Subtract 2½ inches (6 cm) for the seam allowances. This is your final pattern measurement.

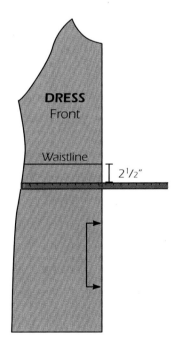

Now measure yourself over the tummy area, about 2½ to 3 inches (6 to 7.5 cm) down from your waist, depending on your figure. (To find your honest measurement, see the Quick Class "Measurable Results" on page 16.)

If the final pattern measurement isn't 4 inches (10 cm) larger than your personal measurement, you need to use larger cutting lines at the side seams in the tummy and high hip area.

KNOW THYSELF The amount of ease needed for a garment varies. For example, for a fitted garment such as a skirt and some dresses, you need 2 inches (5 cm) of fitting ease for the tummy. This ease, or extra fabric, makes it possible to move comfortably when you're wearing the garment. Simply put, the fitted garment should measure 2 inches (5 cm) larger than your tummy area.

For example, if the final pattern measurement is only 1 inch (2.5 cm) larger than your personal measurement, you need 3 more inches (7.5 cm). Divide the amount that you need (3 inches or 7.5 cm) by 4, which equals ¾ inch (2 cm). Add ¾ inch (2 cm) to each side seam on both the front and back patterns.

Make the addition all the way to the hem. Even though you may not need the addition at the hip, the dress will be more flattering if you add material all the way from the tummy to the hem. To start, tape tissue paper to the side seams, then smoothly taper in the addition from the tummy to about 3 inches (7.5 cm) above the waist at the side seams.

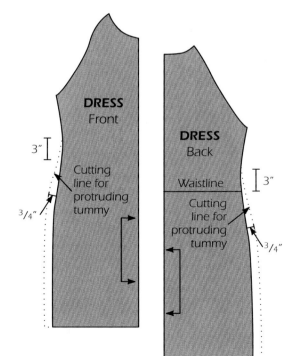

Large or Small Hips

Most of us are pretty familiar with the pear-shape figure. We tend to buy separates because our shoulders, bust, and waist are small in proportion to our hips.

Ideally, the dress should be 4 inches (10 cm) wider at the hips than your personal measurement. If it isn't, you can widen the pattern with an alteration, as explained in "Protruding Tummy" on page 169.

On the dress front and back patterns, you'll transition between sizes around the waist.

For example, if you need a size medium at the bust and waist but a size large at the hips, use the size medium cutting lines at the bust but the size large at the hips, gradually shifting

from the smaller size to the larger size starting slightly above the waistline. At the waist, it may be necessary to cut a bit outside the size medium cutting lines so that the transition is smooth, which is necessary for smooth seams.

If you're larger on top than through the hips, transition to the smaller cutting lines in the hip area. When finished, the dress will have a wedge shape, which is flattering to your figure.

Dress Length

Choose one of your dresses that has a nice length and has a neckline that sits at the base of the neck at center back. Measure the finished length from the base of the neck at center back all the way down to the hem. Use this to determine the length of your new dress.

You may not need to alter the dress length if your measurement matches the one listed in "Finished Lengths and Hem Widths" on page 208. But if you do, add 1½ inches (3.5 cm) to this measurement to determine the hem allowance. Now measure and mark your new hem cutting line on the dress front and back patterns.

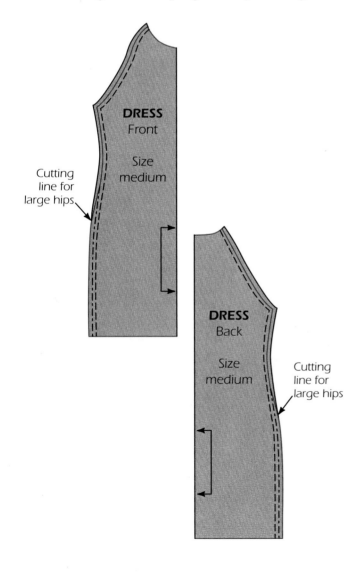

Cutting line for large hips

DRESS Front

Size medium

DRESS Back

Size medium

Cutting line for large hips

CLEAN FINISH YOUR EDGES Sergers are great time-savers and are definitely worth the investment if you sew a lot. If you don't line your dress, finishing the seam allowances with serging is a nice, professional touch. This is also called clean finishing.

If you don't own a serger, pinking or scalloping with the appropriate shears is another seam finish option, but serged seams look professional.

Right after the garment is cut out, serge around all the cut edges of each pattern piece. Now sew your seams together according to the instructions. Your seams will automatically be finished as soon as they are pressed open.

QUICK CLASS

The Long and Short of It

The photo on page 164 features a tunic, dress, and lounge robe. These were all created from my dress pattern in the Rodale Designer Collection. In addition, they were all assembled in the same manner. They're just different lengths, which is shown by the two extra cutoff lines on the front and back patterns.

How to Lengthen or Shorten

1 You've probably read my warnings in other chapters not to lengthen or shorten at the hem because this distorts the garment's silhouette. In some cases, it's okay. If the silhouette of your dress, skirt, or pants is a straight line from the hips to the hem, the hem area doesn't flare out or taper in. The first step when deciding whether you can lengthen or shorten at the hem is to inspect the side seams of your pattern to make sure that they are straight from about midthigh to the hem.

2 Determine the desired length that you want for the garment. Compare this figure to the finished lengths for the pattern. For my garments in the Rodale Designer Collection, look at the numbers that I compiled in the table "Finished Lengths and Hem Widths" on page 208. (If you're measuring a pattern, remember to subtract the hem allowance to come up with the correct finished length.) The difference is the amount that you add or subtract from the cutting line at the hem. Fold the pattern or tape paper to the hem and mark the new cutting line.

3 Measure and mark a new cutting line for the hem on the appropriate patterns. For the dress, this means that you mark both the front and the back.

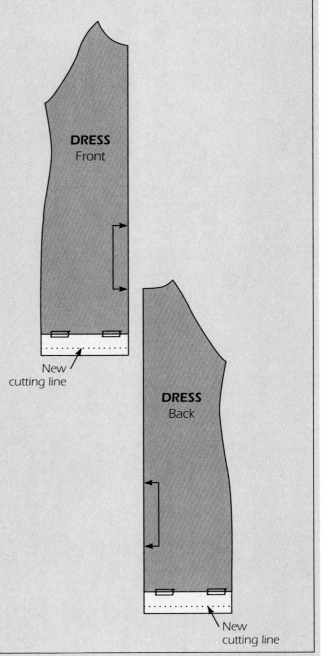

DRESS
Front

New
cutting line

DRESS
Back

New
cutting line

Prepare the Fabric and Pattern Pieces

30 MINUTES

This is a fairly simple process that shouldn't take you more than half an hour. There's nothing to interface, only a few patterns, no tailor's tacks to make, and very few notches. In some sizes and fabric widths, the most difficult part is refolding the fabric to cut out the remaining patterns.

1 Pretreat your fabric in the same manner that you plan to clean the finished dress. If you plan to line your dress, remember to pretreat the lining fabric as well.

2 Straighten the crosswise grain on both ends of your fabric. At the edge of the fabric, snip through the selvage. (The selvages are the tightly woven edges that run along both lengthwise edges of your fabric.) Some fabrics can't be torn, so you'll have to pull a thread close to each edge. If it breaks, just pull on the thread next to it. The idea is to draw the thread until the fabric puckers. Now cut the fabric along this pucker, or tear off a strip of fabric from selvage to selvage (starting at the snip), so that you have a straight edge that's on-grain. If you have a knit fabric or a woven on which it's hard to find a crosswise-grain thread, you need to use a different procedure. See the Quick Class "When the Going Gets Tough" on page 78.

3 Position the pattern pieces on your fabric as shown in the pattern layout for your size and fabric width on the opposite page. Place pins in all the corners and along the gaps. If your fabric has a nap or one-way design (a pattern or motif that has a top and bottom), make sure that all of your patterns are going in the same direction. Note that both the front and back patterns are placed lengthwise on a fabric fold. The layouts all include the pattern for the cowl collar. If you don't plan to make a cowl, use the layout specified for your size and fabric width, and exclude the cowl pattern.

4 Cut out the pattern pieces. As you cut, use smooth long motions whenever possible, holding the pattern flat against the fabric with your opposite hand. Before taking the pattern tissue off the fabric pattern pieces, snip into the seam allowance to mark the notches.

5 If you're using lightweight fabric, you may want to underline the fabric pattern pieces for your garment. (See the Quick Class "Underline Your Style" on page 125.) Now pink or serge all of the cut edges of your pattern pieces. See "Clean Finish Edges" on page 170.

PATTERN LAYOUT KEY		DRESS	
Right side of fabric	■	**Name**	**Number**
Right side of tissue	□	Front	24
		Back	25
Wrong side of tissue	▨	Sleeve front	26
		Sleeve back	27
		Cowl*	28

*The cowl (pattern 28) is optional. Only cut it out if you plan to include a cowl on the dress, as featured in "Cowl Collar" on page 182.

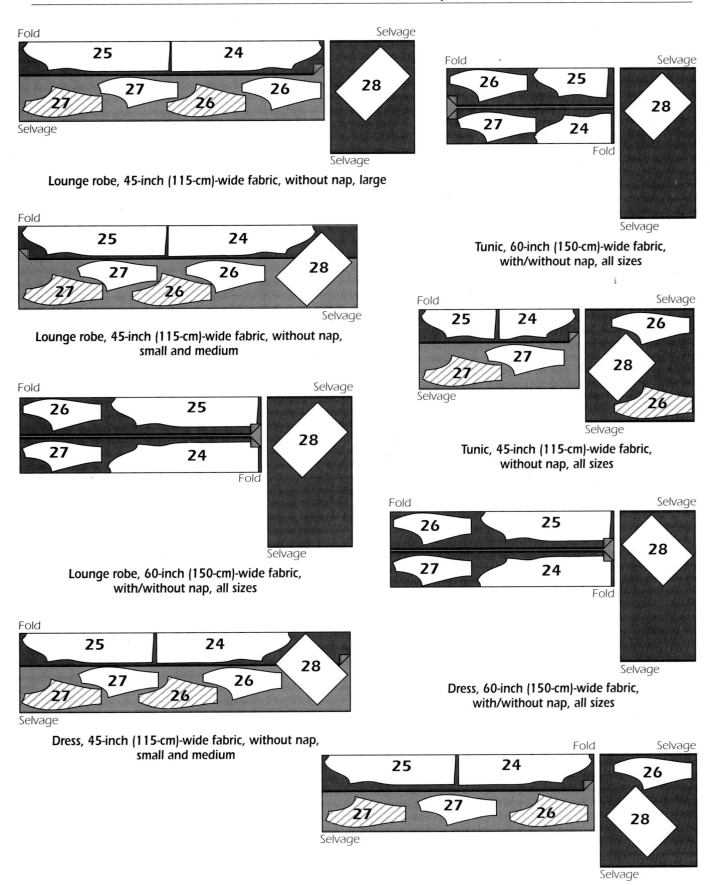

Lounge robe, 45-inch (115-cm)-wide fabric, without nap, large

Lounge robe, 45-inch (115-cm)-wide fabric, without nap,
small and medium

Lounge robe, 60-inch (150-cm)-wide fabric,
with/without nap, all sizes

Dress, 45-inch (115-cm)-wide fabric, without nap,
small and medium

Tunic, 60-inch (150-cm)-wide fabric,
with/without nap, all sizes

Tunic, 45-inch (115-cm)-wide fabric,
without nap, all sizes

Dress, 60-inch (150-cm)-wide fabric,
with/without nap, all sizes

Dress, 45-inch (115-cm)-wide fabric, without nap, large

Construct Your Dress

2 HOURS

You'll love constructing the raglan sleeve in this dress. Since the seams in my dress in the Rodale Designer Collection are almost straight lines, the pieces fit together effortlessly. To stabilize the size of the neckline, I use a technique that you may recognize from the T-shirt instructions.

Assemble the Shoulders

1 All the seam allowances are ⅝ inch (1.5 cm) wide, and the stitch length is medium (10 to 12 stitches per inch or 2.5 on a 0-to-4 stitch length setting), unless otherwise indicated.

With right sides together and cut edges and notches matching, sew both of the sleeve fronts to the dress front. With right sides together, join the sleeve backs to the dress back. Press all of the seam allowances open.

Dress Front

2 If you serged or pinked the cut edges of your pattern pieces, you're ready for Step 3. But if you want to use flat fell seams, see the Quick Class "The Fastest Mock Flat Fell Seam" on page 39.

3 With right sides facing and cut edges even, sew the front to the back at the shoulders. If you have a broad back and narrow upper chest and have resized your pattern accordingly, sew

with the longer pattern piece nearest the feed dogs. This will help take up the extra fabric. Press the seam allowances open.

Stabilize the Neckline

1 Since the neckline is a single thickness of fabric and may stretch, stabilize it with twill tape cut to the same measurement as the long edge of the cowl pattern minus 1¼ inches (3.2 cm). Even if you don't want a cowl on your dress, use the pattern for the measurement.

2 Place the twill tape on the wrong side of the fabric so that the farthest edge is ³/₄ inch (2 cm) from the cut edge of the neckline. Most of the tape is in the seam allowance.

3 Pin the tape to the neckline so that the neckline matches the length of the twill tape. If your fabric is unstable (as is often the case with stretchy or loosely woven material), the neck may seem larger than the twill tape. Distribute any fullness evenly. Staystitch the twill tape to the neckline with the fabric closest to the feed dogs and the twill tape against the presser foot. The feed dogs will ease the neck to fit the tape.

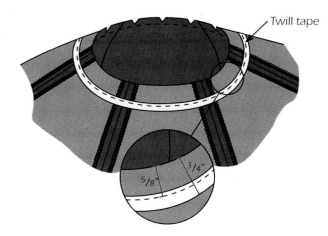

Twill tape

4 Clip into the fabric seam allowance at 1-inch (2.5-cm) intervals. Don't cut through the stitches and don't clip into the twill tape. Often sewers are reluctant to snip far enough into the seam allowance. Make sure that your snip goes almost to the line of stitching. Press the seam flat. Trim the seam allowance to ¹/₄ inch (5 mm).

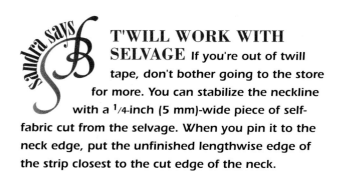

Sandra says

T'WILL WORK WITH SELVAGE If you're out of twill tape, don't bother going to the store for more. You can stabilize the neckline with a ¹/₄-inch (5 mm)-wide piece of self-fabric cut from the selvage. When you pin it to the neck edge, put the unfinished lengthwise edge of the strip closest to the cut edge of the neck.

Trim the Neckline

1 Cut a 1¹/₄-inch (3.2-cm)-wide strip of trim fabric. I suggest that you use a knit fabric. It can be cut on the crosswise grain because this direction has the greatest stretch. If you're using a woven for the trim, cut the woven strip on the bias. (The bias is at a 45-degree angle to the selvages on your fabric.) Your strip needs to be the same length as the long edge of the cowl pattern minus 1³/₄ inches (4.5 cm).

2 With right sides facing and using a ⁵/₈-inch (1.5-cm) seam allowance, join the two short ends of the trim together to make a circle. Press the seam allowances open, and trim them to ¹/₄ inch (5 mm).

1¹/₄"

3 Position the trim seam on the dress back so it aligns with the cut and serged edge of one of the sleeve seams. Place the right side of the trim against the right side of the back. Because the trim is smaller than the neckline, stretch the trim to fit the neckline. The trim will lay flat against the neck on the finished dress. Using a ¹/₄-inch (5-mm) seam allowance, sew the trim to the neckline. This is done by sewing right on top of the line of stitching that you used to attach the twill tape to the neckline.

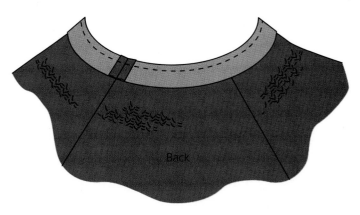

Back

4 The procedure for attaching the trim varies according to your fabric. If you're using a woven strip for the trim, turn under ¼ inch (5 mm) along one long edge. This isn't necessary for knit fabric because it doesn't ravel. Enclose the cut edges of the neckline and the seam allowances by wrapping the trim from the outside to the inside of the neckline. Let the unattached cut or folded edge of the trim extend just past the seamline on the wrong side of the neckline. Pin the trim to the neckline in the well, or "ditch," of the seam. If you're using a knit, place the pins on the right side of the dress. If you're using a woven, place the pins on the wrong side of the dress. Make sure that the seam allowances are tucked inside the trim so that the cut edges will be completely enclosed after you sew down the trim. See Step 5 if you're using knit strips; otherwise hand stitch the woven edge in place.

5 For knit strips, sew the trim to the neckline. This is done by stitching in the well of the seam from the right side of the dress. When finished attaching the trim, cut off the excess trim that extends beyond the stitching line on the wrong side of the garment.

thread TALES

I'm often asked for a simple procedure for lining a garment.

A lining is a good idea because it prevents the garment from stretching in places like the seat and it cuts down on wrinkling.

Besides, since you don't have to finish the seams on a lined garment, it really isn't more work than sewing an unlined piece of clothing.

It's easy to make a lined version of this dress. I assembled the dress following the general instructions for applying twill tape to the neckline on page 174. I didn't attach trim. I also hemmed the dress and the sleeves. The lining was cut and assembled in exactly the same manner, except I didn't include hem allowances and I didn't use twill tape on the lining pattern pieces.

Next I slipped the lining inside the dress with wrong sides together and basted them together at the neckline.

Now finish the neckline with trim or a cowl, including both the dress and the lining in the seams.

Align the side seams of the lining and the dress at the underarm, and pin for 2 inches (5 cm). Anchor the lining to the dress at the underarm seams by lifting the sleeves and sewing in the well of the side seam for 2 inches (5 cm).

Now hem the lining by turning it under ½ inch (1 cm) twice so that the cut edge of the lining is enclosed and topstitching it close to the top fold.

Sandra

Refine the Fit

1 With right sides facing and the cut edges even, pin a side and sleeve seam together, starting at the hem of the dress, and continuing past the underarm to the end of the sleeve. Machine baste both seams, using ⅝-inch (1.5-cm) seam allowances.

2 Pin up the dress and the sleeve hems. Insert a pair of shoulder pads, and try on your dress. It's best to do this while wearing whatever shoes you'll wear with the finished garment. Look in the mirror and decide if you need to take in or let out the side seams. Machine baste again to refine the fit of the dress before you permanently sew the seams.

BASTE IN HASTE Sometimes it isn't necessary to remove basting, especially if the stitches are on the seam line. But if you will need to take them out, use a different color of thread in the bobbin. Thread in a contrasting color is much easier to single out from the threads in the fashion fabric.

3 You may also decide to raise the underarm curve a bit. Simply sew straight up from the side seam an extra inch before curving out to the sleeve. Clip the seam allowances along the length of the curve.

Restitch if necessary

4 Sew the side seams permanently, and press the seam allowances open. If you're using flat fell seams, finish the seams.

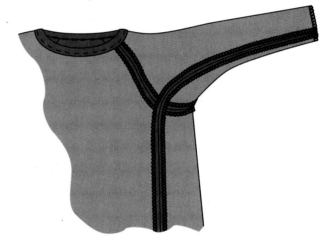

Hem the Dress and Sleeves

1 Again try on your dress with the shoes you plan to wear with it. Make a final decision about dress length. Pin-mark or chalk the finished hem.

2 Take off the dress, and lay it flat. Cut off any excess fabric at the bottom of the hem, remembering to allow a 1¾-inch (4.5-cm) fabric extension beyond the finished hem mark for the hem allowance (the amount that you'll turn to the inside of the dress).

3 Sew a row of stitches ¹/₄ inch (5 mm) from the cut edge at the bottom of the dress. As you run this ease line around the cut edge of the dress, push at the fabric behind the presser foot with your finger. (See the Quick Class "Crowd Your Stitches" on page 154.) Use a longer stitch—almost a basting stitch—for heavy fabric and a shorter stitch for lightweight fabric.

4 Press up the 1³/₄-inch (4.5-cm) hem allowance. If you eased too much, the hem allowance won't lie flat. Snap a thread in the ease line and let the hem allowance relax.

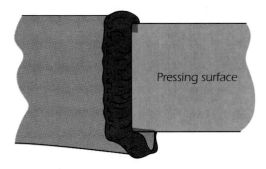

If the hem allowance seems too full so that little tucks are needed to get rid of the excess, run another line of ease around the hem allowance to ease in more fabric. Both rows of ease don't have to be right on top of each other.

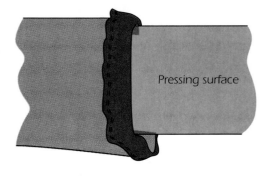

5 Once the hem fits the dress smoothly, serge or pink the cut edge of the hem allowance, enclose it with Seams Great, or use bias tape. (See "Hem the Pants" on page 19 or the Quick Class "Wrapping It Up" on page 126.)

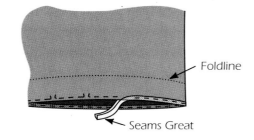

6 Hem the dress by hand using the blind hem stitch. For an invisible hem, take one thread from the garment, move forward ¹/₄ inch (5 mm), and take one thread from the hem. Never pick up garment and hem threads at the same time.

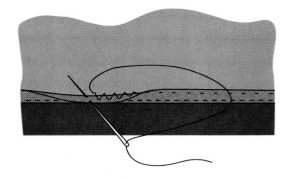

7 Hem the sleeve as you did the dress, or cut off the hem allowance and trim it in the same manner as the neckline. However, it isn't necessary to stabilize the sleeve edge with twill tape. Cut the trim 1¹/₄ inches (3.2 cm) wide and to the length of the sleeve circumference minus ¹/₄ inch (5 mm). Don't forget to stretch the trim slightly as you sew it.

Decorative Sleeve Seams

45 MINUTES

This detailing looks great and helps draw the eye up and away from the hips. Piping at the shoulder seams adds visual weight to this area, thereby balancing the lower half of the body. It's a super alternative to using shoulder pads.

I added piping to this lounge robe that was created from the dress pattern. The shoulder detailing works well with the striped fabric. To make the piping, I wrapped a solid-colored knit fabric around oversize cotton cable cord.

Add to Your Shopping List

- ⅛ yard (.1 m) of contrasting or complementary knit fabric
- 2 yards (1.8 m) of ½-inch (1-cm)-wide cotton cable cord

Appropriate Fabric

Cotton knit, stretch velour, and wool jersey all make attractive trim for the decorative piping on the sleeves.

USE WHAT YOU HAVE If you don't have any suitable knits in your fabric collection for trim, but you do have a matching woven, you may want to use it rather than make another trip to the store. My preference is knit fabric because it has more "give," but woven strips can work; they just need to be cut differently. If you use a woven fabric, cut your strips on the bias. You'll need ¾ yard (.7 m) of fabric. (See the Quick Class "Bound to Succeed" on page 58.)

Make the Piping

1 Measure the shoulder seam from the neckline to the end of the sleeve. Since you have two sleeves, cut two lengths of cord to this measurement. Set one aside.

SLEEVE
Front

2 Cut two fabric strips, each 3½ inches (8.5 cm) wide and the same length as the cord. This will make enough piping to decorate the top of the two sleeve seams.

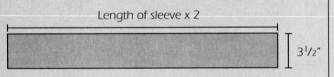

Length of sleeve x 2

3½"

3 Enclose the cord in the fabric strip. When you do this, the wrong side of the fabric strip is against the cord.

SANDRA SAYS

PULL TO AVOID THE PUSH On very lightweight fabrics, sewing machines want to push the fabric through the hole in the needle plate and down into the bobbin. To prevent this and to keep the fabric from bunching up behind the presser foot when you start, slightly pull the thread ends behind the machine as you begin sewing.

4 Install a zipper foot on your sewing machine, and insert the fabric strip under the presser foot with the cord to the left of the needle. Sew the fabric together close to the cord without catching the cord in the seam. Repeat for the remaining piece of cord.

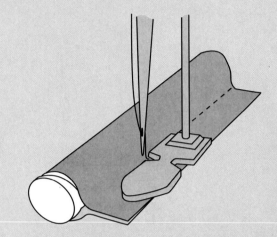

Assemble the Dress

1 Join the sleeve fronts to the dress front. Do the same for the back of the garment, sewing the sleeve backs to the dress back.

2 Trim the seam allowances on the piping so that the distance between the cut edge and the stitching line is exactly ⅝ inch (1.5 cm).

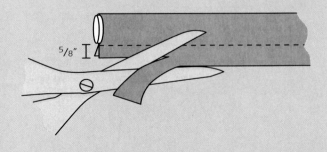

⅝"

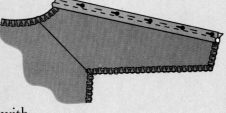

3 Pin one piece of the piping on the right side of the front shoulder seam with the cut edges of the piping and the sleeve shoulder seam allowance matching.

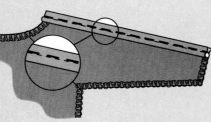

4 Machine basting piping to a garment shortens the seam. Your best bet is to hand baste the piping in place by sewing right on top of the machine stitches that enclose the piping.

5 With right sides together and cut edges matching at the shoulder seams, lay the dress front on the dress back. Pin the shoulder seams together so that the hand basting is visible. Place the pins in the dress front seam allowance. With the zipper foot still on your sewing machine, sew the shoulder seams, using the hand basting as a guide. The object here is to get the piping into the seam as tightly as possible without sewing over the cord. You may need to lengthen your stitch to avoid tiny stitches as you sew through the multiple layers of fabric.

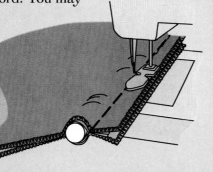

6 Temporarily secure the cord in the piping at the end of the sleeve by pinning it to the fabric. To avoid bulk at the neckline seam, pull out ³/₄ inch (2 cm) of the cord at the neckline from

the end of the piping fabric. Cut it off. Pull the shoulder seam to allow the end of the cord to slide back inside the piping. Pin this end of the cord to the piping ³/₄ inch (2 cm) from the neckline edge.

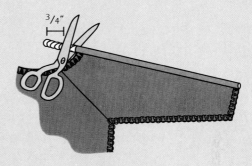

7 To avoid bulk in the sleeve hem, remove the pin and pull 1¹/₄ inches (3.2 cm) of the cord out of the end of the piping fabric. Cut it off. Pull the shoulder seam and allow the end of the cord to slide back into the piping, 1¹/₄ inch (3.2 cm) from the bottom of the sleeve.

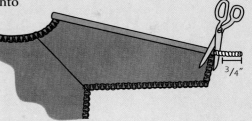

8 Since the ends of the neckline and sleeve piping are now empty, flatten them so that half of the casing is on each side of the seamline. Pin them in place. This will help the piping sit upright when the garment is finished.

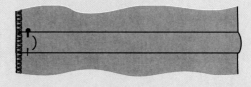

9 Finish assembling your dress, starting with "Stabilize the Neckline" on page 174.

Cowl Collar

45 MINUTES

Wrapping a soft piece of fabric around your neck is a nice way to frame your face. I do it all the time with scarves. But sometimes I prefer to have this effect in the garment itself. In this case, I add a cowl collar to the neckline. You can use these same instructions to add a cowl to any garment.

The cowl collar is meant to be soft and drapey, so inter-facing isn't required for this pattern piece. Because it's cut on the bias, it will drape nicely.

Add to Your Shopping List

Before you purchase additional fabric to make your cowl, take a look at your yardage. There's a very good chance that you can squeeze the cowl into your existing pattern layout.

	Fabric Yardage for Cowl Collar		
Fabric width	Small	Medium	Large
All fabric widths	7/8 yard (0.8 m)	7/8 yard (0.8 m)	7/8 yard (0.8 m)

WASH IN TIME You're better off spending an hour preshrinking fabric. If you don't you may spend several hours restitching hems and seams if your fabric shrinks after the garment is sewn.

Rayon challis, acetate slinky knit, and velour can be machine washed and dried.

Machine laundered rayon velvet looks antique. Cut off a fabric strip and throw it in with your next load of laundry. If you like the results, then wash the yardage.

Make the Cowl

1 Cut out the cowl pattern piece on the bias, which is at a 45-degree angle to the selvages. With right sides together and short ends matching, form a circle and sew a seam. Press the seam allowances open, and trim them to ¼ inch (5 mm).

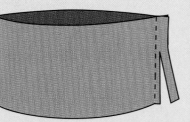

2 Press a ¼-inch (5-mm) fold to the wrong side of one edge of the circle. This will go on the inside of the garment.

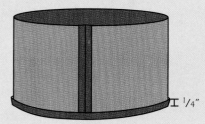

Prepare the Dress and Add the Cowl

1 Alter your patterns and prepare your fabric, following the general instructions in "Fit Your Dress Pattern" on page 168 and "Prepare the Fabric and the Pattern Pieces" on page 172. Partially assemble the dress, following the instructions in "Assemble the Shoulders" on page 174 and "Stabilize the Neckline" on page 174. Don't make or attach the neckline trim.

2 Place the right side of the cowl against the right side of the dress with the cowl seam at center back. Pin the cowl in place from the dress side so that the cowl won't stretch when the neckline is sewn. Sew, using a ⅝-inch (1.5-cm) seam allowance on top of the stitching line that attaches the stabilizing twill tape to the neckline. Trim the seam allowance to ¼ inch (5 mm).

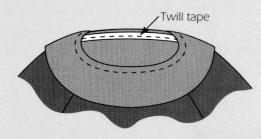

Twill tape

3 Fold the cowl to the inside of the dress so that the folded edge extends just past the neckline seam. Hand stitch the cowl foldline to the neckline seam. The twill tape you attached to stabilize the neckline may be slightly visible. If desired, you may instead attach the cowl by sewing in the well of the neckline seam from the right side of the dress.

Twill tape

Hand-Knitted Collar

3 HOURS

If you like to knit as well as sew, here is an opportunity to combine both elements into a single garment. The knitted collar is a simple rectangle made of (knit 1, purl 1) ribbing. It's such a basic stitch that you may want to give it a try even if your knitting skills are limited.

This dress is made from hand-woven yardage that is very dear to me. I wanted the rest of the garment to be just as special, so I found a complementary yarn and hand knit the ribbing that's attached to the neckline. If you'd like to knit your own ribbing, make it 5 inches (12.5 cm) deep and the length of the cowl collar pattern minus 1¼ inches (3.2 cm).

Add to Your Shopping List

The amount of yarn you'll need varies depending on the type you select. Ask a salesperson to determine the amount that you'll need once you've selected the yarn.

Appropriate Fabric

Choose a dress fabric that has some visual weight and texture. Fabric with a very obvious weave is good.

Any type of yarn is suitable for this collar, but make sure that the knitted collar is a weight suitable for the fashion fabric that you're using for the tunic. For example, I discovered that my heavyweight, hand-woven dress fabric works best with a bulky yarn. For a medium-weight fabric, you may prefer a worsted weight yarn.

I LIKE IT HOT Get into the habit of pressing as you sew. Your completed garment will look more professional. If you have an iron with an automatic shutoff, get rid of it. It's faster when your iron is always hot and ready.

Prepare the Dress and Add the Collar

1 Alter your patterns and prepare your fabric, following the general instructions in "Fit Your Dress Pattern" on page 168 and "Prepare the Fabric and the Pattern Pieces" on page 172. Make the dress, following the instructions in "Assemble the Shoulders" and "Stabilize the Neckline," both on page 174, and in "Trim the Neckline" on page 175. I recommend that you finish the neckline edge with trim before you attach the knitted collar so that the inside of your garment will have a nice finished look.

2 Measure one long side of the cowl collar pattern. (You aren't using this pattern, but it's a good way to determine the length of your knitted collar.) If you're knitting in the round, subtract 1¼ inches (3.2 cm) since your cowl doesn't need seam allowances.

3 Make your (knit 1, purl 1) ribbing, either as a rectangle or by knitting in the round. For guidance, you can turn to the staff at the store where you bought the yarn, or refer to *Rodale's Visual Encyclopedia of Needlecraft* (Rodale Press, 1996). The length or circumference is the number you determined in Step 2, and the depth is 5 inches (12.5 cm). Your knitting gauge (the number of stitches and rows per inch) doesn't matter because you're knitting to the finished dimensions. Cast off your knitting.

4 If you didn't knit in the round, sew the short ends of the rectangle together to make a circle. This seam will be positioned at center back.

5 With the right side of the ribbing on the right side of the dress, overlay the knitted ribbing on the neckline so that one edge of the ribbing just covers the neckline trim. Run a length of doubled thread through beeswax, and then press it. This will strengthen the thread and prevent it from knotting frequently. Using the doubled thread, hand sew the ribbing to the neckline, making your hand stitches as invisible as possible. This isn't difficult since the thread sinks into the hand-knitted ribbing.

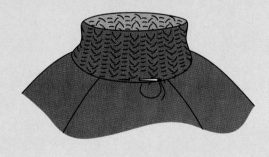

6 Now finish assembling the dress following the instructions in "Refine the Fit" on page 175 and "Hem the Dress and Sleeves," also on page 175.

Oblong
SCARF

Your Number One Accessory

My assortment of scarves gives me great pleasure. Some of them date back ten years, and I'm still wearing them. You'll do the same with the ones you make. Therefore, it makes sense to buy scarf fabric you really love. Chances are that you'll have the finished scarf a long, long time.

My first rule about selecting yardage is to never choose fabric unless you can see yourself in front of a mirror. The fabric's color must flatter your complexion. A plain scarf is infinitely more versatile than a print, but certain prints can be irresistible. Just make certain that the scarf isn't so busy that it competes with you. After all, the main purpose is to draw attention to your face, not overpower it.

An oblong scarf is my favorite shape. It covers up an unflattering or boring neckline. It fills in an opening on a coat, directs the eye upward toward your face, and enables you to wear a garment color that isn't your best by putting a flattering color next to your face. In addition, a scarf adds vertical style lines to break the silhouette into smaller parts so that your figure "reads" slimmer. And it provides a finishing touch for an outfit.

In just a few minutes, you can also have a great reversible scarf to coordinate with your wardrobe. All you need to do is straighten the edges of the fabric that you brought home from the store, and then stitch it up. The sewing won't take you longer than 20 minutes, even if you do it by hand.

What You Need

This accessory takes so little fabric that you should consider splurging on luxurious, more expensive material. Two yards (1.8 m) of any width fabric will make one scarf that is constructed completely by machine or two scarves if you hand hem them.

"*Test your fabric for drapeability by unwinding a few yards off the bolt. Hang the loose fabric around your neck. Can you envision this as a beautiful scarf or does it just look like a piece of fabric hanging around your neck? If the fabric is too heavy, it'll look bulky.***"**

Fabric Yardage for Scarf

Fabric width	One size
45 inches (115 cm)	2 yards (1.8 m)
60 inches (150 cm)	2 yards (1.8 m)

Note: You may need more or less fabric if you choose to vary the length of this scarf. Two yards (1.8 m) makes a 72-inch (183-cm)-long scarf. The finished width is half the width of your fabric, as measured from selvage to selvage.

Sandra says

SKIP A STEP Preshrinking your fabric isn't necessary. Realistically, very few people ever preshrink their fabric. If your fabric does shrink a few inches in either direction, it won't matter for a scarf. Trust me—you'll never notice the difference.

Appropriate Fabric

Silk, silk, and silk. Beyond a doubt, a scarf that is made from silk is the most luxurious and the most flattering accessory that you can own. But choosing the right silk is just as important as deciding to splurge on silk. Selecting a high-quality fabric is a must for two reasons: The fabric must drape well and it must be wrinkle resistant.

Silk crepe de chine, silk chiffon, silk charmeuse, and silk georgette are traditionally used for scarves. If the fabric is drapey enough, a polyester chiffon will also work. China silk is a bad choice because it wrinkles very easily.

Notions

- ✂ Matching cotton or polyester thread
- ✂ 10/70H sewing machine needle
- ✂ Miscellaneous supplies, as listed in "The Sewing Basket" on page ix

TRY A LITTLE TENDERNESS Most silks can be hand laundered. To preserve this fabric's fluid nature, hand wash it in shampoo and warm water.

If you fear that the color of your silk is going to bleed, which is more common with darker colors, try washing a swatch to see if the color loss is too great. If it is, then set the color by rinsing the yardage in a mixture of cold water, 1/4 cup (57 ml) of salt, and 1/4 cup (57 ml) of white vinegar before the shampoo wash. Air-dry the silk on a hanger, and press it while it's still damp.

On printed silks, the colors often run together, creating a muddy appearance. If you wash a small test swatch and this happens, the silk must be dry-cleaned.

Prepare Your Scarf Pattern Piece

10 MINUTES

Since you are using the entire piece of fabric, no cutting is necessary if the ends of your fabric — the crosswise grain — are straight. When the fabric is cut off the bolt at the store, not all salespeople take the time to cut perfectly straight ends. But straight ends are necessary for a beautiful scarf.

1 To straighten the cut ends of your fabric, snip into the selvage (the selvages are the tightly woven edges that run along both lengthwise edges of the fabric) near one end.

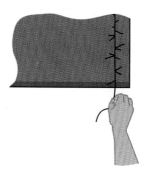

2 Pull a crosswise thread all the way across to the other selvage until the fabric puckers slightly. Using this drawn thread as a guide, cut off the uneven ends.

Construct Your Scarf

20 MINUTES

Your scarf is now half finished and you haven't sewn a single seam yet. (Now you know why I like making scarves to give away as gifts.) It should only take about 20 minutes to sew and press the scarf fabric and seam allowances. All that's left to do is slipstitching the opening closed.

1 The seam allowances are ⅝ inch (1.5 cm) wide and the stitch length is medium (10 to 12 stitches per inch or 2.5 on a 0-to-4 stitch length setting), unless otherwise indicated. Fold your fabric in half lengthwise, so that the selvages and the right sides are together. Pin all of the edges together. Place two pins 6 inches (15 cm) apart and at right angles to the selvages in the middle of one long side.

2 Don't sew between the pins. This opening enables you to turn the scarf right side out.

Don't be tempted to use a smaller opening. You'll end up tearing fragile fabric if you pull it through an opening that's too small.

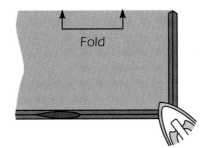

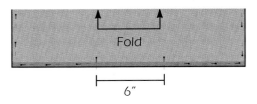

3 Sew a seam around the pinned areas, except for the 6-inch (15-cm) opening. For sharper points, hand walk two stitches diagonally on the two corners. (See "Let Your Fingers Do the Walking" on this page.)

4 Trim all four corners by cutting off ½ inch (1 cm) of the seam allowances diagonally to the stitches. Press the seam allowances open by pressing one seam allowance back onto the scarf fabric. Press the seam allowance on the 6-inch (15-cm) opening back as well.

5 Trim all the seam allowances to ¼ inch (5 mm). Turn the scarf right side out by reaching in through the opening, and pulling it through.

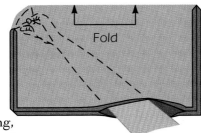

6 If you push out a point with your scissors, you're going to make a hole in the fabric. Instead, push the corners out with a point turner. Slipstitch the opening closed. (See the Quick Class "Slipsliding Away" on page 193.)

QUICK CLASS

Let Your Fingers Do the Walking

You'll have far sharper points on a corner that is hand walked than on one where you sewed seamlines at right angles. If you don't believe me, sew one corner by hand walking and do another by sewing at right angles. You be the judge.

How to Hand Walk

1 Sew to the corner, stopping before you sew into the seam allowance. Leave the needle down in the fabric.

2 Lift the presser foot. Pivot your fabric so it's on a diagonal. Put the presser foot down. Turn the hand wheel on the machine so that you sew two stitches diagonally. Leave the needle down in the fabric.

3 Lift the presser foot. Turn the fabric and sew the other side of the corner.

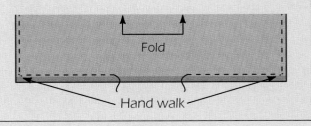

Reversible Scarf

20 MINUTES

*Another great idea for a scarf is to make it reversible. To do this,
you need 2 yards (1.8 m) of two different fabrics. Each reversible
scarf needs the entire length, but only half the width of the fabric,
so your yardage will make two reversible scarves.*

*This scarf features silk charmeuse on one side and cut
velvet on the other. In the past I have also successfully
combined two different colors of silk charmeuse, with
one on each side of the scarf.*

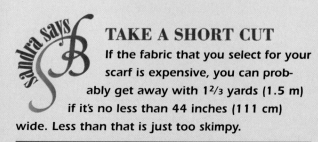

TAKE A SHORT CUT

**If the fabric that you select for your
scarf is expensive, you can probably get away with 1²/₃ yards (1.5 m)
if it's no less than 44 inches (111 cm)
wide. Less than that is just too skimpy.**

1 Straighten the crosswise grain (cut ends) of
your fabrics by making a snip into the selvage about an inch from the end, and tearing
off the last inch of fabric. If your fabric won't
tear, pull a crosswise thread until the fabric
puckers, then cut along the pucker. If the
thread breaks as you pull it, just pull on the
next thread.

2 Fold one of the pieces of fabric in half
lengthwise with the selvages and cut ends
even. Don't press the fold. Make a snip at one
edge of the fold. Open the fabric and, at the
snip, pull on a thread that extends the length of
the fabric. Pull the thread gently to slightly
pucker the fabric down the length of the fold.
Using this drawn thread as a guide, cut the
fabric in half. Do this for both fabrics.

3 Place one length of each of the two different
fabrics together with right sides facing. Pin
them together with the bulk of the fabric to the
left of the pins and with the heads of the pins
facing you. Place two pins perpendicular to the
seam 6 inches (15 cm) apart to mark an opening
needed for turning.

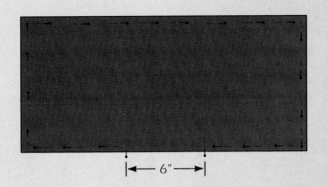

|← 6" →|

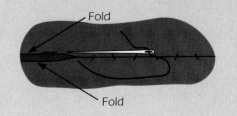

4 Sew all around the scarf. Be sure to leave the opening for turning. Press one seam allowance back onto the scarf fabric. However, if you are using velvet, steam and finger press it instead. Pressing directly on velvet will make the fabric shiny. Hold the iron ½ inch (1 cm) away from the fabric surface and allow the steam to permeate the fabric. Then flatten the edges with your fingers.

5 Trim the seam allowances back to ¼ inch (5 mm). Trim the corners diagonally. Now turn the scarf right side out. (See Steps 5 and 6 on page 191.) Slipstitch the opening closed. (See the Quick Class "Slipsliding Away" on this page.)

6 Press again to flatten the edges. If one side of the scarf is velvet, steam and finger press the edges flat. (See Step 4 on this page.)

QUICK CLASS

Slipsliding Away

It's easy to invisibly secure openings with a hand-stitched slipstitch.

How to Close an Opening with Slipstitches

1 Knot your thread and hide the knot inside the opening. Slide the needle along the fold for ¼ to ½ inch (5 mm to 1 cm) and bring the needle and thread up out of the fold, catching both sides of the opening with the needle.

2 Continue moving the needle forward another ¼ to ½ inch (5 mm to 1 cm) within the fold to make more stitches.

3 At the end, take a few tiny stitches and break your thread. Press the opening and pound it flat with a tailor's clapper.

Fold

Fold

Putting It All
TOGETHER

The Ultimate Wardrobe

Now that you've made a pair of full pants and slim pants as well as a vest, T-shirt, tuxedo shirt, jacket, skirt, dress, and scarf, how do you put the items together and integrate them into your wardrobe for maximum versatility and impact?

The first step is learning how to combine your new clothes. In "Create Style to the Max" on page 196, I list my garments from the Rodale Designer Collection and detail the clothes that you probably already have that you can wear with them.

Once you have a well-coordinated wardrobe, you can turn your attention to your total presentation. "Discover the Beautiful You" on page 200 is full of advice on color selection, makeup, and hairstyles.

Just like me, you're probably very busy so you need a closet full of items that really work. When you're in a hurry, there's nothing worse than trying to dig through clothes and accessories that don't fit or work together. I prevent this problem by cleaning out my closet and drawer clutter once a year. My advice on how to do this, as well as how to shop to avoid future mistakes, is also in this chapter. See "Get Things under Control" on page 204.

I want to guide you to great garment combinations and show you how to choose accessories that give you a polished, pulled-together look. One of my favorite ways to finish off an outfit is to add a scarf. The one that I'm wearing here is reversible, with cut velvet on one side and satin on the other. You can make one like it by following the instructions on page 192.

Create Style to the Max

My garments for the Rodale Designer Collection were designed to mix and match. To expand your wardrobe options, many of them can be combined with clothes that you probably already have in your wardrobe. The lists that follow are my suggestions for stylish outfits.

"Here I combine a favorite chamois skin blouse with a pair of slim pants from the Rodale Designer Collection. Whenever I sew a new item, I try to coordinate it with other garments that are already hanging in my closet. I think about more than color combinations because the overall silhouette of the combined pieces and the accessories that I choose affect the look."

Full Pull-On Pants

These pants are really very versatile. You can wear them with many blouses, sweaters, and jackets that you probably already have in your closet. Depending on the fabric that you choose for your full pants, the effect can be dressy or casual. For appealing silhouettes, try combining the full pants that you make with the following garments:

- A loose-fitting T-shirt that is untucked
- A bodysuit or close-fitting T-shirt (if you have the curves)
- A long, loose sweater that coordinates with the pants fabric
- A jacket over a tucked-in shirt that is belted at the waist
- A long, fitted jacket that is buttoned
- A shawl collar jacket that is buttoned or unbuttoned

Slim Pull-On Pants

These pants look great combined with any oversize top because the narrow leg balances the volume of your upper body. When selecting a top, keep in mind that it needs to be crotch length or longer. The pants aren't flattering with tucked-in tops or short sweaters unless you're an aerobics instructor. Consider combining your slim pants with the following garments:

✂ An oversize blouse that is untucked

✂ An oversize jacket over a tucked-in top

✂ A long, fitted jacket that is unbuttoned over a tucked-in top

✂ A long, fitted jacket that is buttoned

✂ An oversize sweater

✂ A loose T-shirt lengthened to cover the crotch

✂ A tuxedo blouse that is untucked

✂ A vest over a shirt that is longer than the vest

CHECK THE FIT   Your figure doesn't need to be perfect to wear close-fitting garments, but you may find that they show off areas that might be better unnoticed. If you choose to wear a body suit, for example, make sure that your bra isn't so tight that bulges show.

Oversize T-Shirt

Once confined to only the most casual outfits, the T-shirt is now worn with many other garments. In fact, I believe the loose T-shirt should be considered a basic piece of your wardrobe. It's very easy to make, so you may want to sew up several versions of the garment in a variety of fabrics. The T-shirt can be worn with the following garments:

✂ Full pants with the T-shirt loose or tucked in

✂ A gored skirt with the T-shirt tucked in

✂ A straight skirt with the T-shirt loose or tucked in

✂ Slim pants, if the T-shirt is crotch length or longer

Tuxedo Shirt

This shirt looks good with any combination of clothes. It can be worn over absolutely any bottom, so don't worry about how you'll wear it. In addition, the tuxedo shirt can be worn open as a jacket if you combine it with a fitted bodysuit or blouse. Try these bottoms with an untucked tuxedo shirt:

- ✂ Full pants
- ✂ Slim pants
- ✂ A gored skirt
- ✂ A raglan-sleeve dress under the open tuxedo shirt

MIX AND MATCH

The items you make from the patterns in this book will become your good friends. You'll wear them often, always finding new ways to put them together in your wardrobe. Don't ever be afraid to experiment.

Gored Skirt

The skirt in this book is certain to become such a favorite because it can be worn with so many items. You'll love the way it drapes across your body and flatters your figure. Use the skirt as a starting point for outfits that use the following garments as building blocks:

- ✂ A loose sweater (on a less-than-perfect figure)
- ✂ A bodysuit (if you're an aerobics instructor)
- ✂ A long jacket (if you have a tummy)
- ✂ A short jacket (if sit-ups are starting to show results)
- ✂ A tuxedo shirt as a jacket with a smaller, fitted top underneath
- ✂ A shawl collar jacket with a fitted top underneath

Raglan-Sleeve Dress

Length makes all the difference with this garment. Extend the bottom so that it's floor length and you have a lounge robe. If you stop the pattern at mid-calf, you end up with a dress. Go shorter still and you have a tunic. So, with a few adjustments, you can make several items to wear with the following garments:

- ✂ A vest, worn over the dress
- ✂ Full pants, worn with the tunic
- ✂ Slim pants, worn with the tunic
- ✂ Tuxedo shirt, worn open over the dress
- ✂ A straight skirt, worn with the tunic

Shawl Collar Jacket

I call this my wear-with-almost-everything jacket. The style is very versatile, and the cut works with many tops that you may want to wear underneath it. For example, the dolman armhole accommodates a variety of sleeve styles. In my opinion, the jacket looks best if the sweater or blouse underneath is shorter than the jacket. It can be worn over the following garments:

- ✂ A raglan-sleeve dress
- ✂ Full pants and a loose or fitted top
- ✂ A gored skirt and a loose or fitted top
- ✂ A straight skirt and a loose or fitted top
- ✂ Tailored pants and a loose or fitted top

Oblong Scarf

This accessory is so important that I dedicate an entire chapter to it. As I explain in the introduction to that chapter, the most useful scarf is oblong. Whether you make a reversible scarf or a single-sided version in several color options, you'll find the scarf is a great wardrobe extender. It can be worn with the following garments:

- ✂ A coat, to fill in a neckline
- ✂ A jacket, under the collar to add more interest
- ✂ A sweater, to bring the eye up to the face
- ✂ A T-shirt, in a fabric that matches the pants or skirt to encourage vertical movement of the eye

Coordinating Vest

Think of the vest as an alternative to a jacket. Because it has deep armholes, it can go over the raglan-sleeve dress, the tuxedo blouse, the T-shirt, a bodysuit, and an oversize blouse. To lengthen and slim your silhouette, make the vest and your bottom garment, either pants or a skirt, in a color-coordinated fabric. Try wearing your vest with the following garments:

- ✂ Full pants and a bodysuit
- ✂ Slim pants and a loose top
- ✂ A raglan-sleeve dress
- ✂ A loose jacket and full or slim pants

Discover the Beautiful You

Before we start the fun part of accessorizing, take a good look in the mirror. How do you feel about yourself today? A positive attitude is the first and last thing someone remembers about you. Focus on the positive things, and develop a plan to get the negatives moving along and out of your life.

Coiffed and Confident

Beyond personality and the way you feel about yourself, there are specific things that you can do to refine your presentation as well as feel good about how you look every time you get dressed. Your hairstyle, makeup, accessories, and the colors you wear all have great impact.

How long has it been since you changed your hairstyle? Many women look like they are in a time warp because they're still wearing their hair in the same cut that they had in their teens or twenties. Styles change and so should hair.

For many years, wash-and-wear permanents were acceptable. They're easy, but do they look that good? Clean, shiny hair will always look good, even if it's flat. And rinses might improve the color of white or gray hair, but is blue hair an asset? If you're at a loss about how to improve or update your hair, do what I do. When I see someone walking down the street with a great haircut or terrific color, I stop her and ask who did her cut or color. Don't feel shy because the woman will be flattered by your inquiry.

If you are truly convinced that no hairstyle will flatter you, get into hats. I have a friend with very thin, fine hair, but she looks great in a hat! Who cares if few people wear them because you will look very pulled together. Why do you think fashion models usually wear hats? Because a hat finishes the outfit. Besides, a hat can be a great friend on a bad hair day, and wearing one helps to upgrade you to first class when you travel. Even if you don't book first class, you'll look as if you ought to be there.

SANDRA SAYS

LOOK YOUR BEST Try to wear makeup whenever you're out in public. Makeup boosts your confidence because you know that you look your best, even if you're only wearing mascara and a touch of lipstick.

Colorful Options

What are your best colors? If you don't know, it's time you found out. Have your colors done. And if it's been a decade since you last visited a color consultant, go again. You need to find out what looks good on you now because coloring changes as you age. You may discover that colors that you thought were your best do nothing for your current complexion. (Now you have an excuse to make some new clothes.)

Besides, having your colors done is fun because the results open up whole new vistas. A periodic update will get you out of a rut and prevent you from wearing the same two (or more) colors all the time.

My favorite book on this subject is *Color with Style* by Donna Fuji (Graphic-Sha Publishing Company, 1991). I like it because the book isn't limited only to the well-known "four seasons" color theory. Instead, Donna offers 25 extensive color palettes, each one based on the complexions of women from a broad range of ethnic groups.

After you have consulted an expert or worked your way through a book, what happens if you don't like your colors? You can still wear your favorite colors; just add a scarf in a flattering color near your face.

I'm a "fall," so I look best in warm browns, rusts, and other rich, dark colors. Yet I love the "winter" palette. The jewel tones, black, and white are so appealing to me that I wear these winter colors even though they're not part of the fall scheme. Yet no one ever gives me a compliment when I'm wearing the winter palette, which I do from time to time. I call these times my color rebellion periods. But when I'm wearing my colors—the warm browns and rusts—I get lots of attention.

In addition to selecting suitable colors, you should also consider the placement of the colors on your body. If you are heavier than you would like to be (who isn't?), stay away from color blocking. You're color blocking if you wear different, unrelated colors on the top and bottom halves of your body. Color blocking adds weight without the pleasure of overeating.

A good example of color blocking is wearing a white blouse with a navy skirt. The eye is not encouraged to move up and down the body. Rather, it stops between each piece. This cuts the body in half, which adds width. If you are tall and slim, you can get away with color blocking, but the rest of us can't.

If this is you, it's better to wear garments in several hues of the same color, or colors of the same value. This encourages the eye to move vertically, thus making you appear taller and slimmer. Should a tall, slim person dress in hues of the same color? Can someone ever be too tall or too slim?

A Polished Face

Do you wear makeup? No? Why not? Very few women over 35 look their best without it. You don't have to wear a lot, just enough to bring out your best features. If you lack makeup application skills, take a lesson from a cosmetician who makes up one side of your face and then coaches you while you do the other side yourself.

A trained cosmetician can guide you to makeup that will enhance your complexion as well as work with the colors that you like to wear. Consulting an expert will save you a fortune by eliminating trial-and-error shopping. You'll immediately have colors that complement your coloring and clothes, and you'll be able to throw out all the unflattering lipsticks.

You may have to practice applying your new makeup a few times. But after you're comfortable with your products and tools, you'll find that applying makeup won't take up a lot of your time. In fact, makeup that used to take me 20 minutes to apply now takes me only 5 minutes to do.

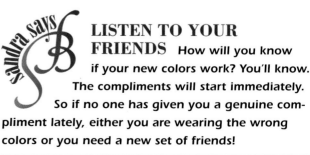

LISTEN TO YOUR FRIENDS How will you know if your new colors work? You'll know. The compliments will start immediately. So if no one has given you a genuine compliment lately, either you are wearing the wrong colors or you need a new set of friends!

The Finishing Details

Before evaluating your accessories, focus for a few minutes on the strengths and weaknesses of your body. This will help you determine how to use accessories to focus on your body's positive features.

For maximum effect, each ensemble should have two focal points. Avoid the temptation to wear an eye-catching bracelet, detailed shoes, and a hand-painted scarf at the same time. A definite focus isn't established when you wear too many accessories, so the eye wanders all over the body. This might be acceptable if your figure liabilities are minimal, but you lose the impact of one or two strong focal points.

Frequently, the focus in my outfits is on parts of the garments that I'm wearing. Since I tend to enjoy construction details, I look for simple, well-designed accessories. For example, while I may be attracted to a belt with a thousand doodads on it, I will pass this up for a belt with a simple sterling silver buckle that's elegant and understated. On the other hand, if your wardrobe is full of simply styled garments in solid colors, and you happen to have a small waist, go for that fancy belt. You'll wear it with practically everything you own.

I often recommend belts for both accenting and hiding figure variations, depending on how you use them. Regardless of your shape, you can find a look that's suitable for you. Here are the guidelines that I've developed during my years of teaching.

- ✂ Draw attention to a small waist with a great belt. If you also want to draw attention to your face, go ahead and wear some great earrings.
- ✂ An undefined waist looks best with a belt that has a significant buckle. This will draw attention away from the waistline.
- ✂ Your waist will look smaller if your belt, bodice, and skirt are the same color.
- ✂ Any size waist can wear a belt inside a jacket. Make sure that the waistline of the garment or your belt is not too tight. This makes the tummy bulge and look larger.

When sorting through your accessories, keep an eye out for flexible leather belts that can be worn more than one way. These belts are great because they're so versatile; they can be worn at the waist or loose on the high hip. The way that you wear one depends on your garment's silhouette.

At the waist, a belt can be worn inside a jacket even if you ordinarily avoid belting your clothes. You may want to try a belted waist when you're topping the outfit with a jacket. The belt adds visual interest, yet the jacket streamlines the look, thereby covering a multitude of sins. I promise—you won't look too "hippy."

QUICK CLASS

To Pad or Not to Pad

Are shoulder pads in or out of fashion? Who cares! If they make your clothes hang better, you should be wearing them. I recommend a soft-sculptured raglan pad that works in any garment.

You don't need to buy a set for every piece of clothing that you own. It's easy to add removable shoulder pads to a garment, so that you can take them out when you want.

How to Attach Shoulder Pads to a Garment

1 Before sewing the Velcro to the shoulder pads, you may want to cover them with self fabric. This is only necessary if your garment is unlined and the shoulder pads will be visible if you take the garment off in public, which is most likely with a jacket or vest. For complete instructions on covering a shoulder pad with fabric, see "Cover the Shoulder Pads" on page 133.

2 Cut a 3-inch (7.5-cm)-long strip of Velcro. Pull the hooked side away from the loop side. Center the hooked, or prickly, side on the top of the shoulder pad. Hand sew it to the shoulder pad using a whip stitch.

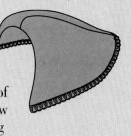

3 Cut the looped, or soft, side of the Velcro in half lengthwise. (Keep one half and toss out the other half.) Using a narrower strip of looped Velcro reduces bulk at the shoulder seam on your garment.

4 Put your garment on and check that both of the shoulder seams fall correctly on your shoulders. If your garment doesn't have shoulder seams or if the style has a shoulder seam that sits in front of the natural line that runs from your neck to your shoulder, insert a pin to mark the spot where the shoulder seam would be. Take off the garment.

5 Position one of the narrow looped Velcro strips at the shoulder seam with pins on the wrong side of the garment. One edge of the Velcro strip should be 1 inch (2.5 cm) away from the top of the arm hinge. Whip stitch both sides of the strip to the shoulder seam.

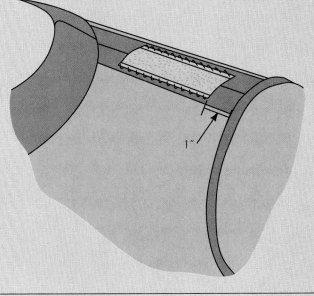

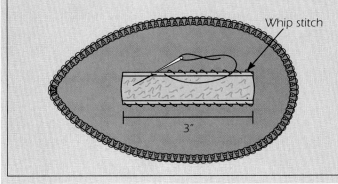

Whip stitch

3"

Get Things under Control

If you haven't taken a long, hard look through your closet, drawers, and jewelry box for a while, now is the time to do so. I do this every year to make sure that I'm not ignoring any of my garments and accessories. Sometimes I'm surprised by new combinations.

Closet Clutter

Organize your closet by color and get rid of anything that doesn't fit or isn't flattering. A typical closet that's effective has three or four color groups. This is a workable palette that you should aspire to.

My closet isn't typical, and I pay a price for this. I love color and make clothes in any fabric that pleases me. This also means that I don't wear a lot of the clothes in my wardrobe because the colors aren't flattering on me. But it sure was fun sewing them. To prevent things from getting out of hand, once a year I do a purge and the uncomplimentary clothes travel from my closet to happier homes among all of my friends.

While you're cleaning out your closet, ask yourself how often you wear each garment. If you haven't worn something in two years, there's a reason. Put a note on anything that needs a mate: The jacket that goes with nothing, the skirt that's the wrong color for the sweater you bought. Identify orphans now. Make a list of companion pieces or accessories that are needed to pull a look together.

If you haven't the time to go on a sewing frenzy, you can expand your options and give your wardrobe a lift by trying different color combinations of the clothes that you already own. For example, have you ever tried combining purple and fuchsia or navy and lime green? Keep an open mind. The first step is to buy a color wheel at an art supply store and learn how to use it. (See the Quick Class "Customize Your Colors" on the opposite page.)

FOCUS ON CLOTHES
Sandra says
Garments can also be considered accessories. Think of a brocade or sequined dinner jacket, a one-of-a-kind arty sweater, or a highly embellished vest. I once attended a wedding where the mother of the bride wore a beautiful kimono over a basic column dress. To this day, the thing I remember most about the wedding is how beautiful that kimono looked as the mother of the bride was being seated.

Hidden Treasures

You may have some terrific accessories that are pushed to the far back of your jewelry box. We all get in the habit of wearing two or three pairs of earrings because we know what they go with. I think you should move things around a bit so you can find a few new favorites.

A Jewel of an Idea

Dump out your jewelry drawer. Poke through the contents and look for significant pieces. Set aside earrings that are smaller than a quarter because they're too small to draw attention to your face, which is the main reason you should be wearing earrings. Also pick out any large, interesting pins and one-of-a-kind necklaces, especially long ones because they add vertical lines to your silhouette. Give away anything you haven't worn in three years. Polish all of the

QUICK CLASS

Customize Your Colors

After you have your colors done, you'll receive swatches that exemplify your best color options. Unless you want to wear a monochromatic color scheme (different tones of the same color) all the time, you need to learn how to combine colors in an interesting and attractive fashion. This is where a color wheel can help.

How to Use a Color Wheel

1 For a subtle approach, try an analogous color scheme. This is where any three colors that are side by side on the color wheel are used in an ensemble. An analogous color combination creates much the same harmony as a monochromatic scheme, although the results are more interesting. The eye passes easily between colors because they are so similar. If you'd like to make more of a statement, use colors that are exactly opposite each other on the color wheel. Keep in mind that you need an outgoing personality to carry off this dramatic color statement.

2 Very interesting combinations are possible with a triad color scheme. To allow this color scheme to work effectively, use the colors in uneven proportions and make sure that the shades of each color are of equal value.

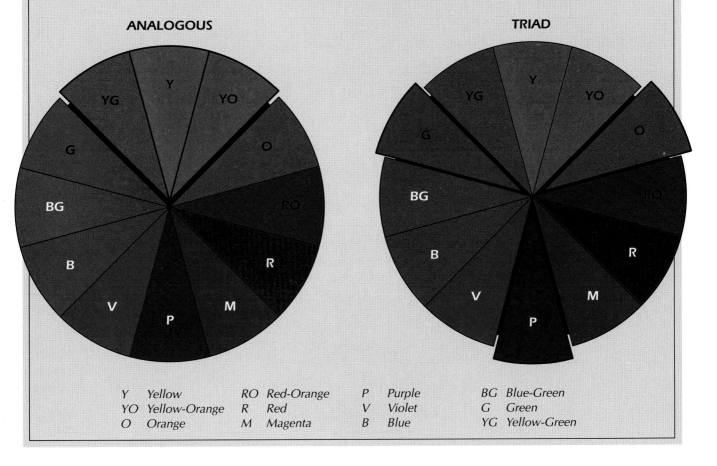

ANALOGOUS   TRIAD

Y	Yellow	RO	Red-Orange	P	Purple	BG	Blue-Green
YO	Yellow-Orange	R	Red	V	Violet	G	Green
O	Orange	M	Magenta	B	Blue	YG	Yellow-Green

silver pieces. Get any broken items fixed.

When you're finished sorting, rearrange the drawer, putting the newly chosen pieces in front so you can find them easily.

Take a look at your watch. What does it say about you? This is an accessory you wear every day. It makes a statement, so make sure it's a good one. Wouldn't it be fun to buy a new watch? Stores are full of attractive "retro" styles, so you should try a few on.

How many rings are you wearing? Too many rings on one hand devalues each. Think about wearing your rings on a rotating basis so that you can enjoy them one at a time.

By now you probably identified some really special accessories. Consider building outfits around them as I do. In addition, I often start with an accessory and shop for fabric and a pattern with it in mind. Limit the number of accessories you wear. Big earrings, a big necklace, and a bracelet are too much. But big earrings can work with a pin and a bracelet. I love accessories and have to remember occasionally to take one off.

Little Essentials

Most sewers I've met have a shoe fetish. Perhaps this is because it's easier to get a good fit in shoes than clothes, or maybe it's because no one expects us to make our shoes. I also love shoes, and pay the price for having too many in my closet. There's always clutter! If your budget is limited, buy two pairs a season, either in black, brown, gray, or taupe—whatever works best with the majority of your clothes. One pair should be casual, like short boots, loafers, flats, or sandals. Another pair should be slightly dressier, with a heel. The heel needn't be high.

Buy a good quality shoe in a "new-looking" style. A quality shoe holds its shape longer. If you don't know what the new trends are, ask a sales clerk. The styles for dressy shoes rarely change so on the few occasions when you really get decked out, wear the dressy shoes you bought a few seasons ago.

There's one other color that you should include in your shoe wardrobe—your hair color.

These are some of my favorite pieces. As you can see, I like bold jewelry that draws the eye up to the face. Since my clothes are dramatic, I also choose jewelry with character. These pieces are such an important part of my wardrobe that after I sent them to the photographer, I felt lost. I made my editor promise to store them in a locked drawer.

This ivory pin is incredible. I purchased the antique disk in Japan, then a friend worked it into this design. To really showcase it, I made the chamois skin blouse. You can see the entire blouse on page 196.

I've always believed that it's flattering to repeat your hair color in a shoe or boot.

Years ago, a woman shopped for shoes and a purse at the same time because these had to match. In today's fashion picture, the shoe and purse only need to coordinate with the outfit. However, purse styles change every third or fourth season and bounce back and forth between soft and structured. I rarely buy structured purses and then only smaller ones that go with my evening wear. The structured purse isn't suitable for many uses. Shopping with a structured purse, for example, is a nightmare. It's constantly bumping people or knocking items off counters. Plus, these stiff-structured bags never seem to hold enough. Consider investing in a soft leather tote instead.

Gloves are used less to keep your hands warm and more as another way to give your outfit a shot of color. Once again, buy good quality or forget them. If you live in a cold climate, cashmere-lined gloves will serve you well. Seasonally speaking, cloth or crocheted gloves are worn in spring and summer, while leather or suede gloves are worn in fall and winter. To really look well dressed at night, gloves are a must.

The Ultimate Accessory

Your last chore before going on a shopping expedition is to browse through your scarf drawer. Empty it. Look for oblong scarves that are either incredibly beautiful, have a very flattering color, or possess a great texture in a favorite color. Take these special ones over to your closet. Do these scarves work with garments that you already own? Keep these scarves in a visible place so that they won't be forgotten.

Now that you've picked out your favorites, it's time to make tough decisions about the ones that you ignored. Perhaps your remaining scarves need to find a home with someone else. Why not invite your friends over and let them take their pick?

Your collection may include a few large squares that can be used as shawls. Mine doesn't. I limit my scarf purchases to oblong shapes, since these are more versatile and easier to wear.

Ready, Set, Shop

Now you're ready to shop for accessories. Fetch a large carryall bag to take with you to the store. Fill it with the dress that needs a belt, the jacket that needs a pin, the blouse that needs a skirt or pants, and the sweater that needs a scarf or necklace. Taking these items with you will ensure that you'll get exactly what you need. And don't forget your shopping list.

---

thread TALES

I allow myself two terrific accessories a year. Because this is a limited amount, price is no object. When I fall in love with something, I ask myself, "Is this better than anything else I have in the same category?" For example, if I'm attracted to a large pair of silver earrings, I run a mental checklist of my jewelry. Why would I need another pair if I already own an incredible pair of silver earrings? Sometimes, however, the piece I'm considering buying is so spectacular, I give in. I try not to do this very often because the things I like are often expensive.

Sandra

Size Table for the Patterns

Guaranteed success with my patterns hinges upon only one thing: honest body measurements. Even if you already know your measurements, you should take them again to make sure they're still accurate and also to compare them to the ranges in the table below.

Before you even cut out your fabric pattern pieces, you need to take your measurements so that you can choose the right size pattern. It's very important that you do this because my sizing is different from other patterns and from ready-to-wear clothes. Don't just assume that you're a specific size because that's what you've worked with in the past.

Since my patterns are multisized, you can use different sizes for different parts of your body. I explain how this is done in each chapter.

	Body Measurements		
Size	**Small**	**Medium**	**Large**
Bust	30½–34 inches (77.5–86 cm)	34½–37½ inches (87.5–95 cm)	38–43 inches (96.5–109 cm)
Waist	23–27 inches (58–69 cm)	27½–31 inches (70–78.5 cm)	31½–36 inches (80–91 cm)
Hips	32½–36 inches (82.5–91 cm)	36½–40½ inches (92.5–103 cm)	41–46 inches (104–117 cm)

Finished Lengths and Hem Widths

In order to get a perfect fit—one that's both comfortable and flattering—you should fine-tune your patterns by adjusting the cutting lines to suit your body shape. To save you time, I've listed the pattern information in a table, so that you don't have to measure the areas on the patterns.

After you compare your body measurements to the sizes I use for my patterns, the next step is to evaluate the fit in particular areas. This is where the finished lengths and hem widths come in handy. First you compare your body measurements and those of your favorite clothes with key locations on the patterns. (A full explanation is included in the fitting section of every chapter.)

Even experienced sewers often skip this step but regret their decision later on. The old saying "a stitch in time saves nine" is very appropriate here because the few minutes that might be saved by ignoring the finished lengths and hem widths could add up to hours of fussing over the fit when you're sewing the garment together.

If you've enjoyed this book,
you may be interested in these other titles from Rodale Press.

Christmas with Jinny Beyer

DECORATE YOUR HOME FOR THE HOLIDAYS WITH BEAUTIFUL QUILTS, WREATHS, ARRANGEMENTS, ORNAMENTS, AND MORE
by Jinny Beyer

Renowned quilt designer Jinny Beyer shares her ideas and techniques for making over 50 holiday projects, suitable for any skill level. Complete instructions and full-color illustrations accompany every project.

Hardcover   ISBN 0-87596-716-7

High Fashion Secrets from the World's Best Designers

A STEP-BY-STEP GUIDE TO SEWING STYLISH SEAMS, BUTTONHOLES, POCKETS, COLLARS, HEMS, AND MORE
by Claire Shaeffer

Nationally known sewing expert and author Claire Shaeffer reveals the sewing secrets of fashion industry legends from Ralph Lauren to Yves Saint Laurent. You'll also discover that high-fashion sewing does not have to be difficult! Available February 1997.

Hardcover   ISBN 0-87596-717-5

Sew It Tonight, Give It Tomorrow

50 FAST, FUN, AND FABULOUS GIFTS TO MAKE IN AN EVENING
edited by Stacey L. Klaman

Make one-of-a-kind gifts in no time at all. The projects, from golf club covers and a tea cozy to crib bumpers and holiday ornaments, are appropriate for sewers of all levels.

Hardcover   ISBN 0-87596-645-4

The Experts Book of Sewing Tips & Techniques

FROM THE SEWING STARS OF AMERICA—HUNDREDS OF WAYS TO SEW BETTER, FASTER, & EASIER
edited by Marya Kissinger Amig, Barbara Fimbel, Stacey L. Klaman, Karen Kunkel, and Susan Weaver

Learn the trade secrets of the top sewing experts in this easy-to-use guide. Hints and tips, from appliqué to zippers, are covered in alphabetical order.

Hardcover   ISBN 0-87596-682-9

Rodale's Visual Encyclopedia of Needlecrafts

UNIQUE LOOK-AND-STITCH LESSONS AND PROJECTS
by Carolyn Christmas

Full-color photographs and step-by-step directions accompany this comprehensive guide to the most popular needlecrafts, including appliqué, crochet, cross-stitch, duplicate stitch, embroidery, knitting, patchwork quilting, and plastic canvas.

Hardcover   ISBN 0-87596-718-3

Sewing Secrets from the Fashion Industry

PROVEN METHODS TO HELP YOU SEW LIKE THE PROS
edited by Susan Huxley

Learn the same tips and techniques that the industry professionals use in their sample rooms and production factories. Over 800 full-color photographs accompany the step-by-step directions.

Hardcover   ISBN -0-87596-719-1

FOR MORE INFORMATION OR TO ORDER ONE OF THESE BOOKS,
CALL **1-800-848-4735** OR FAX US ANYTIME AT **1-800-813-6627.**

Index

▬ Pattern Measurements

Size	Small	Medium	Large	Hem Depth
Full pant length from waist to hem at side seam	40¾ inches (103.5 cm)	40¾ inches (103.5 cm)	40¾ inches (103.5 cm)	1¼ inches (3 cm)
Full pant width at hem	26 inches (66 cm)	28½ inches (72.4 cm)	31 inches (78.7 cm)	N/A
Slim pant length from waist to hem at side seam	35 inches (88.9 cm)	38½ inches (97.8 cm)	41½ inches (105.4 cm)	1 inch (2.5 cm)
Slim pant width at hem	11 inches (27.9 cm)	12¼ inches (31.1 cm)	13½ inches (34.2 cm)	N/A
Vest length at center back from neck to hem	24 inches (61 cm)	25 inches (63.5 cm)	26 inches (66 cm)	N/A
T-shirt length at center back from neck to hem	25 inches (63.5 cm)	26 inches (66 cm)	27 inches (68.6 cm)	1 inch (2.5 cm)
T-shirt circumference at hem	41½ inches (105.4 cm)	46 inches (116.8 cm)	51 inches (129.5 cm)	N/A
Tuxedo shirt length at center back from neck to hem	30½ inches (77.5 cm)	31½ inches (80 cm)	32½ inches (82.6 cm)	N/A
Tuxedo shirt sleeve length	21¾ inches (55.2 cm)	23 inches (58.4 cm)	23¾ inches (60.3 cm)	1¼ inches (3 cm)
Shawl collar jacket length at center back from neck to hem	28 inches (71.1 cm)	29 inches (73.7 cm)	30 inches (76.2 cm)	2 inches (5 cm)
Shawl collar jacket sleeve length from neck to hem	27½ inches (69.9 cm)	28½ inches (72.4 cm)	29½ inches (74.9 cm)	1½ inches (3.5 cm)
Gored skirt length	32¼ inches (81.9 cm)	36¼ inches (92 cm)	38¼ inches (97.2 cm)	1 inch (2.5 cm)
Gored skirt circumference at hem	106½ inches (270.5 cm)	112½ inches (285.8 cm)	115½ inches (293.4 cm)	N/A
Dress, tunic length, at center back from neck to hem	23½ inches (62.2 cm)	24½ inches (62.2 cm)	25½ inches (62.2 cm)	1¾ inches (4.5 cm)
Dress, mid-calf length, at center back from neck to hem	43¼ inches (109.9 cm)	43¼ inches (109.9 cm)	43¼ inches (109.9 cm)	1¾ inches (4.5 cm)
Dress, lounge robe length, at center back from neck to hem	54¼ inches (137.8 cm)	54¼ inches (137.8 cm)	54¼ inches (137.8 cm)	1¾ inches (4.5 cm)
Dress circumference at hem	39½ inches (100.3 cm)	45 inches (114.3 cm)	49½ inches (125.7 cm)	1¾ inches (4.5 cm)
Dress sleeve length from neck to hem	27¾ inches (70.5 cm)	29½ inches (74.9 cm)	30¼ inches (76.8 cm)	⅝ inch (1.5 cm)